AF322580

also by
W. MICHAEL FARMER

The Iliad of Geronimo: A Song of Blood and Fire
The Odyssey of Geronimo: Twenty-Three Years a Prisoner of War
Trini! Come!: Geronimo's Captivity of Trinidad Verdín

The Apache Kid Chronicles
Army Apache Scout • Vanished Outlaw

Chato's Chiricahua Apache Legacy
Proud Outcast • Desperate Warrior

The Life and Times of Yellow Boy, Mescalero Apache
Killer of Witches • Blood of the Devil
The Last Warrior

Legends of the Desert
Mariana's Knight: The Revenge of Henry Fountain
Knight's Odyssey: The Return of Henry Fountain
Knight of the Tiger: The Betrayals of Henry Fountain
Blood-Soaked Earth: The Trial of Oliver Lee

The Vanishing Trilogy
Hombrecito's War • Hombrecito's Search
Tiger, Tiger Burning Bright: The Betrayals of Pancho Villa
Conspiracy: The Trial of Oliver Lee and James Gilliand

Nonfiction
Geronimo: Twenty-Three Years as a Prisoner of War
Apacheria: True Stories of Apache Culture 1860-1920

AN APACHE ILIAD

★ ★ ★

TRUE STORIES OF GERONIMO'S WAR AND RESERVATION LIFE 1877—1886

W. MICHAEL FARMER

Otterford

Otterford

an imprint of
Roan & Weatherford Publishing Associates, LLC
Bentonville, Arkansas • Heber City, Utah
www.roanweatherford.com

Library of Congress Cataloging-in-Publication Data
Names: Farmer, W. Michael
Title: An Apache Iliad: True Stories of Geronimo's War And Reservation Life 1877—1886
W. Michael Farmer, Author
Description: First Edition. | Bentonville: Otterford, 2026.
Identifiers: LCCN: 2025947309 | ISBN: ISBN: 979-8-89299-102-5 (hardcover) |
ISBN: 979-8-89299-103-2 (trade paperback) | ISBN: 979-8-89299-104-9 (eBook)
Subjects: HISTORY/Native American | HISTORY/Military/United States |
HISTORY/United States/19th Century
LC record available at: https://lccn.loc.gov/2025947309

Otterford hardcover edition April, 2026

Jacket Design & Interior Design by Casey W. Cowan
Editing by Don Money

For Corky, my best friend and wife,
the wind beneath my wings

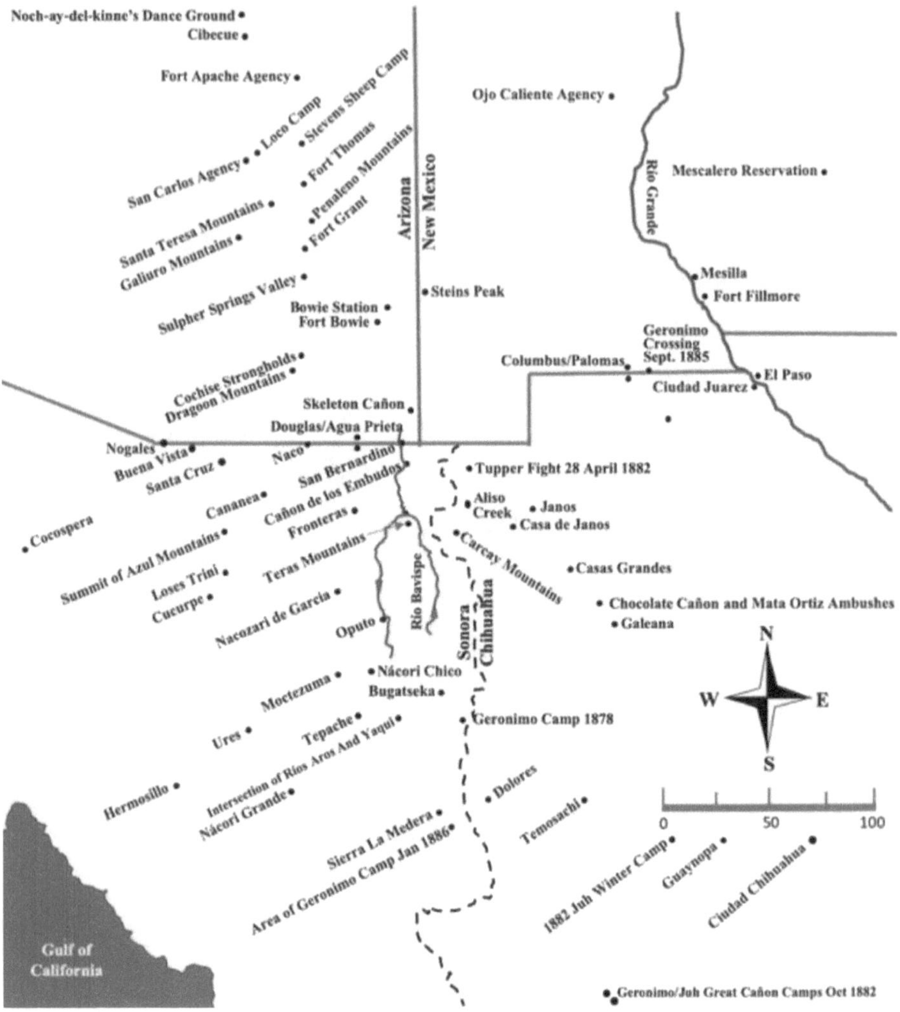

APACHERIA

★ ★ ★

Approximate locations for points of interest in An Apache Iliad *beginning with the deceitful capture of Geronimo at Ojo Caliente Reservation, New Mexico, in 1877 and ending with the Trojan Horse of lies in General Nelson Miles surrender terms at Skeleton Canyon, Arizona, September 4, 1886, when the Geronimo-Naiche band of Chiricahua Apache surrendered to become prisoners of war. Modern locations are provided for common reference.*

CONTENTS

ACKNOWLEDGEMENTS

I AM INDEBTED to the support of numerous contributors to this work who range from editors, to archival librarians, to historians whose research has helped make this work possible, to friends who have opened their home to me for work in the southwest, all of whom deserve special mention.

Lynda Sánchez has shared rare photographs from her collection developed over years of research and her support of Eve Ball, and she has been a guiding light in understanding the Apache People.

Most of the photographs in this work are from the National Archives and Library of Congress. Their work has given the public access to historical images that would not have been possible even twenty years ago.

Histories I found particularly helpful included those by Angie Debo, Robert Utley, Eve Ball, Nora Henn, and Lynda Sánchez, Alicia Delgadillo and Miriam Perrett, Lynda Sánchez, Sherry Robinson, and Edwin Sweeney.

I especially owe a note of thanks to Pat and Mike Alexander in Las Cruces, New Mexico, who opened their home to me while I rambled through the surrounding countryside doing research, giving lectures, and signing books.

To the many readers of the original drafts of these vignettes, I owe my sincere appreciation for their support and comments.

The patience, encouragement, and support of my wife Carolyn made this work possible, and it is to her that this book is dedicated.

PREFATORY NOTE

FIVE THOUSAND AMERICAN soldiers, three thousand Mexican soldiers, and hundreds of civilians in posses across southern Arizona and New Mexico and northern Sonora and Chihuahua chased and fought Chiricahua Apache led by Geronimo with seventeen warriors and twenty-two women and children for five months in the spring and summer of 1886. During that time, not a single Apache was wounded, killed, or captured.

Near the end of August 1886, Geronimo and his warriors agreed to discuss surrender terms with Lieutenant Charles B. Gatewood, representative of General Nelson A. Miles. According to Lieutenant Gatewood, General Miles said that if they did not surrender, he would chase and kill them all even if it took fifty years. If, however, the band surrendered, then General Miles offered to reunite them with the rest of their families within five days after they surrendered, to unite all the Chiricahua and leave them alone on a common reservation with good water and grass for cattle, to wipe their records clean of wartime killings and thefts, and to protect them from revenge-minded settlers and the Apache retaliating, which would continue the war, by holding the Apache in Florida while President Cleveland decided what to do with them. The warriors assumed they would be in Florida no longer than two years because Miles's predecessor, General George Crook, had offered that five months earlier. None of these surrender terms were met, and the Chiricahua Apache were prisoners of war for twenty-seven years. Geronimo was a prisoner of war for twenty-three years until he died. The story of the

Geronimo and Chiricahua years in captivity is told in *Geronimo: Prisoner of Lies* and in the novel, *The Odyssey of Geronimo*.[1,2]

Iliad is a Greek word meaning a series of exploits or woes and trials suitable for an epic. *The Iliad* as told poetically by Homer is an ancient Greek story of an epic ten-year war fought between Greek and Trojan heroes. It is a tale of a long series of exploits and woes and trials the Greeks endured who fought to overcome an implacable enemy behind the walls of the great, impregnable Trojan fortress, Troy. The Greeks finally overcame and destroyed Troy by deceiving the Trojans into believing that they had given up and returned home. As a sign of their acceptance of defeat, the Greeks left a huge wooden horse as a tribute to the gods who had decided against them and for the Trojans. However, the Greeks deceived the Trojans by only sailing their ships out of sight of Troy's walls and waiting for a signal to return from warriors hidden inside the horse. The Trojans accepted the horse as a Greek gift to the gods and pulled it inside Troy's walls as part of a great celebration for winning the war. Beware of Greeks bearing gifts. While the Trojans slept, passed out from too much celebratory wine, the Greek warriors left their hiding place in the horse to signal the Greek fleet to return, and then opened the city's gates to those who had waited ten years for Trojan blood. The destruction of Troy was the end of the Trojan War, and the end of the Trojans.

The last ten years of the Chiricahua Apache war with the United States is an epic story that bears remarkable similarities to *The Iliad* of Homer. From the only time Geronimo was captured until he surrendered to General Miles was about ten years, the same duration as the Trojan War. It was a time of great, legendary chiefs, leaders, and warriors such as Victorio, Loco, Nana, Juh, Naiche, Chihuahua, Ulzana, Kaytennae, Chato, Mangas, and the great warrior of the Apache Iliad, who like the Greek hero Achilles, was their greatest fighting man and the best-known Apache war leader, at least to the American public, Geronimo. Like the Greeks, the Americans had their heroes too. They included John Clum, General George Crook, Major Albert Morrow, Captain Emmett Crawford, Captain Wirt Davis, Captain Harry Haskell, Lieutenant Marion Maus, Lieutenant Britton Davis, Lieutenant Charles Gatewood, Al Sieber, Archie McIntosh, and George Wratten.

The Apache believed their "fortress," the great Sierra Madre Mountains in Mexico, was impregnable to the Americans just as Troy had been to the Greeks. The Apache beliefs about their safety in the Sierra Madre arose from the facts that the American army couldn't cross the border until Mexico gave its approval, and even if they did cross into Mexico, they couldn't find Apache camps except by pure luck in an area covering over fifty thousand square miles in some of the most rugged terrain on earth. General Crook managed to breach the walls of the Sierra Madre Apache fortress by gaining border crossing approval from the Mexican authorities and by using his fundamental belief, "It takes an Apache to catch an Apache," as a strategy to use Apache scouts for betraying camp locations or tracking "renegade" Apache to their hidden camps.

Geronimo's surrender to Generals Miles came as a result of a deception, more subtle than the Trojan Horse, but just as deadly to the Apache way of life. The surrender terms given the Chiricahua in general and Geronimo's band in particular were not kept. Beware Americans bearing gifts. Like the Trojans believing Greek sincerity through the gift of the great horse, the Chiricahua believed American sincerity in a commanding general's surrender terms made lies by their commanders and bureaucrats who cared little about the value of verbal commitments given by their generals facing reality on the ground and not policy made two thousand miles away.

Although the Greeks attempted to destroy the Trojans, they failed. The Romans claimed descent from the Trojan war hero, Aeneas, who escaped the destruction of Troy and whose culture and skill at war helped form the early Romans. In a kind of karmic justice, Rome conquered Greece in the centuries that followed. The Americans attempted to destroy the Apache culturally through American education of their young but failed. Individual commitment of Apache youth to their People as a tribe and tribal customs and beliefs was too strong even if their tribal customs and beliefs were only faint memories when the children returned to their parents.

An Apache Iliad tells the epic Apache story of the Apache war from 1877 to 1886. It was a time when the Chiricahua and Chihenne Apache at war with Americans and Mexicans gave no quarter and asked none as they killed everyone in their path, took what they needed when they needed it, and set the countryside ablaze with the fires made in their deadly raids. Those ten years of war and peace encompassed great victories, humbling defeats, and many sorrows. It was a time when the history for *An Apache Iliad* was recorded in American and Mexican military and civilian documents and Apache oral history as ten years of blood and fire punctuated by what amounted to two short times of peace.

Geronimo, after his final surrender in 1886, was one of the most photographed and interviewed First Nations people in America. Many details and events in his life as a prisoner of war have been recorded and photographed. But, his last ten years of Apache war with the Americans is a time dimly recorded with few photographs and little understood in the twenty-first century except through many twentieth century novels and movies that have portrayed Geronimo, and the Chiricahua and the Chihenne Apache, as little more than blood-thirsty savages or to the other extreme as Apache super patriots fighting for their land. But in truth, it was a time when the Chiricahua Apache under Naiche, a son of Cochise, Chihuahua, a protégé of Cochise, and Mangas, son of Mangas Coloradas, great Chief of the Chihenne people, and the Chihenne Apache under Victorio, Nana, and Loco struggled to accept the reservation life offered them by the overwhelmingly innumerable and devastatingly armed *Pindah Lickoyee* (White Eyed Enemies).

At first offered and accepting reservations on land they wanted and valued, the Chiricahua and Chihenne Apache were later herded by bureaucratic edict onto the San Carlos Reservation in eastern central Arizona. San Carlos was, to use Lieutenant Britton Davis's description, "forty acres of hell," and filled with long-time tribal enemies ready to spill each other's blood. It was only a matter of time before these people, used to freely roaming southwest plains, deserts, and mountains, escaped their forty acres of hell to live as they wanted, and the Pindah Lickoyee, determined to force them back, began a war that lasted ten years. For the famous Chiricahua war leader and *di-yen* (shaman or medicine man), Geronimo, the war was punctuated by two peace times that lasted a year or two, and two times when he agreed to surrender but changed his mind. To see this war through Geronimo's eyes and to understand it as an *Iliad*-like epic involving heroes on both sides of the war helps bring clarity to how an epic era in the southwest ended. Geronimo was neither hero nor villain. He was simply a man of his time.

W. Michael Farmer
Smithfield, Virginia
September 2020

DRAMATIS PERSONAE

Apache

Geronimo's Family

- **Goyale:** *Apache spelling of Geronimo's given Apache name*
- **Taklishim:** *Geronimo's father*
- **Juana:** *Spanish name for Geronimo's mother*
- **Alope:** *Geronimo's first wife and mother of his first three children all killed by Mexicans*
- **Chee-hash-kish:** *Wife to Geronimo, mother of*
  - **Chappo:** *Son of Geronimo*
  - **Dohn-say:** *Daughter of Geronimo*
- **She-gha:** *Wife to Geronimo*
- **Shtsha-she:** *Wife to Geronimo*
- **Zi-yeh:** *Wife to Geronimo and mother of*
  - **Fenton:** *Son of Geronimo*
  - **Eva:** *Daughter of Geronimo*
- **Ih-tedda:** *Wife to Geronimo, taken in 1885, divorced in 1889, and mother of*
  - **Lenna:** *Daughter of Geronimo*
  - **Robert:** *Son of Geronimo but unknown to him until 1904*
- **Thomas Dahkeya:** *Grandson of Geronimo, mother Dohnsay, father Mike Dahkeya*

- **Daklugie:** *Nephew of Geronimo, married Ramona Chihuahua at Fort Sill*
- **Jason Betzinez:** *Geronimo's cousin and an acolyte*
- **Fun:** *"Brother of Geronimo" (second cousin), Segundo in Naiche-Geronimo Band; After Aliso Creek, the Apache named him, "Yahechul," which means "Smoke Comes Out," because his rifle was always smoking*
- **Perico:** *"Brother of Geronimo" (second cousin), major warrior in Naiche-Geronimo Band*
- **Jelikinne:** *Father-in-law (Zi-yeh's father) to Geronimo*
- **Jasper Kanseah:** *Youngest Warrior in Naiche-Geronimo Band (orphaned nephew of Geronimo)*
- **Yanohsha:** *Major warrior in Naiche-Geronimo Band (Brother of She-gha, a wife of Geronimo) and training warrior for Kanseah*

Apache Leaders

- **Ah-dis:** *Nednhi Apache warrior who survived the murder of Nolgee by the Nakai-yes*
- **Ahnandia:** *Geronimo war leader and close friend of White Eye interpreter George Wratten*
- **Chihuahua:** *Sub-chief of Chokonen Apache, protégé of Cochise*
- **Gordo:** *Friend of Geronimo and famous war leader*
- **Juh:** *Chief of Nednhi Apache*
- **Kayihtah:** *Scout who talked to Geronimo about surrender*
- **Kaytennae:** Segundo *(number two) to Nana and later leader of the Chihenne Apache*
- **Loco:** *Peace chief of the Chihenne Apache*
- **Mangas:** *Chihenne chief, son of Mangas Coloradas, named Carl Mangas by the army*
- **Martine:** *Scout with Kayihtah who talked to Geronimo about surrender*
- **Naiche:** *Chief of Chokonen Apache, youngest son of Cochise*
- **Nana:** *Married to Geronimo's sister, Nah-dos-te, leader of the Chihenne Apache,* segundo *(number two) to Victorio*
- **Noch-ay-del-kinne:** *The prophet who brought the "Ghost Dance" to the Apache*

- **Nolgee:** *A segundo of Juh, murdered by federal Mexican soldiers during peace negotiations*
- **Victorio:** *Great war chief and leader of the Chihenne (aka Mimbreños)*

Anglos

- **John C. Fremont:** *Governor of Arizona Territory 1878–1881*
- **General George Crook:** *Commander of Department of Arizona and later Department of New Mexico. Directed the war against the Chiricahua from 1871–1875 and 1882–1886. Known to the Apache as* Nant'an Lpah *(Gray Leader).*
- **General Oliver Otis (One Arm) Howard:** *Negotiator of the Cochise peace and reservation in 1872.*
- **General Nelson Appleton Miles:** *Replaced General Crook in 1886 and made surrender terms to the Chiricahua that were never kept.*
- **General August V. Kautz:** *Commander of Department of Arizona from 1875–1878*
- **General Orlando Bolivar Willcox:** *Commander of Department of New Mexico from 1878–1882*
- **General David Sloan Stanley:** *Commander of Department of Texas from 1884–1892*
- **Colonel Edward Hatch:** *New Mexico Army Department commander, 1880*
- **Colonel Eugene A. Carr:** *Commander at Fort Apache who arrested Noch-ay-del-kinne in 1881*
- **Colonel Luther Bradley:** *Commander the District of New Mexico, 1885*
- **Lieutenant Colonel George A. Forsyth:** *Commander of Cavalry Detail Chasing Chihenne People after leaving San Carlos in 1882.*
- **Major Albert P. Morrow:** *Commander Ninth Cavalry, 1880*
- **Captain Harry L. Haskell:** *Emissary from Gen. Willcox to Juh and Geronimo*
- **Captain Emmett Crawford:** *Army officer acting as San Carlos Agent in 1883, 1884 and as a field commander during the last Geronimo campaign.*
- **Captain Adna R. Chaffee:** *Army officer acting as San Carlos Agent in July 1879–July 1880.*
- **Lieutenant Marion P. Maus:** *Second in command to Captain Crawford,*

who after Crawford's murder by Mexican paramilitary Tarahumara negotiated Geronimo's March 1886 meeting with General Crook.

- **Lieutenant Charles B. Gatewood:** *Chief of White Mountain Apache scouts. Carried General Miles surrender terms to Geronimo in 1886.*

- **Lieutenant John Anthony Rucker:** *Led the surprise raid on Geronimo's camp in southwestern New Mexico in January 1877 that drove Geronimo to lead his band to Ojo Caliente where he was given support by Victorio and issued supplies by the government until arrested by Clum.*

- **John Clum:** *San Carlos Agent 1874–1877. Captured Geronimo by a deceit. Known to the San Carlos Reservation Apache as* Nant'an Be-tun-niki-yeh *(High Forehead Leader)*

- **Clay Beauford:** *John Clum's Chief of Apache Police*

- **Lyman Hart:** *San Carlos Agent 1877–1879. Freed Geronimo and his war leaders from the guardhouse upon arrival at San Carlos in 1877*

- **Joseph C. Tiffany:** *Agent at San Carlos 1880–1882*

- **George Wratten:** *Trusted interpreter for Apache*

- **Tom Jeffords:** *Former Agent to Cochise and Advisor to Commanders of New Mexico*

Mexicans

- **Luis Terrazas:** *Governor of Chihuahua 1878*

- **Francisco Prieto:** *Mexican Council at Tucson, 1878*

- **Colonel Joaquin Terrazas:** *Chihuahuan Army Commander who tried to trap and execute Juh.*

- **Colonel Lorenzo García:** *Chihuahuan Army Commander who led the fight at Aliso Creek*

- **Major Mauricio Corredor:** *Tarahumara Indian, a major in the Mexican National Guard who claimed to have killed Victorio and was in charge of the attack that killed Captain Crawford in January 1886.*

- **Juan Mata Ortiz:** *Commander of the Chihuahuan Army Galeana Garrison, famed Indian fighter and segundo to Colonel Joaquin Terrazas when Victorio's band was destroyed. Killed in the Chocolate Pass ambush led by Juh.*

APACHE & SPANISH WORDS AND PHRASES

- *Alcalde:* mayor (Spanish)
- *Ayúdame:* help me (Spanish)
- *Bosque:* forest (Spanish)
- *Casa:* house (Spanish)
- *Cena:* supper (Spanish)
- *Commandante:* commander (Spanish)
- *Comida: lunch (Spanish)*
- *Comprende:* understand (Spanish)
- *Cortinas:* drapes (Spanish)
- *Dahndáh:* start
- *Desayuno:* breakfast (Spanish)
- *Dispare:* shoot (Spanish)
- *Di-yen:* medicine woman or man
- *Dueña:* guardian (female) (Spanish)
- *Enjuh:* good
- *Espere:* hold on (Spanish)
- *Googé:* whip-poor-will
- *Habla Espanol?:* Do you speak Spanish? (Spanish)
- *Hacendado:* wealthy landowner (Spanish)
- *Hija:* daughter (Spanish)
- *Iyah:* mesquite bean pods
- *El Jefe:* the chief or leader (Spanish)

- *Llano:* dry prairie (Spanish)
- *Mujer:* woman (Spanish)
- *Mujercita:* little woman (Spanish)
- *Nakai-yes:* Mexicans
- *Nakai-yi:* Mexican
- *Nant'an:* big chief
- *Nish'ii':* I see you
- *Nkáh:* We will go
- *Nt-ah:* Wait
- *Pindah-lickoyee:* White-eyed enemies
- *Pesh:* iron
- *Por favor:* please (Spanish)
- *Puta pequeña:* little whore (Spanish)
- *Reata:* thin rawhide rope (Spanish)
- *Río Bavispe:* Bavispe River (Spanish)
- *Río Dolores:* Dolores River (Spanish)
- *Río Grande:* Great River (Spanish)
- *Río Altar:* Altar River (Spanish)
- *Río Magdalena:* Magdalena River (Spanish)
- *Río San Miguel:* San Miguel River (Spanish)
- *Sí, muy bien, gracias:* Yes, very well, thank you (Spanish)
- *Tsach:* cradleboard
- *Teniente:* lieutenant (Spanish)

Reckoning of Time & Seasons

- *Harvest:* used in the context of time, means a year
- *Handwidth (against the sky):* about an hour
- *Season of Little Eagles:* early spring
- *Season of Many Leaves:* late spring, early summer
- *Season of Large Leaves:* midsummer
- *Season of Large Fruit:* late summer, early fall
- *Season of Earth is Reddish Brown:* late fall
- *Season of Ghost Face:* lifeless winter
- *Time of Shortest Shadows:* noon

PROLOGUE

FROM THE TIME they were off their *tsach* (cradleboard) Apache children of both sexes, already trained to be silent, learned to hide where there was no place to hide, to hunt where game was scarce, to pray to the great god Ussen who filled their lives with supernatural Power (power is capitalized to indicate supernatural power), to use weapons such as knives, slings, bows and arrows, and lances without hesitation, and every day, without exception, to survive in a harsh, unforgiving land where every living thing could be deadly, where there was little water, and where one mistake on any account could mean death. By the time they were eight or nine, boys and girls once playmates and close friends no longer trained together. The girls learned family life skills from their older sisters, mothers, and aunts, and the boys learned hunting, raiding, and making war with their older brothers, fathers, and uncles.

Every day was a training day for both boys and girls to increase stamina and fitness. Boys learned to run miles across scalding hot deserts while holding water in their mouths (forcing them to breathe through their noses). If they didn't run fast enough, then an older man ran behind them with a switch. As the seasons changed and slicks of ice formed overnight on still water in the bends of nearby streams, they wrestled in snow, and plunged into the icy water and swam before racing nearly naked to gather a fire's warmth before doing it all over again and again.

Girls also learned to run long distances, trained with weapons (women were camp defenders when the men were gone), and grew in strength carrying heavy burdens over long distances as their People escaped enemies, roamed the mountains and deserts, and gathered food such as the heavy bulbs of mescal, and baskets filled with nuts, berries, and other desert plants.

Apache boys and girls learned to suffer any burden, bear any pain, and have the patience to hunt and to overcome their enemies.

By the time pubescent girls had their womanhood ceremony where they became marriageable women, the boys were nearing the age for their warrior novitiate when they became acolytes to support proven warriors on their raids for livestock and supplies from Anglos, Mexicans, and farming Indians. Like European pages in service to knights in the Middle Ages, the acolytes supported the warriors by taking care of camp duties like cooking, caring for livestock, and carrying supplies and weapons taken in raids. Successful participation with the warriors in four different raids yielded invitations to become warriors and thus marriageable men, and to ride in raids that helped yield enough wealth to pay a woman's parents a suitable bride gift and to establish a family. It was into this culture that Goyale (Geronimo's Apache name and spelling and its meaning are disputed—some say his name was Goyahkla, meaning "one who yawns," others his name Goyale probably meaning "shrewd, intelligent, clever") was born.[1]

By the time he was fourteen, Goyale was supporting his widowed mother, Juana. At seventeen, Goyale, who had completed his novitiate and been recognized as a warrior, loved and wanted the beautiful Bedonkohe Apache woman, Alope, for his wife. The bride gift her father asked for her was beyond reason for a beginning warrior—many ponies—only something an older much more experienced warrior, who her father would want for a son-in-law, might provide. Without a word, Goyale left her father's lodge after learning the bride gift price. He returned a few days later with many ponies. As her father stared in disbelief, Alope left his lodge, swung up behind Goyale and rode away with him as his wife.[2] In the ten years that followed, Alope bore Goyale three children, and through tactical skill and bravery he became a recognized war leader under the great Chihenne (also known as Mimbreño) chief, the most powerful and commanding Apache leader of his time, Mangas Coloradas (Red Sleeves).

Around 1850, Goyale took his family, now with three children under age ten, Alope, and his mother, on a trading trip with Mangas Coloradas and other warriors and families to a village in northern Chihuahua, Mexico. The Apache called the village Kas-ki-yeh (probably Janos). The Mexicans at Kas-ki-yeh and Mangas Coloradas had an understanding that allowed him to raid in Sonora and trade plunder in Kas-ki-yeh. One day while the men were off trading in Kas-ki-yeh, soldiers came from Sonora and destroyed the Apache camp then occupied with old ones, women, and children. The soldiers slaughtered Alope, Goyale and Alope's children, and his mother, leaving them in a blackening pool of blood. The destruction of his family left Goyale stunned and with an unquenchable thirst for revenge against Mexicans that lasted a lifetime.[3,4]

Mangas Coloradas didn't have the men or weapons to immediately retaliate against the Mexicans who had killed the old men and women and children in the camp. He led a retreat north back across the border and took a year to prepare for blood revenge. During this time, Ussen gave Goyale his first gift of supernatural Power—guns couldn't kill him and Ussen would guide his arrows. As Mangas prepared his revenge raid, Goyale passed among the bands recruiting even distant relatives such as Cochise to help him take the revenge Mangas Coloradas was planning.

The Mangas Coloradas's revenge raid began when the Apache advanced in three columns toward Arizpe, about seventy miles south of the border at Naco in Sonora, Mexico. The Apache somehow knew the soldiers who had attacked their camp the year before were stationed there. The first column of Apache were Chihenne led by Mangas Coloradas, the second column, Chokonen led by Cochise, and the third column, Nednhis led by Juh. At Arizpe, Goyale, because he had lost his entire family in the Mexican camp, was given the honor of directing the fight. It was bows and arrows, lances, and slings against rifles. Many Apache were killed, but after a two-hour battle, they held the field littered with Mexican dead. It was here that legend says the Apache Goyale became known, even to his own people, as Geronimo. His new name was a remembrance of the soldiers fighting against the ferocious attack of the Apache calling on Saint Jerome to save them.[5]

In the years that followed, Geronimo's reputation and supernatural Power grew. He married Chee-hash-kish, a Bedonkohe girl, who later gave him a son, Chappo, and a daughter, Dohn-say. He also soon took a second wife, Nana-tha-thtith, who had one child. Having more than one wife and children was a sure sign that Geronimo was growing in power and wealth. Cochise had his "Cut-Through-the-Tent" confrontation with American army Lieutenant Bascom in 1861, and the army murdered Mangas Coloradas in 1862. Geronimo often rode with Cochise in his ten-year war with the Americans. Some believe that when Cochise negotiated his peace terms and reservation location with General Oliver Otis (One Arm) Howard, Geronimo served as an interpreter translating Apache to Spanish for the treaty and during the talks developed a deep respect and like for General Howard as a man of his word.

Cochise let Geronimo and Juh use a section of the reservation as their own. One side of their section was on the border, which allowed them to enter Mexico and raid as they pleased without interference from American soldiers who wouldn't come on the reservation without a request from the agent. True to their promise to General Howard, Geronimo and Juh left American settlers alone. Geronimo's increasing supernatural Powers allowed him to see the future and events that happened at great distances. He was also said to be gifted with the Power to detect the direction from which enemies came, and the Power to heal certain illnesses.[6]

By the beginning of An Apache Iliad, Geronimo was about fifty-four, a well-known war leader, a *segundo* (number two) to the great chiefs like Cochise and Juh, and a *di-yen*, a medicine man or shaman, of great Power, but never a chief as many White Eyes (even the man who wrote his autobiography, S. M. Barrett) have since called him.[7] He had visions that reliably told his chiefs and leaders when and where they would be attacked or what would happen to someone experiencing his curing ceremonies. He often used brilliant tactical strategies in raids and war. He was feared for his raids in Mexico that killed many, and against farming Indians in the United States who lost much property. There were few who did not know him and many did not like and feared him, but all respected him.

AN
APACHE ILIAD

★ ★ ★

TRUE STORIES OF GERONIMO'S WAR
AND RESERVATION LIFE 1877—1886

Geronimo, 1884. Photograph by Frank Randall,
courtesy of the National Archives

PART ONE: CAPTURED

Geronimo surrendered to the White Eyes three times. He was taken by force of arms (captured) once and that by a clever deception employed by his captor, San Carlos Indian Agent, John Clum. Geronimo was captured in the camp of the great Chihenne chief, Victorio, and taken in leg irons and chains with three of his war leaders (Fatty, Ponce, and Jatu (son or son-in-law of Nana)) to the San Carlos guardhouse.[1] Clum told him that he could expect the immediate arrival of the Tucson sheriff, who would take them to Tucson to dance on air choking at the end of a rope while White Eyes watched and laughed.[2] Through a seemingly miraculous series of events (Geronimo later claimed they were the result of his prayers to Ussen), Geronimo and his war leaders were released from the San Carlos guardhouse after a three month stay to rejoin their families and live peacefully at San Carlos. His time in the guardhouse made Geronimo paranoid, perhaps justifiably so, about anything the White Eye agents told him and was a major reason behind his two escapes from San Carlos and one from Fort Apache. Part One of An Apache Iliad tells the story of Geronimo's only capture and the beginning of his last ten years of war with the Pindah-Lickoyee, the White Eyed Enemies.

ONE

John Clum, Geronimo's Only Capturer

ULYSSES S. GRANT was elected President of the United States in 1868. Prior to and after Grant's election, government investigation had shown appalling and corrupt treatment of Indians who had been forced onto reservations and practically starved to death by politically appointed agents in the Bureau of Indian Affairs. The agents often stole a large portion of the rations due the Indians, this in order to line their pockets from sales on the black market. To stop this bureaucratic plundering, President Grant developed his Peace Policy. The Peace Policy gave responsibility for Indian agent appointments to different protestant church denominations thereby taking reservation management out of the hands of the Bureau of Indian Affairs. Tribe assignments were drawn in a lottery. The Dutch Reformed Church (German Presbyterians) "won" the Apache. The San Carlos Apache Reservation, one of the most dangerous in the west, was in their portfolio. With fear and trembling the church picked a young church member, John Clum, as the San Carlos agent. A native New Yorker, who had been in the west since the fall of 1871, collecting weather data for the Meteorological Service of the U.S. Army Signal Corps in New Mexico, he was three months shy of twenty-three and had virtually no experience with First Nations people. Clum arrived at San Carlos August 8, six months after his appointment on February 27, 1874.[1]

Clum was shorter in stature than many of his Apache charges, but large in ego and drive. He was prematurely bald with a fringe of hair hanging over his ears and on the back of his head. He made himself look older by growing a big mustache soon after he arrived at San Carlos. Once at San Carlos, he quickly demonstrated he was an innovative and competent administrator. He had unbounded honesty, a

1877 Photograph of John Clum posing with members of his Apache police.
Photograph by Henry Buehman, courtesy of the Arizona Historical Society.

conscience, iron nerves, and a desire to observe and understand Apache culture. The Indian Ring, contractors and merchants who most profited from the reservation and black-market sales of government supplies stolen from the Indians, and the army soon discovered Clum couldn't be manipulated or bullied. They relentlessly attacked Clum from every side. To their fury and embarrassment, they learned that Clum was also an astute politician who had the wits and insight to know when and where to strike in the bureaucracy to get his way.

When Clum arrived at San Carlos, the reservation had seven hundred Apache who regularly drew rations. The army was still in full control of the reservation and defiantly refused to let any agent appointed through the Bureau of Indian Affairs have responsibility for the reservation. After three weeks of burning up the telegraph wires with wrangling messages between all levels of government and Clum making some fast and intelligent arguments of his own, word finally came from Washington that Clum was to have full responsibility for San Carlos Reservation, and the army garrison was forced to accept its reduced role of keeping the peace and assisting in the capture of renegades.[2]

Clum went to work ensuring that the Apache got the rations they were due. He showed them how to keep sickness away by keeping their camps and wickiups clean and free of garbage. He told them that he trusted them to manage their own affairs, helped them establish a law court with their own judges, and served as their chief judge. He began an Apache police force with four men he asked the chiefs to pick for him. Most importantly, he put the once idle Apache to work.

The Apache were an active people who needed to be kept busy. He used a large portion of his budget to start a major building program for reservation support facilities and hired the Apache as construction workers and craftsmen. The work fulfilled the Apache's need for activity, rewarded them with pay, and greatly improved the physical facilities at San Carlos. The Apache began calling him *Nant'an Be-tun-niki-yeh* (High Forehead Leader) and treated him with the same respect they showed their own leaders.

By showing he cared for and respected the Apache, he was able to accomplish management feats other agents had thought impossible. For example, Clum talked the Apache into turning in their guns after he promised they could check them out whenever they wanted to go hunting. It didn't take long for him to see trouble like quarreling, fighting, even killing resulted from the brewing and drinking "gray water" or a corn beer, they called *tulapai* (the White Eyes called it *tizwin*). He banned *tulapai* brewing and drinking outright and for the most part made the rule stick.[3]

When Clum had first traveled to the San Carlos Agency on his way from Tucson he stopped overnight at Fort Grant where he met the Apache chief Eskiminzin being kept there in chains to ensure he didn't escape confinement. Clum had a long and serious talk with him and promised he would do what he could to get the chief returned to San Carlos. It was not long before Eskiminzin returned to San Carlos where he developed a strong, supportive friendship with Clum.

Clum enlarged his police force into an elite and highly loyal strike force of several dozen men who were trained by Clum's clerk and general assistant, a retired cavalry sergeant named Martin Sweeney. Within two months, Clum and Sergeant Sweeney had San Carlos functioning, despite occasional bumps, smoothly in a way Washington bureaucrats, the Indian Ring, and the army would not have believed possible before his arrival.

The dispute with the army over who had final authority at San Carlos Reservation continued to fester, especially when Clum stood up for the Apache when they were unjustly harassed by the army. The Apache saw him take their side and their loyalty to him increased even more. In the days that followed, Clum would need this loyalty when bureaucrats in Washington decided to implement a "consolidation policy."

Ignorant bureaucrats in the Department of Indian Affairs assumed that San Carlos was a fine place to live, that all Apache got along well between bands, and that their individual band reservations covered far more land than they needed, this when they had been used to roaming over hundreds of miles in a season. Under these assumptions, the bureaucrats decided that consolidation of several Apache reservations into a single large one would save the government a lot of money and give arriving settlers land they wanted.

The consolidation policy was a blunder of major proportions. It failed to recognize Apache cultural divisions and that some bands, despite both being Apache, were deadly enemies. Forcing the unfriendly bands to live elbow-to-elbow on the hot, dusty gravel flats where deadly snakes and mosquito borne diseases, malaria and yellow fever were rampant, contributed to every subsequent reservation outbreak and was a major reason why the Chiricahua left with Geronimo in his escapes from the reservation. Clum welcomed the new bands forced to move to San Carlos as part of his "happy family," ignoring the fact that many who refused to go to San Carlos slipped away and roamed the countryside as "renegades."

In March 1875, General Crook, arguably one of the best Indian fighters the army had, was transferred to fight the northern plains tribes led by Sitting Bull, Crazy Horse, Red Cloud, Gall, and many other famous warriors and chiefs. In Crook's stead, came General August V. Kautz and General Orlando Bolivar Willcox. General Crook, who had put many of the Apache on their separate reservations in the first place, was strongly opposed to the idea of a consolidation policy but was too far away fighting the plains tribes to effectively fight against the Washington bureaucrats and their politics pushing it. Captain John Bourke, Crook's long-time aide, later wrote, "It was an outrageous proceeding, one for which I would still blush, had I not long since gotten over blushing for anything the United States Government did in Indian Matters."[4]

The first tribes to be moved to San Carlos were some western Arizona Apache and non-Apache tribes who were in fact bitter enemies. The army began herding 1,476 of these people toward San Carlos, February 27, 1875. Clum received 1,361. Some of the missing 115 could be accounted for, but most had disappeared into their old hideouts. The White Mountain and Coyotero Apache at Fort Apache Reservation sixty miles north of San Carlos were collected next by Clum who rode up to Fort Apache "on a big white horse" showing a paper from Washington and talked those tribes into moving. A few scouts and their families stayed behind. Clum now had under his supervision forty-two hundred Indians of unrelated tribes, many hostile to each other.

The next band to be moved was the Chokonen Chiricahua on the Cochise reservation under agent Tom Jeffords. Clum was instructed by his Washington superiors to carry out the transfer.

An Apache

Painting by Frederic Remington, 1891.

TWO

Geronimo and Juh Escape
the Chokonen Chiricahua Reservation

IN 1872, GENERAL Oliver Otis Howard agreed with Cochise, chief of the Chokonen band of Apache, on his choice for the site of the Chokonen Chiricahua reservation and for its agent, Tom Jeffords, a man Cochise trusted. Although Apache didn't normally have hereditary chieftains, Cochise groomed his first-born son, Taza, to take over when he, Cochise, rode the ghost pony. Taza's younger brother, Naiche, who enjoyed dancing, women, drinking, and fighting, was not groomed to be a chief. Cochise wanted Naiche to support his brother, not compete with him. Two years after the reservation began, Cochise died in 1874, but not before making Taza and Naiche promise to avoid, if at all possible, any war with the White Eyes.

With the passing of Cochise, the Chokonen chose twenty-one-year-old Taza to become their chief, and he competently led them. Naiche was seventeen. Skinya, one of Cochise's leading warriors, contested Taza as chief, saying he was too young and inexperienced to lead the band. Skinya was supported by his brother, Pionsenay, and about a dozen followers in this view and a factional dispute broke out. Skinya and his followers left the majority of the band to live in their own camp in the Dragoon Mountains. Taza and the rest of the Chokonen camped near the Sulphur Springs agency run by Jeffords.

On June 4, 1876, Clum arrived at the agency with fifty-four of his armed Apache police, shadowed by a military force supplied by General Kautz that was ready to lend support should trouble break out. That day, sometime before Clum arrived, Skinya and his followers went to the Sulphur Springs camp to argue for Taza's camp to reject Taza as chief and to follow him. A firefight ensued. Naiche shot Skinya and killed him. Taza wounded Pionsenay, and six other members of the band were killed. That was the end of anyone contesting Taza's leadership.[1]

The next day, Clum met with Taza and Naiche at the Sulphur Springs agency. They remembered the promise they had made to Cochise, and Clum (with cavalry nearby) convinced them to move the Chokonen to San Carlos. Jeffords informed Clum that another band under Geronimo, Juh, and a warrior named Nolgee also lived on the reservation. They had been included in General Howard's settlement and wanted to meet with Clum. The meeting was held two or three days later on June 7 or 8 at the agency. Clum assumed that Geronimo was the leader because he was spokesmen. Juh, chief for the Nednhi band of Apache, stuttered badly when he was excited. He had asked Geronimo, his *segundo* (number two), who spoke excellent Spanish, to speak for them.

After initial talks, Geronimo told Clum that they were willing to go to San Carlos, but that their people were about twenty miles away. He asked permission to bring them in and Clum agreed but sent some of his police to shadow them when they returned to their camp. The shadow followers later reported to Clum, that upon returning to their camp, Geronimo and Juh gave brief orders to kill the camps' dogs (to keep them from barking), break camp, and run for Mexico. By the time the Apache police reported this back to Clum, it was too late to even think about stopping the Juh-Geronimo band from slipping across the border.[2]

Once in Mexico, Juh and Nolgee camped in their Sierra Madre strongholds. Six weeks later, on July 21, 1876, Geronimo with about forty followers appeared at the Ojo Caliente (also known as Hot Springs) Reservation in west central New Mexico. He had many relatives there and probably wanted to relocate from Mexico where fighting between political factions in both Sonora and Chihuahua made the prospects dim for some kind of peace deal, which Juh wanted, with the Mexicans in either state.

Ojo Caliente was the reservation for the Chihenne Apache band led by the famous chiefs Victorio and Loco. Old, arthritic Nana was Victorio's *segundo* and his son-in-law. Loco, whose left eye drooped from being scarred defending himself with only a knife against a bear, was later to be known as the Chihenne peace chief. Victorio was the war chief and primary Chihenne leader.

Although the agent at Ojo Caliente had been instructed to issue rations to refugees (members of Gordo's and Chato's bands) from the Chiricahua reservation after the Skinya fight, Geronimo stayed a short time at Ojo Caliente, then returned to Mexico and met with Juh. He was unable to convince Juh to move to the Chihenne reservation. Juh and Victorio were not enemies, but neither liked the other. Juh believed Victorio was too impulsive and would start a needless war. Victorio thought Juh was too slow to act when quick action was needed.

Juh and Geronimo decided to try to make a peace deal for their 209 followers with the town of Moctezuma on the Sonora River. They enlisted the services of the infamous "White Apache," Zebina N. Streeter, to open negotiations with Moctezuma's prefect. While Streeter was negotiating, Geronimo and a chief, Nat-cul-bey-e (also known as José María Elías) leading fifty-three people, split with Juh and sent peace feelers to the towns of Bavispe on the north flowing fork of the Río Bavispe on the western side of the Sierra Madre and to Janos on the eastern side.

The governor of Sonora, General Mariscal, instructed the prefect of Moctezuma to make a deal with the Apache under the conditions that they live within one league of any of five military presidios scattered throughout the state, that they surrender their arms, that they be counted daily, that they could not leave the area without permission from an agent who was assigned them, and that they had to live in peace with Mexicans and all other inhabitants of Sonora and not enter another country for the purpose of raiding. In return for satisfying these conditions, the governor agreed to provide the Apache food and clothing, and if they wanted to grow crops, he would protect them against all attacks.

Streeter met with Colonel Elías, the military commander of the northern presidios, who told him that he would offer the Apache a reservation at either Santa Cruz or Bacoachi and would allow them eight days to come in. The Apache never showed. Streeter then went to Ures and then Guaymas where he met with Governor Mariscal in December.

Unknown to Streeter, Juh's patience with the peace negotiations had worn thin. Juh went south up into the high country along the Río Aros where Mexican soldiers were reluctant to go. In early November, Juh's warriors had killed ten and wounded four people on a raid in the Sonoran district of Sahuaripa. In mid-November, a Mexican patrol surprised Juh's camp at Chamada overlooking the Río Aros, killed two Apache, and recovered a large amount of plunder and seven animals. Even so, Governor Mariscal told Streeter he would still make a treaty if Juh complied with the terms given the prefect of Moctezuma. Streeter returned to Juh's camp with the offer, but Juh decided to reject it.[3]

Geronimo left Juh in November and joined the warrior Esquine camped in southwestern New Mexico. While camped with Esquine, Geronimo with several Bedonkohe Apache decided to raid in southern Arizona. On December 2, 1876, General Kautz was notified that Indians had taken twenty-one horses from a ranch near camp Crittenden. Kautz forwarded the report to Fort Bowie. Second Lieutenant John Anthony Rucker with ten troopers and Company C of thirty-four Pinal Apache scouts, whose reservation home was San Carlos but were stationed at Fort Bowie, were sent after the raiders on December 11, 1876. Rucker's scouts had found the raider's trail by December 16. Geronimo led Rucker north and then doubled back south before Rucker had to return to Fort Bowie and resupply on December 30.

Geronimo made the bad assumption that Rucker had abandoned his pursuit, but Rucker, still following the Apache trail, left Fort Bowie on January 4, 1877. Rucker's scouts found the raider's rancheria on January 8 near the northern part of the Animas Mountains in southwestern New Mexico. They attacked the rancheria at daybreak the following morning. The scouts had to charge the rancheria three times before they drove the Chiricahua away and captured a nephew of Geronimo, who was about five years old. Geronimo described this event in his autobiography saying that "United States troops surprised and attacked our camp. They killed seven children, five women, and four warriors, captured all our supplies, blankets, horses, and clothing, and destroyed our tipis. We had nothing left. Winter was beginning, and it was the coldest winter I ever knew. After the soldiers left, I took three warriors and trailed them back to San Carlos."[4]

THREE

Geronimo Camps with Victorio at Ojo Caliente

IN HIS AUTOBIOGRAPHY, Geronimo said that he heard Victorio was holding a council with the white men near Hot Springs (Ojo Caliente). "We easily found Victorio and his band, and they gave us supplies for the winter. We had not the least trouble with Mexicans, white men, or Indians."[1] Geronimo's brother-in-law, Nana, the family of Jason Betzinez (his father, Nonithian, was Geronimo's first cousin) and friends and relatives welcomed them and shared their belongings and provisions to provide sanctuary for him and his followers.

The Chihenne lived in peace with their neighbors, but the arrival of Geronimo and the Chiricahua in 1877 changed everything. Nana and Loco tried to warn Victorio that the newcomers "will get us in trouble," but Victorio shrugged them off saying, "These people are not bothering us."[2]

GENERAL KAUTZ LEARNED hostile Chiricahua had sought shelter at Ojo Caliente. He wrote Agent Davis there for information about them. Davis, who had run out of patience with the surly, uncooperative Apache had left the agency, leaving Acting Agent Walter Whitney to take over temporarily. Whitney answered Kautz's request for information, writing that 250 Chiricahua had come into Ojo Caliente, but that 100 were then present. Receiving Whitney's letter, General Kautz sent Lieutenant Austin Henely to Ojo Caliente to investigate the situation.

Henely met with Agent Whitney on March 16, 1877, at agency headquarters. After the meeting, he recognized Geronimo, who he knew from his days at Fort Bowie, "indignant because he could not draw rations for the time he was out."

Geronimo, Gordo, Chato, and Ponce had just returned to the reservation with a herd of a hundred stolen horses. Henely believed that about thirty-five Chiricahua (Bedonkohe and Chokonen) and about fifteen Chihenne had formed the raid in southern Arizona that had killed nine men in February. He reported this to General Kautz who wired his report to Governor Safford. The governor wired Edward P. Smith, the commissioner of Indian Affairs in Washington, included Henely's letter to Kautz, claimed that the agent at Ojo Caliente had lost control of the reservation, and that all Indians should be removed to San Carlos or a new agent appointed who could control them.

Commissioner Smith, losing patience with the turmoil at Ojo Caliente, telegraphed Agent Clum at San Carlos on March 20, 1877. Smith's instructions to Clum said, "If practicable, take Indian Police and arrest renegade Chiricahua at Southern Apache Agency. Seize stolen horses in their possession; restore the property to rightful owners; remove renegades to San Carlos and hold them in confinement for murder and robbery. Call on military for aid if needed."[3]

Clum was delighted to accept the commissioner's directive. Although Smith referred only to taking renegade Chiricahua to San Carlos, Clum believed he could convince Indian officials in Washington that it might be best to extend the orders to move the Chihenne to San Carlos as well. He knew Washington officials would give him the jurisdiction he needed without bothering to ask the Apache how they felt. Clum exalted in the idea that, with the Chihenne also at San Carlos, he would have all the Apache west of the Río Grande under his control at San Carlos.

It took Clum about a month to prepare for his operations at Ojo Caliente. During this time, he and General Kautz were in a bitter feud over how the other carried out their duties. Clum decided to cooperate with the army in New Mexico since General John Pope, commander of the Department of the Missouri, had ordered his command to assist in arresting Geronimo. Clum arrived mid-April at Fort Bayard, ten miles east of Silver City, New Mexico, with one hundred Apache Police. He sent a message to Major James Franklin Wade who was to lead three companies of cavalry and meet him on April 21, 1877, at Ojo Caliente. Clum had learned from a "dependable" scout that Geronimo with eighty to one hundred followers had received rations on April 14. By Agent Whitney's account, he had provided rations for 599 Apache at Ojo Caliente. On April 15, Clum wired Commissioner Smith requesting authorization to expand his mission. He wrote, I advise movement of all to San Carlos. On April 17, Smith approved Clum's suggestion if the military authorities concurred. Clum never bothered to discuss the move with the military.

Three Apache. 1903 Photograph by Edward Curtis,
courtesy of the National Archives.

Clum arrived with his police about twenty miles west of Ojo Caliente and went into camp at noon, April 20, 1877. Clum sent a note to Whitney asking how many how Apache were at Ojo Caliente and his opinion on removal of them all to San Carlos. Whitney answered that they would not be happy to leave but that they would probably go without a fight and that some would leave before being taken to San Carlos. Clum decided to take his twenty-two mounted police and go on to the agency, and to let the remaining seventy-eight, who had come on foot, rest until the next day.

FOUR

Geronimo Captured For the First and Only Time

SAN CARLOS AGENT John Clum arrived at Ojo Caliente in the early evening of April 20. A telegram awaited him saying the cavalry couldn't arrive until April 22. Clum knew if he delayed making any arrests, the "renegades" (Geronimo and his war leaders) would leave. He reasoned that the renegades might have seen only twenty-two policemen and sent word to his chief of police, Clay Beauford, camped twenty miles away that the rest of the policemen needed to come up that night. Beauford and his men arrived about 4:00 a.m. on the morning of April 21.

The adobe agency buildings at San Carlos were arranged in an "L" shape. The Agency building, on the west edge of the parade ground, faced east. On the south side was a large commissary building. On the north and east sides were deep ravines.[1] Clum had Beauford conceal his men in the commissary building and at sunrise sent a messenger to Geronimo's camp about three miles away inviting him and his war leaders in for a talk. Geronimo thought it was a friendly invitation, and since it was ration day, he came in that morning shortly after sunrise with about fifty men, women, and children.[2]

Clum with a rifle in the crook of his arm and Beauford standing behind his shoulder were on the agency porch facing the parade ground as Geronimo and his warriors, fully armed, with Ponce and five or six war leaders in front, gathered to hear what Clum had to say. Three of Clum's policemen were spaced out on his left to the north of the agency porch and three to the south toward the commissary building.

Clum addressed all the warriors, but mainly directed his charges at Geronimo. He accused them of failing to come in as Geronimo and Juh had promised in June

Agent John Clum with his Apache Police ca. 1876. Merejildo Grijalva, the bearded man
standing to the left and once captive to the Apache served as Clum's interpreter.
Photograph courtesy of the National Archives/Commons Wikimedia.

of the previous year when Taza and Naiche had agreed to move to San Carlos and
of killing men and stealing cattle in violation of the agreement Geronimo and
Cochise had made with General Howard to create the Chiricahua Reservation.
Now, Clum said, he had come to bring them in.

Geronimo grimly shook his head. "We are not going to San Carlos with you,
and unless you are very careful, you and your Apache police will not go back to San
Carlos either. Your bodies will stay here at Ojo Caliente to make food for coyotes."[3]

At that, Clum gave a prearranged signal. The commissary doors burst open
and the hidden policemen came out running single file, rifles at the ready to
form a line along the south side of the parade ground. Geronimo, his war leaders, and warriors were caught in potential cross fire. A few stragglers started to
move away but were stopped by Beauford's raised rifle. A woman ran from the
watching crowd and jumped on Beauford throwing her arms around his neck
and shoulders and pulled down his rifle. He threw her off, and by the time he
raised his rifle again, all the policemen with their rifles aimed and ready were in
place ready to stop any attempt to escape.

Clum saw Geronimo's thumb creeping toward the hammer of his rifle, but with the policemen in place, it moved back, and Clum realized he had control of the situation. He gave his own rifle to one of the policemen standing near him and ordered Geronimo and his leaders to lay their rifles on the ground. They shuffled their feet and made no move to obey. Clum signaled to Beauford who aimed his rifle directly at Geronimo. Then Clum stepped off the agency porch, walked to Geronimo, and jerked the rifle out of his hands. Clum in later years said that for the rest of his life he never forgot the look of concentrated hatred in Geronimo's face. Beauford then came and snatched the rifles out of their leaders' hands and ordered their warriors to lay their rifles on the ground, which they slowly did. Clum then asked Geronimo and his war leaders to come up on the porch for a conference, and the main group, including men, women, and children, dispersed over the parade ground.

The leaders squatted on the porch facing Clum who had just berated Geronimo for leaving the year before. He informed them they were prisoners and ordered them to the guardhouse. Geronimo and the war leaders jumped to their feet as did most of the warriors in front watching the porch. Geronimo's hand slowly reached for the knife in his belt. Clum could see the indecision in his eyes whether to surrender or draw the knife and die fighting. When he hesitated, Rip, one of the policemen, jumped forward and snatched the knife from Geronimo's belt while the other policemen cocked their rifles as they pointed them at the leaders on the porch. Geronimo, eyes flashing, looked around in defiance at his captors. But then he relaxed and said, *"Enjuh"* (All right).

Clum had forgotten that the agency had no guardhouse. He decided to use the corral and ordered Geronimo and the leaders marched to the blacksmith shop while their followers watched. Geronimo watched impassively while the irons were being heated. Was he expecting to be tortured? When the irons, connected by chains, were beat to the right size and shape, they were riveted onto Geronimo's ankles first, and then to the war leaders. When the shackling was finished, Geronimo and the war leaders were led back to the corral, given beds of hay, blankets, and food, and placed under strict guard. Beauford with twenty policemen marched the rest of the band back to their camp, made them gather up their belongings, and brought them back to the agency with their stolen horses and cattle. All this before sunset. It was the only time Geronimo was ever captured, and that by a trick. Ten years later as a prisoner of war, he often taunted army officers with the fact that "you never caught me shooting."[4]

After several days of head counts and discussions, Clum talked Victorio and

Loco into moving the Chihenne to San Carlos. Victorio quickly regretted his decision and left the reservation about three months later in a failed attempt to return to Ojo Caliente.

FIVE

The San Carlos Guardhouse

John Clum, agent at San Carlos Reservation, left the Ojo Caliente Reservation in west central New Mexico on May 1, 1877. He traveled 400 miles returning to San Carlos Reservation with Victorio, Loco, and Nana, chiefs of the Chihenne, and their band. With the Chihenne, Clum had Geronimo and his war leaders (Geronimo says there were eight, Clum says seven, but the records name only three) shackled and kept under constant guard. Of all his reservation breakouts (four), it was the only time Geronimo was captured. The other three breakouts ended when he voluntarily surrendered first to General Hatch, then to General Crook, and finally to General Miles.

Geronimo and the other prisoners rode in wagons. Wagons were also provided to carry supplies and any who became sick. Just as they were leaving, Clum discovered a very sick Chihenne who had smallpox. He quickly configured a wagon for a quarantine ambulance and had one of his policemen who had already had the disease look after the sick man.

The three-week trip from Ojo Caliente to San Carlos was uneventful. Geronimo and his men were docile and caused no problems. Four babies were born during the trip and Clum let the mothers ride on baggage wagons. Everyone else walked. The man who had smallpox recovered, but eight died. Along the trail, Clum wrote down hearsay evidence about Geronimo's raids and murders from Apache gossip he heard. He planned to turn Geronimo, his war leaders, and the evidence he had gathered over to the Tucson sheriff and offer to testify. He had no doubt that the prisoners would soon hang. The long train of walking people and wagons reached San Carlos May 20, 1877.

Clum put Geronimo, the other shackled prisoners, and twelve other prisoners in the Agency Guardhouse and told all the other Apache who had come with him from Ojo Caliente that they were free to go and establish their camps anywhere on the reservation on land not already claimed. He told their leaders to bring them in once a week to be counted and receive their food and clothing allotments. Clum recruited four Chihenne for the police force and made Victorio a member of his council of judges. Chihenne continued to die from smallpox, causing those already on the reservation to resent them being there and to scatter to live as small bands in the mountains where the healthy Chihenne had also decided to live in small bands.

The Chihenne sub-agency was built for them on the hot arid flats along the Gila River. The Chihenne felt betrayed. They had left a place they loved for the misery of San Carlos because Clum and his policemen had convinced them that it was a wonderful place. Clum and his police had obviously lied, which meant for Chihenne all promises were off for them to stay at San Carlos.

When the Clum train crossed the Gila River to the agency, he discovered a company of soldiers camped next to the agency under orders to inspect and manage the people for which, he, Clum was responsible. Clum was enraged. He told the commanding officer he was in charge and sent a telegram to the Commissioner of Indian Affairs in Washington. All this resulting from the continued bureaucratic infighting between the army and the Bureau of Indian Affairs over who was actually in charge of managing the reservations (the Apache would later say the army did a much better job than the Bureau of Indian Affairs which was slow to react to problems and had many weak or corrupt agents, although Clum wasn't one of them).

Clum had another grievance which the Indian Office rejected. Clum had been in service for three years. During that time, he had consolidated five reservations into one saving the government $25,000 a year on each and his own responsibility had increased from eight hundred to five thousand people with no increase in salary. On June 9, he sent a telegram that read:

IF YOUR DEPARTMENT WILL INCREASE MY SALARY SUFFICIENTLY AND EQUIP TWO MORE COMPANIES OF INDIAN POLICE FOR ME, I WILL VOLUNTEER TO TAKE CARE OF ALL APACHE IN ARIZONA—AND THE TROOPS CAN BE REMOVED.[1]

When word of Clum's proposal got out, bureaucrats in the War Department were enraged as were Arizona newspapers. A Tucson merchant explained it this way, "What are you trying to do? Ruin my business? If you take the military

San Carlos Guardhouse, ca. 1880.
Photograph courtesy of the National Archives.

contracts away from us, there would be nothing worth staying for. Most of our profit comes from feeding soldiers and army mules." The Department of Indian Affairs rejected Clum's proposal. He angrily resigned and left at the end of July.

While all the machinations between the War Department and the Department of Indian Affairs were going on, Geronimo and his war leaders remained shackled in the guardhouse. Clum wrote down the evidence he thought he had on Geronimo and his war leaders killing and robbing settlers in their raids and had sent word to the Tucson sheriff that the long sought Geronimo and his men were shackled in the San Carlos guardhouse and free to pick up for trial and hanging in Tucson at his earliest convenience (when Geronimo surrendered in 1886, President Cleveland had also planned to turn him and his warriors over to civilian authorities for trial and hanging but changed his mind when he learned Geronimo actually had not been captured but had surrendered under terms which weren't kept).

The Tucson sheriff, for reasons not determined, was a no-show to collect Geronimo et al at the San Carlos guardhouse. Geronimo was still in shackles when Clum resigned two months after returning from Ojo Caliente. A month later, the new agent, Henry Lyman Hart, arrived, reviewed the cases of the guardhouse prisoners, and after a talk with Geronimo was convinced that he would cause no more trouble. Since the sheriff apparently didn't want him, Hart let Geronimo and his war leaders go. Years later, Clum claimed that as a result of the sheriff not coming, Geronimo received no punishment for the murder of at least a hundred men, women, and children. And if he had been hanged, five hundred more human lives would have been saved to say nothing of twelve million dollars (about three hundred and twenty million in today's dollars) and one of the most humiliating military campaigns in U.S. history.[2]

After their release, Geronimo and his war leaders apparently found their families camped with Naiche and his people about fifteen miles upstream on the Gila River where Clum had sent them after he closed the Chiricahua Reservation the year before. Taza, the elder son of Cochise who had taken over as chief of the Chokonen Chiricahua, had died from pneumonia in Washington about ten months earlier on a Clum trip east with nineteen other Apache. Naiche, Cochise's youngest son, then nineteen, was made chief in Taza's place. Naiche didn't have the knowledge or maturity to be a chief, and he knew it. When Geronimo showed up at Naiche's camp to rejoin his family, he began, at Naiche's request, to serve, at first in a minor role, as one of Naiche's advisors. Over the years, Geronimo became Naiche's medicine man and primary consigliere.

Being shackled for four months and living nearly three of those months in the dark San Carlos guardhouse waiting for a sheriff to come take him to a White Eye town where he would be killed dancing on air at the end of a rope had a profound effect on Geronimo. Understandably, he never risked being jailed again. At the first hint of being arrested or abused by corrupt agents, he broke out of the reservation. Neither soldiers nor agents could understand why Geronimo was so quick to believe gossip that was later shown to be untrue. The answer was simple. Geronimo would rather starve, freeze in the cold, burn in the sun's heat, and bleed in battle than to return to captivity in anything like the San Carlos guardhouse.

PART TWO:
THE WAR BEGINS

Despite claims by General Miles and others, years later, the first and only time Geronimo was actually captured was by John Clum at Ojo Caliente. Clum took three weeks hauling his prisoners, shackled in leg irons, and leading Geronimo's followers and Victorio's Chihenne people to San Carlos.

After resigning, Clum left Geronimo and his war leaders in the San Carlos guardhouse expecting to be hanged. It didn't happen. Clum quit as agent at San Carlos over a pay and authority dispute, the Tucson sheriff never claimed Clum's Apache prisoners, and the new agent, Lyman Hart, freed them to live in peace at San Carlos. Geronimo believed all this resulted from of his many prayers to the great creator god of the Apache, Ussen.

Geronimo lived peacefully for a while at San Carlos until he realized the agents were stealing part of the rations intended for the Apache, and the area where they were forced to live gave many of them the "shaking sickness" (malaria and yellow fever brought by swarms of mosquitoes). Geronimo began asking questions out loud all the Apache were thinking and in secret meetings began telling the People to save all the weapons and ammunition and food they could in preparation for an escape from San Carlos.

SIX

The First San Carlos Breakout

AFTER THEIR RELEASE from the dark and stinking San Carlos guardhouse, Geronimo and his war leaders reunited with their families and lived with the Naiche led Chokonen Chiricahua Apache about fifteen miles upstream on the Gila River from the main reservation agency. Within a month of Geronimo's release, Victorio, chief of the Chihenne Apache, led a breakout from San Carlos in an attempt to return to their original Ojo Caliente Reservation. Victorio had tolerated living conditions at San Carlos for about three months as he watched his people suffer through extreme heat, dust, rattlesnakes, clouds of insects, and the shaking sickness. He quickly realized Clum and the Indian police had lied to him and his people about how good life was at San Carlos and vowed never to return, often telling those with whom he later negotiated, "…anyplace but San Carlos."

Living in the camp of Naiche, Geronimo advised him not to follow Victorio's lead to breakout of the reservation, and the young chief (he was about twenty) listened. Lyman Hart heard about the advice Geronimo gave Naiche and was so pleased that he asked Geronimo to be the "Captain" and advisor of the few Chihenne (some estimate about twenty) who had stayed at San Carlos. Geronimo agreed to the arrangement. Some of his close relatives were among the Chihenne who didn't run with Victorio. These included his widowed "sister" Nah-thla-tla and her teenaged children Betzinez (named Jason by the White Eyes when he was sent to Carlisle School) and Ellen. Apparently, Nana's wife, Nah-dos-te, and their son also stayed, although some believe she and her son left the reservation with Nana when he broke out with Victorio. Nah-dos-te was a true blood sister of Geronimo and, therefore, recognized him as the head of their family.

Life continued to get harder at San Carlos. Contractors failed to deliver on beef and flour contracts, others never delivered blankets and other supplies, or supplies were stolen by agents and sold on the black market. The Apache were not getting nearly the rations they needed or what was due them. Things were so desperate that the agents let them hunt and gather the desert's harvest to keep from starving and to augment their rations. Additionally, cases of shaking sickness were increasing and neither the Apache nor White Eye medicine men knew cures for it or from where it came.

Geronimo began to ask questions out loud that the rest of the Apache were only thinking: does the White Eye ever keep his promise; why don't we get all our rations; how long before the shaking sickness takes all of us if we stay here? Geronimo began meeting with small groups and telling them to prepare for a breakout by stealing arms and ammunition and putting aside as much food as they possibly could for when they went on the run.

Juh came up from Mexico, and unseen by the White Eyes helped Geronimo encourage a breakout. Juh told the Chiricahua they could stay with his Nednhi in

Apache Story Telling by Edward Curtis, 1903. Meetings like this illustrate how Geronimo instructed his followers to prepare to escape from San Carlos.
Photograph courtesy of the Library of Congress.

Mexico, putting their lodges on and raiding from his flat-top mountain strongholds in the Sierra Madre. Geronimo told the people at the little gatherings that if they prepared to leave with food and weapons, then Ussen would tell him when it was time to go. A major impediment to a Chiricahua breakout from San Carlos was Naiche. The young chief remembered the promise to his father, Cochise, that he and his elder brother, Taza, would avoid going to war with the White Eyes if it was at all possible. Naiche would not leave the reservation if he could avoid it.[1]

The winter days of the Ghost Face season passed into the early spring season of Little Eagles in the harvest year of 1878. Geronimo and his family were camped in the mountains north of the sub-agency that oversaw Naiche's band. The women managed to acquire enough corn to make *tulapai* for a good drink for all in the camp. Geronimo enjoyed drinking, but getting drunk often brought trouble that led him to do things he later regretted. In this case, Jason Betzinez says that a drunken Geronimo berated his nephew—apparently the son of Nana and Nah-dos-te (but the boy's identity is not known for a fact and this identity is disputed by some)—"for no reason at all."[2] The nephew, with typical Apache sensitivity to disapproval, especially by a family leader, committed suicide. Geronimo blamed himself for the young man's death. With his war leaders, their families, and other irreconcilables, about forty in all, and supported by Juh with a few warriors, Geronimo left the San Carlos Reservation April 4, 1878, and headed for a Juh stronghold in Mexico.

ON THE WAY to the border, the Geronimo escapees encountered a small train of freight wagons, killed the drivers, and took food and ammunition. They were chased by cavalry but managed to fight them off near Steins Peak in New Mexico and continued on into Mexico. In Mexico, Geronimo joined the band of Juh and Nolgee and with them raided in Sonora to sell their plunder in Janos.

The governors of the states of Sonora and Chihuahua decided to put an end to this Apache enterprise by negotiating a treaty with Juh. The terms of the treaty, which were presented to Juh, Geronimo, and Nolgee in early September 1878, basically said the Apache had to give up raiding in Sonora and live on a Chihuahua reservation near the town of Ojinaga on the Río Grande east of Ciudad Chihuahua. Juh had expected a treaty that basically said the Mexican states would give the Apache rations when they needed them in return for no more raiding in those states. Juh knew from Geronimo and from what his own eyes had seen at the San Carlos Reservation that the Apache had suffered much at the hands of the White Eyes. He wasn't about to accept life on a reservation run by Mexicans. After hearing their offer, Juh told the Mexicans he wanted time to discuss the treaty with his people. The Mexicans told him he had until September 25 (about three weeks) to give them an answer or soldiers from the states of Sonora and Chihuahua would join forces to come after the Apache.[3]

Juh waited until September 26 before striking a wagon train struck in Chocolate Pass midway between Casas Grandes and Galena. Juh, Geronimo, Nolgee, and their warriors wiped out twenty-five men, women, and children on the wagon train carrying beans to Silver City, New Mexico, before disappearing into the Sierra Madre. Juh hoped to convince the Mexicans by this example, that paying rations for peace was their best peace option. Nolgee went north to a stronghold near Janos, Geronimo to a stronghold about 100 miles south of Nolgee, and Juh to a stronghold in the Tarahumara country about 100 miles south of Geronimo. Nolgee tried talking to his Mexican friends in Janos for the treaty Juh wanted. Geronimo sent scouts to San Carlos to learn if ration distribution had improved and shaking sickness had decreased in order to determine if it was worthwhile to try to return there, and Juh continued to apply pressure through raiding.

SEVEN

Disasters and Return to San Carlos

NOLGEE, AFTER RETURNING to the Juh stronghold near Janos in late September 1878, continued to extend peace feelers to the Mexicans in Janos, hopeful that they understood their best terms to avoid ambushes like the one on the wagon train in Chocolate Pass were those Juh wanted. After several weeks of talks with the Chihuahuans, Nolgee was led to believe the Mexicans were ready to negotiate the treaty Juh wanted. They invited him and his People to a great celebratory feast where the Mexicans gave them large jugs of high-quality mescal. The feast, a trap set by the Chihuahuan and Sonoran militaries, wiped out two-thirds of the group, including Nolgee, as the mescal put them in a drunken stupor. On the same day, November 12, 1878, a Sonoran army patrol after following Geronimo from a raid at Bacadéhuachi to the northwest of Nacorí Chico attacked Geronimo's camp of about forty people in the mountains southeast of Nácori Chico. Geronimo lost twelve of his band in the battle. He later claimed the Apache killed all the Mexican soldiers (historians say they did not).[1]

Juh and Geronimo met again at Guaynopa southeast of Geronimo's camp and talked more about returning to San Carlos, but bad reports on health and limited rations made them stay in Mexico raiding in Sonora, Chihuahua, New Mexico, and Arizona. Victorio may have joined them, but he and Juh with no liking for the other never joined forces for major raids.

On November 25, 1878, thirteen days after the Apache disasters in Mexico, Loco, who after breaking out with Victorio from San Carlos had returned to Ojo Caliente and stayed put, was forced by irrational bureaucratic edict to return to San Carlos from Ojo Caliente with 172 Chihenne, but only twenty were men.

IN LATE AUGUST 1879, Victorio had planned to settle on the Mescalero Reservation. He left in a rage after dragging the agent, S. A. Russell, around the supply store by his billy goat beard. Russell fearful of any personal initiative getting him in trouble with Washington bureaucrats had refused to give Victorio and his warriors food rations until approval was received from Washington. In his fury, Victorio set southern New Mexico and Chihuahua ablaze and killed anyone in his path wherever he went. With the help of Juh and Geronimo in early September, he took the entire horse herd of the cavalry troop at Ojo Caliente. On October 27, 1879, in rugged terrain a few miles south of the border, Juh and Geronimo joined Victorio in a hard battle with pursuing cavalry. The Apache then turned east and with Juh and Geronimo, Victorio inflicted two massacres on the little town of Carrizal, Chihuahua.

Captain Adna R. Chaffee was put in charge of San Carlos to relieve Lyman Hart, the agent who had started with good intentions when he replaced John Clum but had come to represent the worst the Bureau of Indian Affairs had to offer in terms of crooked agents. Chaffee was a highly competent and efficient administrator and restored honesty and order to the governance of the reservation. Through Archie McIntosh, a chief of scouts with an Apache wife, Chaffee learned that Naiche was willing for Juh and Geronimo to bring their Nednhi Apache to San Carlos and live among his Chokonen. Chaffee passed this information to General Orlando B. Willcox who had relieved General Kautz as commander of the military department of Arizona. General Willcox directed Lieutenant Harry L. Haskell to convince Geronimo and Juh to return to the reservation.

In September 1879, Haskell first verified the Chokonen were willing to share their camp with the Nednhi, then formed his peace party which included: Archie McIntosh, Gordo and Ah-Dis (Nednhi Chiricahua Apache), San Carlos police sergeant Atzebee, Chief Chihuahua, and Chief George (Chokonen Chiricahua Apache). By September 20, Haskell had his base at Camp Rucker in the southeastern Chiricahua Mountains where he met Tom Jeffords, famed friend of Cochise, prospecting nearby.

Haskell sent Gordo and Ah-dis (a warrior who had barely escaped the massacre that killed Nolgee) as scouts to find Juh in Mexico. They didn't find Juh's stronghold near Janos until mid-October. Juh and Geronimo had left a few days earlier to help Victorio. After listening to Gordo and Ah-Dis, the men in camp would not make a commitment without their leader's approval. However, Haskell's

At the Ford, Apache. Photograph by Edward Curtis, 1903,
courtesy of the Library of Congress.

emissaries persuaded two Nednhi men and their families to visit Camp Rucker and determine if they thought the move to San Carlos was a wise one. Sergeant Atzeebee met them at the border and guided them to Fort Rucker where nothing happened for several weeks. Eventually, the men and their families returned hoping for the possibility of serious talks. Haskell finally set out on his own with a small group including the two Nednhi to probe south in the Guadalupe Mountains into Mexico. He teamed up with a scout company under the command of Lieutenant Augustus P. Blockson.

IN EARLY NOVEMBER 1879, Juh and Geronimo parted ways with Victorio and returned to Juh's Carcay Mountains stronghold raiding as they went. Arriving at the stronghold, they were surprised to learn the Chiricahua at San Carlos had come with peace feelers from their own people and the Blue Coats. They wanted the Nednhi to settle at San Carlos and not get caught up in Victorio's war.

When Juh heard Gordo's proposal, he emphatically said, "I'm not going in for anybody." He pulled his gun out. "If they get me, they kill me." Gordo calmed him down enough to listen. "You got lots of children, girl children, and I don't see why you run like a wild man—no sleep, no food, no water. Little children—you carry them around and get them killed and the coyote and crow eat you. When you go back to white man's village, nobody gonna kill you. They give you food, and you not going to starve. Now you can get a good finish. Nobody going to hang you."[2]

Gordo kept the talks going all night, drinking with Juh and remembering old times. Finally, as the gray of dawn was coming Juh said, "You take me back there." Both Juh and Geronimo didn't trust the whites and remained deeply skeptical, suspicious, and unsettled by Gordo's assurances.

ON DECEMBER 12, at San Bernardino Springs, a runner appeared in camp and said Juh and Geronimo wanted to meet with Haskell but that he should come alone without soldiers. Haskell went with the runner and Blockson's interpreter (who some think was Tom Jeffords) to the Nednhi camp in the Guadalupe Mountains about forty miles east of Camp Rucker. A runner had also been sent to Camp Rucker and Archie McIntosh arrived a few hours before Haskell.

A few days before Haskell arrived, Juh and Geronimo had a council talk with their warriors about the Juh and Gordo meeting. All but one of the council agreed to surrender. The talk between Juh and the dissident grew heated and angry. Geronimo ended it by pulling his pistol and killing the dissident.

When Haskell arrived, he spoke to about eighty Nednhi. They had a "big talk" with Jeffords participating. Juh and Geronimo were friendly and said all their people had now joined them. Geronimo again did most of the talking because Juh stuttered so badly. They had one primary concern: "Will my people go to jail if we surrender?"

Haskell answered that General Willcox would treat them well as long as they were "good" Indians and that he would tell General Willcox whatever they had to say. Juh and Geronimo remained suspicious but allowed themselves to be escorted to Camp Rucker and then on to Fort Bowie.

HASKELL WITH MORE Nednhi in tow arrived at Fort Bowie by the end of December. There they had another "Big Talk" where Juh said he wanted a stable treaty. Willcox had wanted the Nednhi to give up their arms but that didn't happen, and the Nednhi talked with Nahilzay, a Nednhi who had surrendered in August 1877, who had suffered no punitive actions from the Americans. At the conclusion of the talks, Haskell wired Willcox that he had 102 "renegades" and eighteen agency Indians, and he expected to arrive at San Carlos in eight days. Thus, Geronimo ended his first San Carlos breakout.

EIGHT

The First Peace

AFTER LIEUTENANT HASKELL convinced Juh and Geronimo that their People would not go to jail if they surrendered, the Nednhi Apache under Juh and Geronimo returned to the San Carlos Reservation and began erecting their wickiups near Naiche's Chokonen Apache People on January 7, 1880. There they lived peacefully through the Season of the Ghost Face and well into the Season of Many Leaves even as Victorio and Nana spread fire and spilled blood on both sides of the border from Texas to Arizona. In late May, Reuben Hood, who operated a trading post at San Carlos, reported that the Nednhi Apache were, "…perfectly content with their new home, and instead of being in sympathy with Victorio's band, they exhibit hostile feelings toward them." He further said that Tom Jeffords was confident they would not assist Victorio even if he should appear there. However, a son of Victorio, a charismatic warrior named Washington, made a fast raid into Arizona, reached a camp of Juh's and Geronimo's People and had a brief skirmish with them. Then they were attacked and pursued by soldiers who suffered some casualties but inflicted no damage on Washington and his warriors who killed and raided on their way back to Victorio's camp in New Mexico. Even as the Chiricahua lived peacefully, significant work was required to maintain that peace.

Five days after Juh's arrival at San Carlos, General Willcox reminded Captain Adna Chaffee, who worked hard to be fair to the Apache, of the importance of keeping the army's word and intent of the surrender terms with Juh. Chaffee answered his general and assured him that the Nednhi seemed content and would remain where they were. However, severe winter weather prevented the contractor from delivering on his ration support contract. Rather than wait

Apache Wickiup at San Carlos. ca. 1890.
Photograph courtesy of the Bullock Museum.

to hear from the Bureau of Indian Affairs in Washington, Chaffee telegraphed General Wilcox and explained the situation. Wilcox immediately ordered the Camp Thomas commander to provide the necessary flour so Chaffee could issue the weekly ration. Soon after that emergency, Chaffee learned that the Nednhi were unhappy with the water quality near the sub-agency overseeing Naiche's and Juh's People. Chaffee let them move up into the mountains above the Gila River where water was free-flowing and more fit for consumption.[1]

MEXICAN OFFICIALS, WANTING the Americans to take firm control of or wipe out Juh while he was reachable on a reservation, let them know they were not happy with the status of Juh's return to Arizona. Willcox assured the Mexican Council at Tucson, Francisco Prieto, that Juh and his followers would be kept at San Carlos where they wouldn't harm Americans or Mexicans, even going so far as to suggest Juh's band might furnish scouts to run down Victorio.

Prieto remained concerned and suggested that the band be treated as prisoners, but Willcox responded that such treatment would be a "breach of faith" of their terms of surrender. That answer failed to appease Chihuahua's governor, Luis Terrazas, who was well acquainted with Juh's raids and maneuvers during the previous three and a half years. Terrazas demanded Arizona Territorial Governor, John C. Fremont, turn over Juh's band to Mexican officials. Fremont requested an answer from Willcox. Willcox in a well-reasoned response that followed a timeline from when Juh and Geronimo left the Chiricahua Reservation in June 1876, until he requested peace with the state of Chihuahua in the summer of 1878, but because Chihuahua had been reluctant to supply rations, the treaty had stalled and Juh's and Geronimo's raids continued. In summary, Willcox pointed out that since the Nednhi had returned to San Carlos their conduct had been satisfactory, and that: 1) they were American Indians; 2) they returned on the promise they would be received and protected; 3) they raided in the United States and Mexico and the Mexicans did nothing about either act; and 4) returning to San Carlos, Juh and Geronimo have separated from Victorio. Therefore, Terrazas demand was denied. When word of Willcox's rejection got out, the editor of the Grant County Herald reported that New Mexico Territorial Governor, Lew Wallace, would have "immediately complied with the [Terrazas] request."[2]

Regardless of Chaffee and Willcox keeping their word with Juh, and the apparent satisfaction of the Nednhi with their reservation arrangements, rumors began to fly in March that Juh was unhappy and already planning a breakout. Apparently, the army had heard the rumors too. In a Tucson speech in early March, Colonel Eugene Asa Carr warned the commander at Fort Bowie to be prepared for a possible break out by Juh. Three weeks later department head-quarters notified Carr that "trouble with the Chiricahua may be serious." In May, Willcox sent Lieutenant Thomas Cruse to Ash Creek "to keep an eye on some malcontents" from Juh's band "who were threatening trouble." Cruse was also supposed to watch out for Victorio who had sent a war party to attack the families of Apache scouts. Geronimo had an argument with Juh, and, with so much uncertainty in the air, left Juh's band and joined that of Esquine who had assumed leadership of Chato's and Gordo's group.

IN EARLY MAY, New Mexico Army Department commander, Colonel Edward Hatch, warned Willcox that Victorio was "en route to San Carlos." Willcox ordered

Carr to move additional troops to the vicinity of San Carlos in case of a breakout and gave Hatch's information to Captain Chaffee who ordered the Chiricahua back to the sub-agency where they had originally camped, and he sent agency police to patrol the eastern edge of the reservation.

The order to return to the sub-agency annoyed Juh and Naiche. Naiche and Juh's People had to camp near the sub-agency where they had found the water unacceptable and cases of shaking sickness increased—this despite the fact that there had not even been a rumor of any of them breaking out to join Victorio. Within weeks or returning from the foothills, cases of shaking sickness had drastically increased and both Naiche and Juh clenched their teeth in anger. Naiche was especially angry; this was the third straight year of sleeping sickness and knew it was somehow related to their living conditions. In his disgust, Naiche was ready to leave the reservation.

ON MAY 7, Victorio and thirty-six warriors came out of the hills to strike George Stevens's ranch on Eagle Creek near San Carlos and "cleaned out" its cattle and horses. They then headed for revenge raids against the scouts and the others who had followed and attacked the Chihenne when they escaped San Carlos in 1877, and they attempted to get their women and children back out of Loco's camp. Victorio and his warriors failed to see or get their women and children but did get a messenger to Juh asking him to join the raid, but Juh wanted no part of it.

The raids of Victorio in New Mexico and around San Carlos left the army and civilian officials on the reservation worried that he might invade the reservation to liberate Loco's band or otherwise incite the then peaceful Chiricahua. They incorrectly assumed that Juh, who had joined forces with Victorio in the fall 1879, might do so again, even though he had clearly demonstrated he wanted no part of Victorio's War.

Willcox had been able, through Lieutenant Haskell, to coax Juh and Geronimo back to San Carlos, and the work of Captain Chaffee had made them willing to stay. This made Willcox believe he had a model he could use to bring Victorio back to the reservation using Juh and Naiche as emissaries. Integral to this plan was the use of Tom Jeffords (former Chiricahua Reservation Agent) and Archie McIntosh (former chief of scouts to General Crook) to act as liaisons between the army and the Apache and then go San Carlos and talk to Juh and Naiche about bringing Victorio back. Working with Carr, who was Captain Chaffee's commander, Willcox requested Jeffords and McIntosh be sent to San Carlos to assure Juh and the skittish Nednhi that the additional troops Carr was sending to the reservation were there to promote peace and understanding.[3]

Chaffee, who thought the Willcox-Carr plan to bring Victorio to the reservation was unwise and that Willcox and Carr were overstepping their authority, refused to allow either Jeffords or McIntosh on the reservation. Carr directed Jeffords to stop at Camp Thomas and asked that he wait there. Jeffords, at Camp Thomas for about a month, gathered intelligence for Carr and learned the Chiricahua were reluctant to bring in Victorio. He met with Naiche who begged off being an emissary because he had two wives, etc. Jeffords predicted Juh would come to the camp and see him as soon as he knew Jeffords was there.

By May 23, Jeffords had met with both Geronimo and Juh and had explained the situation to them. They complained about Chaffee forcing them down out of the mountains to live near the sub-agency after Victorio's May 7 raid. They were very near leaving the reservation on account of being forced to live near bad water and the sleeping sickness they knew they got there. Jeffords persuaded them to wait until the new agent, Joseph A. Tiffany, arrived. Tiffany arrived at San Carlos June 1, 1880. Both John Clum and Tom Jeffords had wanted the agent's job. Clum recommended himself; the army pushed for Jeffords; the Bureau of Indian Affairs appointed Tiffany, who while progressive in his ideas about reservation management and a good organizer, knew next to nothing about Apache.

Two days after Tiffany arrived at San Carlos, General Willcox directed Colonel Carr to visit San Carlos. Willcox wanted to learn Carr's evaluation of Tiffany, the moods of Juh and Naiche, and to obtain an evaluation of getting Chiricahua help to bring Victorio to San Carlos. Carr took Tom Jeffords with him to San Carlos to act as his interpreter, liaison, and advisor. The presence of Jeffords made Naiche and Juh relax and speak candidly as if with friends.

Carr first visited with Tiffany for two days at the end of June 1880 and was impressed. Tiffany was determined to do right and had the ability to carry out his intentions. Carr then went about fifteen miles upstream on the Gila to visit with Juh and Naiche. The chiefs were not happy, complaining that they were more closely confined than others on the reservation. Juh pointed out he had come in voluntarily, and Naiche said he had lived peacefully at San Carlos for four years. He noted the many deaths they suffered from the shaking sickness and wanted to know why they couldn't move away from where they caught it. One third of his band, about 125 people, had died from the shaking sickness since coming to the reservation four years earlier. Carr also asked what the chiefs thought about Victorio being receptive to returning to San Carlos. They thought he would come if not pressed by troops and if given assurances of safe conduct. Victorio was then about sixty years old and very fond of his wife and children at the agency.

As soon as he received Carr's report, Willcox telegraphed Carr to ask Tiffany for "the best measures possible for Juh's and Naiche's bands." Tiffany responded immediately and visited the Chiricahua camps. He counted a total of fifty-nine sick in both camps and noted that within the previous month ten had died. He related the sickness to living in the Gila lowlands and to drinking the water which "is very different from mountain springs." He spoke to Juh and Geronimo and other chiefs who admitted they had thought about leaving the reservation because they were not getting enough to eat. They explained to Tiffany that they had to live on things they obtained in the mountains but being forced to live near the sub-agency left them without the opportunity for gathering their natural foods such as mescal, nuts, and berries to supplement their rations, and they were often hungry. Before Tiffany returned to agency headquarters, he told the chiefs they could move their people from the Gila swamps to the mountains in a fifteen-mile strip between Mount Turnbull and Black Rock in the Santa Teresa Mountains.[4]

The Apache were happy with their new locations, and Willcox was delighted that Tiffany had acted expeditiously. But as problems on the reservation were resolved, the great unknown that could shake the delicate balance of peace apart, Victorio, remained.

NINE

Victorio, Nana, and the Prophet

WHEN VICTORIO APPEARED with about thirty-six warriors near San Carlos in the first week of May 1880, wreaking havoc on ranches, attacking and killing some of the lead White Mountain scouts, but failing to see and take his family back to the New Mexico mountains, he sent messengers to Juh and Geronimo about breaking out of San Carlos, but they stayed and kept the peace. Victorio returned to the New Mexico mountains, where on May 24, 1880, he fought a battle with Major Morrow, his Apache scouts, and his black soldiers in a box canyon. It was Victorio's first tactical defeat. The army killed thirty of Victorio's men, women, and children and Victorio, himself, was wounded. Victorio headed for the border, but before he could cross into Mexico, he faced Major Morrow again on June 5 and lost ten killed and three more wounded in his band (one of those killed was his son, Washington—in fact he lost three sons in his wars with the Blue Coats).

After crossing the border, Victorio raided deep into Chihuahua, at one time coming within thirty miles of Ciudad Chihuahua, the capitol city of the state. In September, plans were laid to make the Nednhi and Chiricahua (bands under Juh, Geronimo, and Naiche) part of what Dan Thrapp called the "greatest manhunt in the history of the southwest." We have no idea what Juh (who disliked Victorio), Geronimo (who had family in Victorio's band), or Naiche (who would likely view supporting the Blue Coats as betrayal) would have done. Fortune saved them all from any commitment one way or the other when Colonel Joaquin Terrazas surprised Victorio, low on ammunition, near the group of three low mountains, Tres Castillos, in eastern Chihuahua.

In the Tres Castillos "battle" Mexicans suffered three killed and ten wounded.

They killed and scalped seventy-eight Apache for bounty, sixty-two of whom were warriors and the rest women and children. They captured sixty-eight women and children to be sold into slavery.[1] Victorio shot his last bullet and then as the Mexicans closed in, stabbed himself in the heart to avoid capture.[2] Seventeen, including a fiery young warrior, Kaytennae, and Victorio's *segundo*, old arthritic Nana who seemed to have supernatural power for finding ammunition, had been out to hunt, and to find ammunition and other supplies. These escaped the massacre. Among the other survivors was the boy Kaywaykla and his mother Guyan, but his baby sister was lost and his grandmother and young girl cousin Siki were among the captives sold into slavery on maguey plantation (their escape along with Huera and one or two others and their return to Fort Apache on foot over twelve hundred miles away from Mexico City with nothing but a knife and blanket some four years later is a story of epic courage and determination).[3,4]

AS VICTORIO DISAPPEARED into history, Juh and Geronimo with their bands lived quietly on the reservation minding their own business. Those in Victorio's band who survived being killed or enslaved gathered around Nana hiding in a Sierra Madre camp to rest and get through the coming Ghost Face with its freezing winds and snow.

With the coming of the Season of Little Eagles (March, April and early May) in 1881, Loco reported to the San Carlos agent that Nana had sent a message that he would come in and join Loco's band and refrain from raiding if they could be assured of protection. Loco said he would be responsible for their future good behavior, but apparently Nana's needed assurances that were not given and Victorio's remnant did not return to San Carlos.

Nana apparently moved his People into the Sacramento Mountains in New Mexico where they made four attempts to contact the Mescalero Agent, but each time were driven off by Blue Coats. Failing to be allowed to join with the Mescaleros, Nana came out of the Sacramentos in mid-July spreading blood and fire across the southwest in vengeance for the massacre of Victorio and his band. James Kaywaykla, with the band as a young boy vividly remembered, "Nana... was not content with an eye for an eye, nor life for life. For every Apache killed, he took many lives." [5] Sometimes riding as much as seventy miles in a day, old and arthritic Nana led an estimated fifteen Chihenne and twenty-five Mescalero warriors striking army units and citizen posses, killing miners and herders, and capturing horses and supplies.

Eight companies of cavalry, eight companies of infantry, and two companies of Apache scouts were sent out to run Nana down.[6] Then in late August, Nana and his warriors disappeared into the Sierra Madre leaving the army in Arizona and New Mexico in a high state of alert.

JUH AND GERONIMO stayed far from Nana's raids, but the heightened alert resulting from the raids led to poor Blue Coat decision making on their commander's part and ultimately the great San Carlos Reservation breakout. The origin of this breakout began with the prophet Noch-ay-del-klinne, described as a "frail, mild ascetic living with his family on Cibecue Creek in the western part of the Fort Apache Reservation." [7]

The White Mountain and Coyotero Apache had discovered white settlers overrunning their land and had seen the boundaries of their reservation moved back several times to accommodate them. Unable to get the agent to give them what was rightfully theirs, they turned to religion. By the Season of Little Eagles in 1880, Noch-ay-det-klinne had convinced himself and the White Mountain Apache that he could commune with the spirits of the dead and even had the power to bring the great dead Apache chiefs back to life. All of which sounds remarkably similar to the Shawnee version of salvation from the White Eyes led by Tecumseh's brother shortly before the War of 1812, and the ghost dance beliefs that swept the Plains tribes in the 1890s.

Noch-ay-det-klinne taught his followers a new dance where those participating were arranged like spokes on a wheel, all facing inward, while he stood at the hub and sprinkled them with sacred hoddentin (golden tule pollen) as they circled around him. The Apache were drawn to him in large numbers and the religious ecstasy with which they were filled scared the White Eyes who saw it. It was reported that Noch-ay-det-klinne tied the return of the dead chiefs to the disappearance of the White Eyes and that this would all happen at the time of the corn harvest.

Daklugie, Geronimo's "nephew" remembered from the time he was a small boy, then probably four or five, that Juh and Geronimo were present when the religious fervor reached its climax. He also said that Geronimo had told him at Fort Sill, shortly before he died, that he never fully understood how Juh and he could have been influenced by Noch-ay-det-klinne's medicine. Nana apparently

Lieutenant Gatewood with his Company A Apache Scouts, Sam Bowman interpreter immediately behind him, and Lieutenant Cruse, back row far left, October 1880. Photograph courtesy of the Arizona Historical Society.

was a stronger believer in the prophet than either Juh or Geronimo. According to Daklugie, as an adult at Fort Sill, Nana had told him that he had visited the prophet and had attended at least one prayer session and that during a misty predawn saw him call up Mangas Coloradas, Cochise, and Victorio. The dancing and emotions were at their height at the same time Nana was spreading death and destruction all over southern New Mexico. No one knew where Nana was until he struck. Daklugie told Eve Ball, "The word of Nana could not be questioned." You might question his vision, but not his visit, and Nana could have visited Noch-ay-det-klinne while gathering his people or trying to return to the reservation.[8]

Colonel Carr tried to calm the situation and warned joking soldiers not to tell the Apache the army was planning to attack them or drive them from the reservation. As the excitement increased, even enlisted scouts at Fort Apache took passes to attend the dances and returned believers. The agent, Joseph Capron Tiffany, who was massively stealing the Apache's rations and was as corrupt as agents came, sent his tribal police to arrest the prophet, but they came back empty handed and complaining about White Eye aggressors. Noch-ay-det-klinne evaded calls from Tiffany and Carr to come in for a conference. Finally, Tiffany sent Carr a demand, "I want him arrested or killed or both." [9]

On August 29, 1881, Carr set out with one hundred seventeen men including twenty-three scouts and arrested Noch-ay-det-klinne who came quietly, but the prophet's followers attacked the soldiers and scouts defected and joined them. In the melee that followed his arrest, the prophet was killed along with eighteen attacking Apache and 8 of Carr's men. Carr managed to get away and return back to Fort Apache, where a small group of the prophet's followers attacked the fort, and other small groups scattered over the reservation killed several soldiers and civilians they found. There was obviously no planned uprising, only People furious over the killing of their prophet.

After their initial angry reaction, the disillusioned Apache settled back down. No miracles had occurred and their prophet was dead. The dream was gone. On the other hand, the entire White Eye southwest trembled in fear of a general outbreak. General Willcox rushed all available military forces from New Mexico and California to the San Carlos area already crowded with soldiers. There were twenty-two companies of soldiers in all. The reservation swarmed with armed men. Apache, like Juh and Geronimo, conscious of their "crimes" in Mexico, grew nervous and feared they were about to be arrested. From his time in the guardhouse in 1877, Geronimo determined he was not about to be arrested again and put in that darkness at the mercy of whatever the resident agent happened to think at the time.

PART THREE: THE WAR EXPANDS

Geronimo was a frequent visitor at the San Carlos Reservation Chokonen Chiricahua Apache sub-agency the summer of 1881, the summer of Nana's raids and the killing of the prophet, Noch-ay-del-klinne. He loafed around and didn't do much of anything. He did use his healing power to cure a seriously ill man by singing over him for several days. The Chiricahua led by Naiche refused to become embroiled in fighting over the Prophet. Geronimo saw the army begin its buildup after the Prophet was killed, and he and Juh grew increasingly nervous about being arrested, sent to guardhouse, and tried and hung for their raids in Mexico. Their fear was a disaster waiting to happen and led to the great Apache breakout from the San Carlos Reservation and the Apache heading for their fortress strongholds in the Sierra Madre.

The army in an attempt to regain control of the Apache "situation" brought General Crook back from the Plains Wars to take over command of Arizona in 1882. Crook listened to the Apache complaints about the weak and crooked agents and how they were being cheated, starved, and made to live on land where they were often infected by shaking sickness. He first made things right for the Apache on the reservation, then in May 1883, in one of the most daring operations ever attempted by the army, led fifty mounted troopers and nearly two hundred Apache scouts into Mexico to "shepherd" nearly seven hundred Apache back to the reservation with a minimum of bloodshed. It was a move that saved many Anglo and Apache lives.

TEN

The Second San Carlos Escape

O N 23 SEPT 1881, Juh and Geronimo rode to the main agency at San Carlos to talk to Agent Tiffany. They wanted to know if troop movements were related to their activities in Mexico—they had been on the warpath but come in on good faith. Tiffany assured them that the army was there only to punish those fighting on Cibecue Creek to protect the prophet, Noch-ay-del-klinne, and for revenge after he was killed. Juh and Geronimo were happy to hear this, then shook hands and left. Tiffany breathed a sigh of relief.

A week later, September 30, 1881, was ration day. The army planned rearrests of the Apache leaders, George and Bonito, and the Cibecue Apache involved in the fight when Noch-ay-det-klinne was arrested. These Apache had been arrested and then freed. Inexplicably, the army wanted them back in custody. George and Bonito had promised to surrender, but George changed his mind. He and Bonito ran to the camps of the Chiricahua—Naiche, Chato, and Juh. George told them the army was coming to murder their women and children and deport the leaders in shackles to a dark, distant place. Chato claimed that upon hearing this Geronimo became "wild as an animal."[1]

THE CHIRICAHUA LEADERS held a council and recalled the betrayal of Cochise at Apache Pass and the shameful midnight execution of Mangas Coloradas at Fort McLane. Juh and Geronimo dominated the council, and Jelikinne, known as Little Chief and who within a year or two would be Geronimo's father-in-law (he was the father of Geronimo's future wife Zi-yeh), supported them.

Renegade Apache
Painting by Herman Wendelborg Hansen, ca. 1902.

According to Chihuahua, during the council Juh became very much excited and decided to leave.

Geronimo told them, "It's more manly to die on the warpath, than to be killed in prison."[2]

Tzoe, later known as "Peaches" by the Blue Coat soldiers and would be a major player in the next surrender, was a Cibecue Apache who had married Chihenne women. He was living with Loco's band at the Agency, and creating even more agitation, claimed he had heard Tiffany who "threatened to have them removed from San Carlos to a distant country."

George's insistence that the Blue Coats were coming to kill the women and children drove Naiche to decide his Chokonen had to leave.

Though a close friend of Juh, Chihuahua, was reluctant to leave, but they all decided to avoid being additional victims of American injustice.

About 375 Chiricahua (74 men and 22 teenagers who could use weapons), which included 200 Chokonen, 89 Bedonkohe, and about 86 Nednhi, decided to leave the reservation. Loco and Zele's Chihenne band, numbering about 270, stayed as did those of George.[3]

★ ★ ★

BY 10:30 P.M., SEPTEMBER 30, 1881, the Chiricahua had gathered their belongings and rounded up their stock in preparation for their race to Mexico. Fewer than a third had horses, but they planned to steal enough stock on the way to mount the entire band. Most of the seventy-four men and twenty-two teenage boys owned Springfield "trapdoor" breech loading rifles and had acquired plenty of ammunition during their stay at San Carlos and from the White Mountains. There was a half-moon for good light and the temperature was perfect for night travel. They followed the road toward Fort Thomas for about twelve miles, then pivoted south dividing into four groups under Juh, Naiche, Chato, and Bonito with plans to rendezvous at Black Rock. Geronimo led a band that stole fifty horses and mules in three raids against two freighters and a rancher. After reuniting at Black Rock, they went about ten miles southeast and camped in the foothills of the Santa Teresa Mountains in late afternoon of October 1. By October 2, General Willcox, slow to learn of the breakout and slow to respond, sent two troops of cavalry to follow the Chiricahua.

Before daybreak on October 2, Juh and Naiche led most of the warriors south while women and children traveled through the Pinaleño Mountains foothills about a mile east of the men. The warriors attacked a twelve-wagon supply train with 108 mules and seven tons of goods headed for San Carlos. The Apache took the train in two hours, with six mules killed, and plundered the wagons taking eight Winchesters, eight revolvers and three hundred cartridges from six men killed. Then the Chiricahua continued down the road toward Fort Grant.

The warriors were engaged by about one hundred cavalry troopers and forty western Apache scouts all under Captain Reuben F. Bernard. The fight went on for about six hours and is called the Battle of K-H Butte. The Apache had to figure out how to get their women and children across the road that the troopers had unknowingly blocked. Jelikinne proposed, and the war leaders agreed, for the Apache to charge the right flank of the soldiers in front of them to create a diversion that would allow the women and children to cross the road a few miles below the battle site. The Apache charged around 8:00 p.m. and got within ten feet of Bernard's positions. They withdrew without losses and maintained sporadic gun fire until they were signaled the main body of women and children had crossed safely. Then they abandoned their positions and rejoined their people near the Galiuro Mountains the evening of October 2. Bernard continued south to Fort Grant with one dead and two wounded.

Early on the morning of October 3, in the Upper Sulphur Springs Valley, the Apache broke camp with the women and children staying near the foothills riding south. No forts were now between them and the border. The warriors took 135 horses from the Sierra Bonita Ranch and fifty-one from a rancher and a wagon freight train. That night they camped at Point of Mountains, seven or eight miles northwest of Willcox. At 2:00 a.m. on October 4, they left their camp and traveled toward the Dragoon Mountains. At about 6:30 a.m., they crossed the railroad tracks at Dragoon Pass and camped before midmorning south of Cochise's east stronghold in Grapevine Canyon. They found a herd of cattle and had slaughtered seventy-nine steers for meat, when to their surprise, the cavalry scouts found them, and they scattered south.

They crossed the border three days later on October 7 and were at last safe from the U.S. Army. In total, 375 Apache had escaped, of which 279 were women and children, and they had covered 216 miles to gain their freedom.[4] Their warriors attacked nearly every party they encountered. The army had responded slowly and was out of position being above the Río Gila after the Cibecue disaster when Noch-ay-del-kinne was killed, so the cavalry couldn't get between the Apache and the border in time to block them. They were pursued by twelve troops of cavalry. The warriors and armed teenagers had taken enough horses and mules so everyone was mounted and had fought two rear guard actions so the women and children could get away. They entered Mexico with 350–500 head of stolen horses and mules after abandoning 100 head when they scattered from the Dragoons. One woman had been killed at K-H Butte, and one woman and three children were captured in the Dragoon Mountains fight. One warrior had been killed between the South Pass post and the Babocomari Ranch. Now in Mexico, Juh led the band to his stronghold west of *Casas Grandes* and took control. Nana and his band raiding and fighting in northern Chihuahua soon joined him.

ELEVEN

The Decision to "Save" Loco and His People
at San Carlos.

THE APACHE TRADED the horses and other goods they had taken in escaping San Carlos with Janos merchants. On November 9, 1881, to keep the wheels of commerce turning, Juh with Geronimo and thirty warriors started peace negotiations on the banks of an arroyo about three miles east of Casas Grandes with Chihuahuans led by Joaquin Terrazas who had 350 troops at Casas Grandes, 100 at Janos, and 100 at Carrizal. Terrazas agreed to talk peace because he wanted no part of chasing Juh in the Sierra Madre. Juh wanted the Carcay Mountains and the plains and valleys on both sides set aside as his country where his people could raise stock, gather wild foods, hunt, and plant. Terrazas said he would send the request to the governor of Chihuahua.

The next day they met again and Terrazas issued cattle, sugar, flour, and other items. He repeated this issuing of goods two or three times during the next two weeks. He hoped to persuade Juh and Geronimo to come into Casas Grandes, but they were too suspicious that the Mexicans would offer them mescal, get them drunk, and murder them. The Mexican government was concentrating troops with the objective of taking the entire band prisoner and hauling them into the interior of Mexico. Their plan was for Terrazas to wait for General Fuero to come up with 200 soldiers, then get the Apache to come into Casas Grandes and capture them while they were drunk.[1]

JUH, GERONIMO, AND Nana avoided the double cross when they abandoned the area. They had confirmed their suspicions of Terrazas's intentions from friendly

Through the Pass
Painting by Henry Farny, 1890.

trading partners. About November 27, Juh led the Chiricahua 140 miles south to winter at his Guaynopa stronghold. Late in November Nana camped with some Mescaleros who were trying to get news on their people enslaved after Tres Castillos. The Mexicans faked interest and then attacked the camp. Nana and most of his people got away and rejoined Juh in the Sierra Madre.

At Guaynopa, the Apache leaders made plans for the coming months. Besides sending raiding parties into Sonora and Chihuahua, they discussed bringing the Chihenne of Loco's, Zele's, and Chiva's bands from San Carlos to the Sierra Madre.[2]

Kaytennae had convinced Geronimo, believing Juh's band needed reinforcements to fight the large concentration of Mexican troops edging into the Sierra Madres, of the need to take Loco and his people from the reservation to fight the Mexicans. There were about 300 Chihenne Chiricahua at San Carlos, 50 of which were fighting men. Juh and Geronimo decided to send emissaries to San Carlos to determine the prospects of getting the Chihenne leaders to abandon the reservation. In mid-December, Bonito and seven warriors slipped into San Carlos to meet with Loco and others. While they were gone, Juh took Naiche, Chato, and about forty warriors and went raiding to the south. Geronimo went into Sonora with Chihuahua, Jelikine, and about forty warriors.

Bonito received a solid "no" from Loco when they first met to discuss the Chihenne leaving San Carlos. When Bonito gave the Guaynopa council this answer, he was sent again to be sure Loco would not change his mind. Again, Loco said he had given his word to the White Eyes and the Chihenne would unequivocally stay at San Carlos. The council sent Bonito back to San Carlos a third and final time with a message and warning.

Bonito and three men reached and entered Loco's camp in late January and returned to Guaynopa in mid-February. They told Loco that a large force of warriors would return in forty days to carry away the entire band if they had not already come voluntarily. Bonito warned they would kill any who refused to leave. Dependents of Nana's warriors and Victorio's wife, whose daughter had married Mangas, were eager to leave. Loco wanted no part of the plan. About a week later, a woman from Loco's camp who had married a western Apache revealed the information to the military.

Willcox was disturbed that Bonito was able to appear on the reservation undetected. On March 22, 1882, he sent Major David Perry with two troops and a company of Indian scouts to establish a base camp in the southern Chiricahua Mountains from which he sent scouting parties along the border to intercept Apache who were attempting to cross unseen.

The Chiricahua began moving north from Guaynopa in the first week of March hoping to make a temporary truce at Janos or Casas Grandes to protect their women and children while most of the warriors went north to San Carlos to "save Loco and his people." On March 14, the Apache made horse raids on Janos and the Ramos Hacienda. The next day, they told the hacienda owners they wanted to make a treaty. After thrust and parry between the Mexicans and Chiricahua, with threats about killing hostages on both sides and more Apache raids for horses and sheep, some exchanges were made, and tentative treaty talks started with the Mexicans trying to get Juh to come into Janos for further talks, but Juh understood what the Mexicans planned all too well.

MAJOR FORSYTH AT Fort Cummings hired Lorenzo Carrasco to go to Janos and Casas Grandes and report on what was happening with the Apache. On March 27, Carrasco arrived at Janos and learned that 450 Chiricahua were camped at Casa de Janos about 25 miles southwest of Janos on the Río Janos, and that about 40 Apache had gone north to the mountains of Fort Cummings to retrieve cached ammunition. Carrasco also learned Mexican militaries in Sonora and Chihuahua were biding their time waiting for an opportunity to exterminate the Apache down to the last child. Mexican generals and colonels were moving their soldiers into place expecting operations to begin on April 20 when "troops from Sonora would be in position." Until then, they directed that the Apache were not to be attacked in any form or fashion to avoid giving away what was planned.

On April 5, Colonel Joaquin Terrazas left *Casas Grande*s with authorization from his commander to take any measures to kill or capture Geronimo and Juh. On April 8, Terrazas met Juh and Geronimo near Casa de Janos. They agreed to return in two days with other chiefs to discuss terms. They returned April 10, as scheduled, but Terrazas decided an attack was not in his best interests. Instead, he promised to issue rations of flour, meat, sugar, and tobacco and to furnish mescal in Janos if they wanted it while discussing peace. The next morning, April 11, Geronimo and all but about thirty warriors rode north for San Carlos. Juh and Nana stayed in Mexico with the remaining thirty warriors and fifteen teenage boys capable of fighting to support and defend 325 women and children.[3,4]

WITH GERONIMO WERE some of the Chiricahua' most famous fighting men including Naiche, Chihuahua, Chato, Kaytennae, Mangas, Sánchez, and Jelikine. A total of seventy-two warriors crossed the border somewhere between San Luis Pass in southwestern New Mexico and San Bernardino in southeastern Arizona on April 12, 1882. They went north through the Animas Mountains and then, according to Al Sieber, abruptly broke west into the Peloncillo Mountains and then north again to the San Simon Valley, which they crossed early in the morning of April 13, 1882. They then moved north toward the Río Gila.

The Long Shot
Painting by Henry Farny, 1891

TWELVE

The Ash Flat Massacre

ON THE MORNING April 11, 1882, Geronimo, with over seventy fighting men including some of the best and most famous (Naiche, Chihuahua, Chato, Kaytennae, Mangas, Sánchez, and Jelikine), left for San Carlos to bring Loco and his people back to the Sierra Madre. They passed through mountains unseen or unreported and on the evening of April 16, arrived at Ash Flat about forty miles east of San Carlos. There are at least four versions of what happened at Ash Flat.[1,2]

The following story incorporates the facts of what happened and includes an imaginative reconstruction for some of what was said. It is told from Geronimo's point of view.

ASH FLAT WAS on the trail we rode to free Loco and his people from San Carlos. We planned to take them with us to our camps in the Sierra Madre where we believed the Blue Coats would never come. We thought we were safe there. Near Ash Flat, we smelled and soon heard many sheep. I smiled when I smelled sheep were nearby. Sheep always meant *Nakai-yi* (Mexican) herders, and it was always a good time for killing *Nakai-yes* (Mexicans) when I remembered what they did to my family many harvests before. Naiche, Chihuahua, and Chato rode with me in the front of our warriors, and they, too, smiled when they smelled the sheep. They said our warriors would be hungry. It was time to stop and eat.

Outriding scouts came to us and said the sheepherders included nine *Nakai-yes* and three White Mountain Apache. Some of the *Nakai-yes* and Apache had their families there. Twelve men with their families posed little danger for us. We were a big war party of maybe seventy warriors. We quietly rode through the brush and appeared like ghosts at their camp where the women worked. I looked the camp over. It was a safe place to take time for a meal and take proper care of the *Nakai-yes*—men, women, and children.

The man in charge came toward us unarmed. A *Nakai-yi,* he looked familiar, and I quickly realized it was Bes-das, once a boy I had taken in a raid in the land of the *Nakai-yes.* He had light behind his eyes. He learned quickly to speak Apache and worked hard around the camp, and I treated him well. I gave him a spotted pony, a saddle trimmed in silver, and shirts to keep the sun from burning his skin, but he was not happy with us. I think he was too old when we took him. It would have been better if I had killed him then and been done with him. I knew I couldn't trust him to stay with us, so I traded him to a White Eye rancher for a pistol, a box of cartridges, and two ponies. The rancher said the boy's *Nakai-yi* name was Victoriano Mestas, which Mestas never told me even though I speak good Spanish. I had not seen him again since I had traded him away. He had grown into a strong man, and his woman had made fancy designs with colored thread on his shirt. It was a very nice shirt. I liked it.

Bes-das walked up to us as we sat quietly on our ponies looking over his camp and deciding what we wanted, but he didn't seem to have much. He waved his arm parallel to the ground and said, "I see you, Geronimo. Welcome to my camp. Do you remember me?"

I swung down from my pony and walked over to him. Every *Nakai-yi* stood still watching us while the sheep milled about nearby making noise, and the children gathered around the skirts of their mothers who held fingers over their mouths to keep from screaming in fear of us.

"I know you, Bes-das. I took you from *Nakai-yes* to raise myself when you were small but growing. You grew into a big *Nakai-yi* after I traded you to the White Eye rancher, and I see you have a woman and three children playing around her. You are the chief of the *Nakai-yes* here? They do what you tell them?"

Bes-das cocked his head to one side and nodded. "*Si,* I am the *jefe* here."

Warriors pushed the sheep herders over by wagon where they made them sit down and then tied their hands together with one rope they found on a wagon, but they left the women free to work.

"I see another little camp of *wickiups* just over there." I pointed toward them with my nose. "They look like Apache, and they have their women with them. Who are they?"

"That's Bylas and three other men. They're White Mountains helping with wether lambs."

"Hmmph. I have lived in the White Mountains. I think I know this man Bylas. My warriors have ridden far. They're hungry." I swung back up on my pony and smiled down at Bes-das. "We can have a few of your sheep?"

Bes-das smiled back, but I saw the fear in his eyes as he turned toward the sheep and spread his arms wide. "*Sí, sí,* Geronimo. Take all you need."

I turned to the warriors and told them to take sheep they needed for a meal and then turned back toward Bes-das. I had seen a fine sorrel pony grazing near his wagon. To Bes-das I said, "That's a nice pony that grazes near your wagon."

The smile left his face. He said, "The pony belongs to *Señor* Jimmie Stevens, whose father owns the sheep. I just ride him once in a while. It's not mine."

"*Enjuh* (Good). I like horsemeat better than sheep." I killed the pony with an easy shot to its head from where I sat on my horse not fifty yards away. The rifle's report made the tied *Nakai-yes* jerk in surprise and look around in fear to see who was shooting. I laughed at them. It was always good to see *Nakai-yes* flinch in fear. "Tell your women to prepare the meal. Is that Bylas's *wickiup* over by those trees?"

Bes-das's fear was leaking out of his eyes and on to his face. He nodded. I said, "I know White Mountains. Bylas probably has some whiskey. I'm thirsty. Maybe he'll give me a drink. Let's go over to see Bylas."

Bes-das told the women to fix whatever the warriors wanted and followed me on foot as I walked my pony over to Bylas's *wickiup* and dismounted. I sat down by his fire and waited for him to come out of his *wickiup*. Soon he came. He smelled of good whiskey and could not walk straight. I said, "I know you. You lived in the White Mountains when I did. You always have some whiskey around. Give me a bottle."

Bylas shook his head as he dropped down in front of me. The whiskey stains on his shirt were still damp, its smell fresh and powerful. "I don't have anymore. I drank it all when I saw you and your war party ride out of the brush."

"Hmmph. Not another bottle you have? None you can give me?"

"Whiskey all gone."

"That's too bad. I was hoping for a drink of good whiskey. You come eat with us. The women cook sheep and horse now. Maybe you remember where another bottle is after you eat."

Bylas and his White Mountains walked behind me as I rode back to Bes-das's wagons where cooking fires burned and the women cooked beans and *tortillas* along with the meat.

I sat with Bylas and his men, one a grown son of one of the men. I said to Bylas, "You still don't remember having any more whiskey?" He looked at his moccasins and shook his head. I spoke of old times with Bes-das, who relaxed a little. I asked Bylas to tell me if things were any better on the reservation while the warriors filled their bellies. After he spoke, I said, narrowing my eyes like I didn't believe his earlier answer, "Still you don't remember having any more whiskey?"

The grown son of one of Bylas's men had not grown enough to control his tongue. He said, "This man Bylas is not a boy for you to talk to this way and keep on asking for whiskey. He won't give you any whiskey." I didn't need a boy to tell me how to act. He didn't look like an Apache to me. He looked like a *Nakai-yi*.

"This boy is a full-blood *Nakai-yi.*" I cocked my rifle. I was ready to kill him, but one of the White Mountains said, "No. He is not a *Nakai-yi.* He's a full-blood White Mountain, and his mother is of the black water clan, so he's of that clan also."

I looked at Bylas and then my rifle, cocked and lying in my lap. "What is he?"

Bylas swallowed, then said in a croaking whisper, "He is White Mountain."

My anger grew. I didn't want to kill a White Mountain. They had many scouts who worked for Crook. Perhaps they needed to know we meant business.

I said to Bes-das, "That's a fine shirt you wear that your woman decorates for you. I think I would like to have it. Why don't you take it off and give it to me so I can keep it clean?"

Bes-das's face froze.

He stood, and his fingers trembled as he unbuttoned the shirt and pulled it off his shoulders. I saw him glance at his woman, his head making a tiny shake most did not see. She spoke to her children, and they climbed under the wagon, squatted there, and watched their father give me his shirt.

I laid it over my knees and took my time to fold it carefully while I knew Bes-das was trembling inside. He knew what was coming. Most of the warriors had eaten and were leaning back on their elbows enjoying their meal, but a group near us sat on their heels with their rifles cocked, wondering what we would do next. I looked at Bes-das and grinned and then said to the waiting warriors, "Tie these *Nakai-yes* together with the others and kill them."

Bylas, who sat near Naiche and Chato while they ate, said, "Why do you want to kill these people after they fed you? You promised Bes-das that you would harm no one."

Bylas's words cooled my heat some, and I held up my hand to stop warriors as Naiche said, "Be straight with these people, Geronimo. They've done nothing to us. They fed us as you wanted. You even took a fine pony to eat. Why don't you pay the women for cooking for you?"

Chato said, "Why would you kill these people? They've done all we asked and nothing at all to harm us. We could have lost many men if we had attacked this camp."

The words of Bylas, Naiche, and Chato had poured cool water on my heat, and my anger was going away when Chihuahua said, "These people are *Nakai-yes,* and they're our enemies. Always the *Nakai-yes* have lied to us and killed our people. You told me what the *Nakai-yes* did to your own family. Remember what Terrazas is trying to do to us now."

Despite what the others had said, the stones in my guts grew hot again. I waved the warriors on. The warriors were on Bes-das before he could take a step toward me. They dragged him and the women, who were screaming and begging to be spared, over to the men who were already tied together. Bes-das's woman screamed at the children under the wagon and told them to run. They ran quick like rabbits leaving a hole taken by a rattlesnake. Warriors looked at me, and I nodded and said, "Yes, even the little ones. They must die like all my children did." They caught two of the three and threw the smallest one on the thorns of a big cactus. It wailed for a long time. It was a strong child like my children must have been. The other child they tied over the coals of a fire to roast. It too screamed a long time.

The warriors smashed the heads of the screaming women with rocks and bashed some of the men with their war clubs. They had knife throwing contests at the bodies of some of the men, and two or three of the throws went straight and true. Those men didn't last long. They found a loaded rifle in Bes-das's wagon and brought it to me. I tried it out on Bes-das, shooting him in his man parts. He screamed and groaned only a little while because he bled so much, and then I put a bullet in his heart.

The warriors found the third child, a boy, hiding under the skirts of Bylas's wife. They drug him away from her while she pleaded for his life. When they looked at me, I nodded and said, "Yes, all must die. Die good in pain."

Jelikine was squatting nearby leaning against his spear watching what was happening and shaking his head saying, "No, good. No good."

Naiche said, "No! There's been enough killing here. Let the boy live."

In my rage, I roared, "He dies! All *Nakai-yes* die like my children died. Kill the woman too. She protected him."

I felt the point of Jelikine's spear push against my chest. "Kill that boy, and you die, Geronimo."

I heard the hammer click back on Naiche's rifle and saw the barrel pointed at me, not two bow lengths from my belly. "Kill that child and woman, and you'll die with them, Geronimo." Naiche was a good warrior, just soft sometimes. Perhaps my thirst for *Nakai-yi* blood was satisfied by now. I was not afraid of Jelikine and Naiche, but I nodded and lifted my hands. "Naiche is chief. I obey Naiche. Let them go."

We took all the supplies we could from the camp, and Bylas and his people went with us on to Dewey Flat and the Old Wagon Road. It was an unexpected gift to eat so well before we raided the reservation to take Loco and his people.

THIRTEEN

Loco and His People Are Saved from San Carlos

TO ENSURE THEY weren't discovered, the Apache left two men at the Ash Flat sheep camp to guard the White Mountain women and compelled Bylas, a White Mountain scout and leader, and the other White Mountain man to accompany them as far as the reservation. That evening they camped on the south side of Ash Flat. There Geronimo made medicine singing four songs to consult his Power to learn if the raid would be successful. Geronimo's Power assured him all was well and helped by sending Loco's people into a deep sleep.[1] The Chiricahua belief in Geronimo's access to supernatural help had added significantly to his rank as a military leader. He had become famous with the Apache by doing his ceremonies and then telling the warriors, "You should go here; you should not go there."

After Geronimo made medicine, the band rode through the night to the reservation and entered it through the *bosque* (brush and trees) along the Río Gila just before dawn. The Chokonen sub-chief and for a time, future scout, Chihuahua, cut the telegraph wires connecting the San Carlos agency, sub-agency for Loco and his people, and the mining town of Globe. To prevent line riders from quickly finding the cut wires so the telegraphy could be reestablished, Chihuahua knew enough to tie the ends of the cut together with a rawhide thong making the line riders check every foot of line until they found the cut.

Geronimo also sent his emissaries to alert their contacts in Loco's camps. About forty Apache policemen had their homes scattered around the camps on the reservation. Geronimo threatened to send three men into every camp and kill them all, but this never happened.

Someone in the band used an Apache trick to learn when daylight was near.

Apache Crossing the Gila River at San Carlos, ca. 1900.
Photograph by Andrew Miller.

He threw a pebble in the air. If he could see it, then it was proof positive dawn approached. At daylight, April 19, 1882, the band of Geronimo's warriors crossed the Río Gila and quietly moved toward Loco's camps lying about three miles east of the main agency on a graveled bench between the Gila and San Carlos Rivers.

A typical lie the agents reported to Congress was that of Apache irrigation works and bountiful crops, but there was little vegetation anywhere near Loco's camps except for cottonwoods and brush along the rivers. Still, Loco had pledged to stay there. But on this daybreak, his people heard shouting and saw a line of armed warriors between them and the agency. Others were on their horses and coming across the river. One of the warrior's leaders was shouting, "Take them all! Shoot down anyone who refuses to go with us! Some of you men lead them out." (Most stories say it was Geronimo). Loco's people did everything they were told to do by the warriors. They were led away on foot with barely enough time to scoop up a few belongings. At gunpoint, some say it was Chato, Loco was forced to lead the evacuation.[2,3] Geronimo rode in front guiding them east long the bottom of the hills north of the Gila. Other warriors stayed behind to stop any help that might come from the agency.

Loco's people hadn't gone far when they heard shooting from near their camp. The telegraph operator at the sub-agency had found the ends of the cut wire and reconnected with the main agency to notify Chief of Police, Albert D. Sterling, the wire had been cut and there appeared to be movement toward Loco's camp. Sterling, aided by one of his policemen, rode for Loco's camp to learn what was happening. Both were killed even though two shots had been fired by the Warm Springs people to warn them. The killing of the policemen filled Loco's people with despair; they had no choice but to keep quiet and try not to escape.

Loco's people were herded along the Gila for a few miles and then turned northeast into the Gila Mountains. As the sun fell behind dark mountains, they were given a short rest near a spring, then began walking and running in the dark. By this time, Loco had been admitted to the council of leaders that included Naiche, Chato, Chihuahua, and others, but with Geronimo clearly in charge. At midnight, they rested again, and some volunteers were sent to raid a sheep camp with instructions for where to rendezvous in the coming morning.

The people moved on, and at sunrise, the raiders came with several hundred sheep. Loco's hungry people ate and were allowed to rest for two days. In the meantime, the council of leaders discussed plans for escaping into Mexico and avoiding fights with the Blue Coats ranging over the countryside looking for them. The band probably consisted of about a hundred twenty warriors and two to three hundred women and children—a very hard group to conceal. They needed to outrun their pursuers to make it to the border, but Loco's people, grown soft living on the reservation from forced idleness, were showing little of the speed and endurance of typical Apache movements. Even the young men in their twenties had no opportunity to train as novitiates or to hunt while they lived at San Carlos. It was a factor Geronimo had neglected to consider in his raid plans. Now, he and the Sierra Madre Apache had to care for poorly conditioned people on the run from well-conditioned scouts and mounted Blue Coats.

SEVERAL WARRIORS WERE sent north up the San Francisco River to raid a ranch for horses and mules for Loco's people to ride. They came back driving a herd and spent another day or two breaking them to ride bareback or with saddles made from bundles of reeds. Farther along the warriors went to another ranch for more mounts while the main group waited out of sight behind a nearby hill. During their wait, one of the girls reached puberty, and the group held a short version of her womanhood ceremony even as shots were heard from the ranch. By this time, the group had killed anyone they encountered, more than fifty people, including ranchers, miners, lone travelers, and wagon train drivers.[4] They hadn't wanted to leave San Carlos. Now, Loco's people were guilty by association.

They traveled again at night but faster mounted. Even surrounded by their captors as they moved, a few managed to disappear from the main group and headed for Navajo country. By morning they stopped to rest at a spring in the Steins Peak Mountains. Twelve warriors were sent out to scout the area while the rest moved about halfway up Steins Peak to await their return.

Lieutenant Colonel George A. Forsyth was on the hunt for the fleeing Apache and discovered the trail of the twelve warriors scouting the area. He sent his own scouts out to find them, but the warriors scouting for the fleeing people ambushed the army scouts and killed four. Forsyth rode to the rescue with six companies of cavalry and attacked the entire force of runaways in a canyon while the women and children watched from the up the mountain. Claiming he had won with his overpowering force, he soon beat a hasty retreat leaving the Apache in possession of the battlefield. The Apache had lost one warrior.

After the battle, the Apache moved down the San Simon Valley. They rode all night until they stopped at daybreak at a rendezvous point in the Chiricahua Mountains southeast of Fort Bowie. There, warriors could get high enough on the nearby mountains to watch Fort Bowie and give advance warning of a coming White Eye attack, but nothing happened. They rested for the day and made another night march through rugged country and entered Mexico where they rested for a day in the Sierra San Luis. At last they thought they were safe. They had left San Carlos and crossed to Mexico with great skill and success. They had escaped the Blue Coats and didn't think much of Mexican fighting ability. Coyote waits. Disaster was about to strike.

FOURTEEN

Blood and Tears at Aliso Creek

A WEEK AFTER beating off an attack in the Stein's Peak Mountains by a much greater U.S. Cavalry force under the command of Lieutenant Colonel George A. Forsyth, the Chiricahua warriors, with Loco's people they had abducted, crossed the border into Mexico and believed they were safe from the Americans. After a short rest, the Apache began a casual night ride across the Janos Plains. They had a good time riding southeast under a river of bright stars, making jokes, singing, calling to each other, and challenging each other for short races.

They stopped at springs along the way for water and by morning were in the middle of the Janos Plains at a small, rough mountain, the Sierra Enmedio. They camped there at a fine spring where to the west and south stretched a level *llano* (dry plains). Between them and the little mountain was a rocky ridge overlooking their camp and a little to the south a small round hill covered with boulders. They stayed in this camp for two days where they rested and relaxed and spent the nights dancing to celebrate their exodus out of San Carlos. The women even collected mescal crowns, dug a pit, and began cooking them for three days. The cooked mescal was a favorite food they had been denied during their stay at San Carlos.

The Apache didn't know that Forsyth had decided to ignore international law and cross the border after them. He had four hundred soldiers and fifty scouts, but he kept them at a safe distance watching and waiting for another attack opportunity. Captain Tullius C. Tupper had independently followed their trail through the mountains and the Janos Plains. Tupper had thirty-nine troopers and forty-seven Apache scouts under the leadership of Al Sieber, who with four scouts saw their campfire from five miles away and reconnoitered the camp undiscovered. After

Pool in the Desert.
Painting by Fredrick Remington, ca. 1908.

learning the lay of the land, Tupper ordered his scouts to man the ridge between the camp and Sierra Enmedio while his cavalry attacked by charging across the open plain. The mescal cooking in the ridge pit saved the band from being wiped out by Captain Tupper with his cavalry and Al Sieber with his scouts.

Just before dawn three women and a young man (Talbot Gooday, grandson of Loco) went to check on the cooking mescal. Laughing and talking they came within twenty-five feet of the hiding scouts. Knowing the attack was about to happen anyway, the commanding officer ordered the scouts to fire and killed all four—except the army record is wrong—one of the women who ran was killed, the others managed to escape.

The Apache had planned to begin an early morning march if the mescal had finished cooking. The shots were an alarm bell, and it put them in instant motion to escape. The scouts fired from the ridge and the charging cavalry from the front. Six warriors were killed. The entire band ran for the little round hill of boulders for cover—the women and children hiding and the men firing from cover. The Apache waited until the charging troopers were within a hundred yards of the little hill when they all fired expecting to wipe out troopers with one blow. Instead being above the plain, they shot just over the trooper's heads enabling most to escape without being hit.

The firing back and forth went on for most of the morning. Early in the afternoon, four young warriors managed to get behind the scouts on the ridge and fired on them from the rear. The scouts pulled back and joined the troopers on the *llano*. This gave the band a chance to escape into the foot hills around the mountain. Tupper, his men exhausted and almost out of ammunition, withdrew. He took the Apache's horses and returned to the previous night's camp. Soon Forsyth arrived and assumed command.

Loco's band had lost fourteen warriors in the day's battle. As the sun was setting, they came out of the hills and gathered together. They had lost everything they had brought with them from San Carlos and had no supplies. The cavalry had taken their horses and many of them were wounded. They drank from a nearby spring and shared what little food they had. Just before they started their march south across the Janos Plains, warriors came in with a few horses they had retaken from the retreating soldiers, but most had to walk. After a time, they were so exhausted they had to stop to rest and sleep for a while. About fifteen warriors with horses including Naiche, Chato, and Kaytennae (who became Nana's *segundo*) rode on. The main band began walking again and by dawn were near their predesignated assembly point after covering twenty-nine miles that night.

BY DAYLIGHT, THEY were in a scattered column two miles long and in a country of low hills paralleling a dry stream bed in an arroyo—Aliso Creek. In the distance, they could see the Blue Mountains, the Sierra Madre. They were in a classic Apache movement formation. A few warriors in the front led the way, the other warriors were in the rear guarding against possible pursuit by the Americans. The warriors in front stopped to rest while those walking passed on.

Suddenly, a Mexican military unit under Colonel Lorenzo García came out of hiding in a ravine and attacked the side of the walking column. García had learned the line of march after he captured a couple of warriors trying to return to Mexico with horses that they had stolen earlier that week for Loco's band but had decided to keep. The Mexicans charged among the women and children shooting them down and stabbing them with bayonets without mercy.

Apache who could run fast headed for the mountains and got away. Betzinez, still a boy, managed to get away and heard Geronimo calling to the men to gather around him and protect the women and children. Thirty-two warriors came to their aid.

Out of sight, sitting under a tree smoking, were the fifteen who had ridden ahead. They heard the shots but made no move to help. No one knows why. Angie Debo makes the point that, "Apache were individualists in their wars; if they trusted their leader they carried out his orders, but he could not enforce obedience." [1] Those who managed to get away from the Aliso Creek fighting went to a rendezvous point on the steep side of a mountain where others were already waiting.

GERONIMO, CHIHUAHUA, AND their warriors assembled in the dry creek bed with a few women and children where the real battle of Aliso Creek was fought. The Mexicans made repeated charges attempting to drive the Apache out of their defenses. The Mexican officers ordered their men to charge with yells like, "Geronimo is in the ditch. Go in and get him!" or "Geronimo, this is your last day!"

The women dug holes in the bank for shelter and the men dug footholds to step up and fire over the edge of the bank. Digging down through the sand the women were able to find water, but it soon turned red with blood. The hero of the battle was the teenager, Fun. He would come over the edge of the bank firing his single shot trap door rifle with his fingers full of cartridges, ducking and running in a zig-zag pattern back and forth as he charged the Mexican line three separate times including one where, as the Apache were running low on ammunition, an old woman drug a heavy satchel full of cartridges back to the creek bank.

Fun was deadly accurate and accounted for many Mexican casualties. He was given the Apache name "Yahechul," which means "Smoke Comes Out" for his abilities that day. The battle went on until dark. Then the Mexicans set the grass on fire to smoke the Apache out and provide light to see them as they prepared to slip out unseen. (In his autobiography Geronimo claimed the Apache fired the grass to provide smoke for cover). Geronimo called out, "If we leave the women and children we can escape." Fun couldn't believe what he heard and asked Geronimo to repeat it. Geronimo told the men to go. Fun raised his rifle and said, "Say that again, and I'll shoot." Geronimo climbed to the top of the bank and disappeared. Some of the groups escaping killed the babies so they wouldn't give away their movements by crying. One mother strangled her baby so it wouldn't grow up in Mexican slavery, others let the warriors do it.

THOSE WHO HAD gotten away earlier and taken refuge on the mountain heard the wailing and mourning for lost relatives throughout a very cold night. They tried to stay warm without fires by covering themselves with grass and sleeping grouped together. There was no help for the wounded and no food. With the morning light they were elated when they saw the Mexican and American soldiers come together far out on the *llano*. They expected a fight, but it didn't happen. Their leaders ordered them to move down the mountain and half way down they met Geronimo and his group coming up. After sharing news of their experiences, Geronimo gave the order to start marching again.

At Aliso Creek, the Apache killed three Mexican officers and eighteen or nineteen men and wounded many more. Seventy-eight Apache had been killed and thirty-three women and children had been taken into slavery. Of those Apache killed, eleven had been warriors, most of the others were women and children killed in the first attack before the warriors came to their rescue.

The War Department was never informed that its forces had invaded Mexico. His superior officer stopped Forsyth's report with the advice, "the less said about it the better." Tupper's report located his fight in the mountains of New Mexico. The Apache later told General Crook they had won the fight on Aliso Creek.

FIFTEEN

Loco's Survivors Gather
with Other Chiricahua in Mexico

UNITED ONCE MORE after suffering through a dark cold night following the Aliso Creek fight, the Apache began moving through the foothills leading to a Juh stronghold in the Sierra Madre. Many were wounded and the band had to move slow. Geronimo sent some warriors to ranches on the *llano* to steal cattle which they drove to the next rendezvous point. There the band made meat, had their first real meal in the three days since Captain Tupper's attack, and rested for two days.

When they again began moving toward Juh's camp they left two men and Martine's wife to care for them while they recovered. One of the men left behind was Kayihtah who was to play a major role in the surrender of Geronimo to General Miles four years later. He was a cousin of Yahnozha (one of Geronimo's best warriors). The other wounded man was a young White Mountain Apache named Tzoe, who had been married to two Chihenne women, remembered as sisters of Chato, and with a little daughter, killed in the attack at Aliso Creek.

Tzoe played a major role in helping General Crook return the Apache in the Sierra Madre back to San Carlos and thirty-four years later was the personal scout of General John J. Pershing when he commanded the Punitive Expedition after Pancho Villa in Mexico. The next evening after the main group had left, Geronimo sent a man back to help them, but he returned saying the place was occupied by Mexicans. The three left behind managed to survive and showed up at Juh's camp a month later fully recovered.

The main group soon found Juh's people high in the mountains about thirty miles southwest of Casas Grandes. When Loco's people arrived in Juh's camp, they had nothing left except the clothes on their backs. There were many strangers in

Apache Ambush
Painting by Frederic Remington, ca. 1900.

Juh's people, but there were also many happy reunions. Loco's people were given food and blankets and spoken to kindly and cheerfully to help get their minds off all they had lost. Geronimo's move to force Loco's people off the reservation and into the Sierra Madre had been costly—twenty-six fighting men were in over a hundred-twenty killed, and there had been great destruction of women and children. Even so, it was the largest number of related Apache gathered together in years. Among them were many powerful warriors, and their mountain camps in the high Sierra Madre had never been invaded by an enemy. When he returned to command the southwest territories, it didn't take General Crook long to realize the Sierra Madre held terror waiting to happen.

The united bands were now led by Juh and Geronimo who soon led them to a stronghold near the San Miguel River. There, after a few days of rest and relaxation, the leaders decided to take a trading trip to Casas Grandes and about a third of the band went. Casas Grandes usually had peaceable relations with Juh and his people and did a brisk business in trade for their raiding plunder. However, the state of Chihuahua didn't recognize any understanding Casas Grandes had with Juh. After the Apache at Casas Grandes had celebrated their trading by getting drunk on good White Eye whiskey, they were attacked by Mexican soldiers, probably Chihuahua soldiers from the town of Galeana about thirty miles to the southeast. Geronimo said, "We fled in all directions." Some of the warriors led by Juh and Geronimo fought the soldiers, but the attack was a disaster for the Apache. The Mexicans killed about twenty (so said Geronimo) and took thirty-five into captivity. Geronimo lost Chee-hash-kish, "first wife" among his women, mother of his beautiful daughter, Dohnsay, and son, Chappo, a novitiate warrior.

The next year, Geronimo kidnapped five Mexican women, one with a baby, to trade for Chee-hash-kish, but General Crook who had just arrived in the Sierra Madre camps, talked the Chiricahua leaders into returning to San Carlos, and returned the women and baby Geronimo had captured back to their village. Geronimo never saw Chee-hash-kish again although it was rumored that she married another captive. There are also stories that Chee-hash-kish was freed by and married the so-called "White Apache" Nathanial Streeter and that she kept two other children (there are no reservation records of them) she had in addition to Dohnsay and Chappo hidden with her in Mexico, but there is little evidence, if any, that these stories are true.

After the disaster at Casas Grandes, the band waited four days for the missing to return and then moved southwest deep into the Sierra Madre and crossed the immense, deep slash across the mountains, Copper Canyon. Camping and moving toward Sonora, they came out on the western slopes of the Sierra Madre and planned a raid with novitiate boys on a Sonora town, which didn't happen because there were too many soldiers nearby. Betzinez says Geronimo asked him to become his apprentice there.[1] There were several other novitiates also in training including Lot Eyelash (who was to accuse Geronimo of being a witch twenty-six years later), Chappo, Yahnozha, and probably the hero of the Aliso Creek battle, Fun.

AT THIS TIME Geronimo, having lost Chee-hash-kish, and needing another wife to help She-gha and Shtsha-she, probably approached the great warrior, Jelikine, and asked for his diminutive daughter Zi-yeh. Jelikine an Apache in every way except blood, had been taken captive as a Mexican born child. He was the warrior who had held a spear to Geronimo's chest and said he would kill him if Geronimo ordered the nine-year-old child of Victoriano Mestas killed during the Ash Flat massacre. Zi-yeh, small and attractive, often outworked the other women. Jelikine agreed to the marriage, which lasted about twenty-three years. Clearly an object of Geronimo's affection, Zi-yeh had a child, Fenton, a boy, before Geronimo's final surrender, and later, in captivity, she had his last child, Eva, at Mount Vernon Barracks north of Mobile, Alabama.

The bands didn't stay together long. After a friendly disagreement between their leaders, the bands split into two groups. Juh, the Nednhi, and most of the San Carlos Apache returned to his stronghold in the heart of the Sierra Madre. Geronimo, Chihuahua, and Kaytennae and their people went on to raid in Sonora. During this time, a child was born to one of Geronimo's other wives, She-gha or Shtsha-she. The raids reached south and west almost to village of Ures on the western side of the Sierra Madre Occidental and to the north where the Río Bavispe turns from flowing north to south. While the warriors plundered villages, stole cattle, horses, and mules, and captured pack trains, their women were safely hidden in the mountains drying beef, gathering wild foods like nuts, berries, and mescal bulbs, and making clothes from cloth taken in their men's raids. The victimized Mexicans were suffering, but it was the best of times for the Apache.

IN THE LATE summer or early fall, they settled in the Sierra Madre Oriental near the turn of the Río Bavispe south. The warriors with nearly new American repeating rifles, were having a hard time finding replacement ammunition in Mexico. Holding a council, they decided to raid across the border for the cartridges they needed. They hid their families, under the protection of old men and novitiate warriors, at the foot of a mountain. It wasn't long before the warriors returned with great quantities of ammunition and "many articles useful for camp life." They had lost one warrior from wounds in the raid and another earlier to a soldier's bullet during a raid to the south. To the Apache these were serious losses, but considering the number of raids and miles covered, they were minor. Little was said in Army reports or local newspapers about this raid. Angie Debo speculates that the Apache had made one fortunate haul, like taking a major freight train, which had caused relatively little disturbance to the surrounding countryside.[2]

Unknown to the Apache, arguably the best Indian fighter in the United States had been sent back to Arizona to straighten out the reservation debacles and to stop raids by Apache coming out of Mexico. General Crook, who believed it took an Apache to catch an Apache and had established the Apache scouts in 1873, had been recalled back from fighting the northern plains tribes to the Department of Arizona and arrived at Whipple Barracks outside Prescott, on September 4, 1882. It was the beginning of the end of the Apache's days of freedom in the Sierra Madre.

SIXTEEN

Revenge and Raids in Mexico
and the United States

THE APACHE IN Mexico had access to some of the best rifles and revolvers of the time. These weapons had been taken in raids on ranches, wagon freight trains, villages and towns, and from the bodies of dead soldiers. The problem in using these weapons was ammunition supply. Once the Apache had used nearly all the ammunition they had stolen with the weapon, they had to find more and that was often hard to do. Thus, in late 1882, after the Chiricahua raid north across the border that quickly provided a large quantity of ammunition and "many articles useful for camp life," they naturally felt they were being guided by their great creator god, Ussen. They saw even more evidence of this as they moved back toward camps deep in the Sierra Madre. Close to Oputo, a village on the south-flowing Río Bavispe, Geronimo's Power led him to tell the warriors that Mexican soldiers were on their trail, and he predicted exactly the time and place where they would appear. The forewarned Chiricahua set up an ambush and captured all the soldiers' horses and supplies, which further convinced them that Geronimo was in fact a man of great Power.[1]

The Chiricahua with Geronimo continued south to camp near the edge of Copper Canyon, a huge, jagged scar across the middle of Mexico slashing through the mountains about 260 miles south of the Arizona border. The Apache called it the "great canyon." A few days after their arrival, Juh's band appeared on the other side, and they were close enough to hear each other's drums across the across the gorge.

Geronimo soon led the band across the canyon to Juh's camp. Even for the Apache in great physical shape it was a hard crossing that took the best conditioned of them about a day to climb down into the gorge and then up the other

A Dash for the Timber
Painting by Frederic Remington, ca. 1900.

side. According to Betzinez, as the two groups met, it was a very happy time for all as they exchanged gifts and memories of past days.

Juh told Geronimo and his band of warriors about a recent battle he and his warriors had with Mexican soldiers. It began with had a two-day running skirmish with Mexican soldiers in pursuit. Their ammunition was nearly gone when Juh led his warriors up a steep mountain leaving a trail a child could follow. A part of the trail ran nearly perpendicular to the ascent up the mountain before it made a switchback turn to climb again. Juh had his warriors hidden above that section and rolled a line of big rocks into place parallel to that part of the trail. They waited for the soldiers to come, slowly watching out for an ambush. When most of the soldiers were on the flat part of the trail, the Apache rolled the boulders down on them. Then Juh and his warriors calmly climbed down from their perch, finished off any surviving soldiers, took their guns and ammunition, and disappeared. Juh had not lost a single warrior.

After camping together for several weeks beside the great canyon, a council was held where it was decided that it was payback time for the attack at Casas Grandes by the Chihuahuan military. Geronimo and others believed that the soldiers had come from Galeana, which was also the home of the *segundo* (number two) for Joaquin Terrazas who had led the attack and destruction of Victorio at Tres Castillos. Terrazas's *segundo* was the famous Indian fighter, Juan Mata Ortiz. Old

Nana, who had not been at the Casas Grandes attack, knew Ortiz lived at Galeana, and still thirsting to avenge Victorio's destruction, insisted on joining the raid.

The Apache traveled north in easy stages holding dances along the way until they came to the mountains from where they could see Galeana in the distance ten or eleven miles away. After meeting in council, the war leaders developed a strategy Apache rarely used—but commonly employed by the Plains tribes—a few warriors lure an enemy into an ambush.

NEAR CHOCOLATE PASS, about halfway between Galeana and Casas Grandes, the road paralleled a ravine and beyond was a depression that could hide a large number of mounted warriors from those on the road. The Apache hid small groups of warriors in the ravine along the roadway and the rest in the depression. A few warriors rode up close to Galeana in plain sight and drove away a small herd of horses up the road toward Chocolate Pass. A small Mexican cavalry troop pursed the Apache who stayed just out of reach as they raced for the pass.

The cavalry was met head on by heavy fire from the hidden Apache riding up out of the depression and from the rear by the groups hidden in the ravine who came up on the road to make a front-to-back crossfire. The retreating Mexican commander swerved off the road to a small, rock covered round hill not far away. At the top, his men dismounted and began desperately piling rocks into a breastworks.

The Apache in the depression rode to another hill close by and turned their horses over to novitiate warriors for holding. Then with the Apache who had sprung out of the ravine, encircled the hill unseen and began crawling up the slope each rolling a stone in front of him for protection. The older men, Juh, Geronimo, Nana, and some of their best marksmen including Kaytennae took a protected position near a lone cedar tree at the base of the hill and fired a few shots to keep the attention of the soldiers. When the warriors reached the breastworks, they charged forward for a hand-to-hand fight. Losing two warriors they wiped out twenty-one soldiers and took their officer, who to their delight was Juan Mata Ortiz. At last, Nana would get his revenge. When the bodies of the soldiers were recovered, Juan Mata Ortiz was a charred cinder.

One survivor got away on a desperate ride for help in Galeana. Geronimo shouted for the warriors to let him go. He would bring more that they could kill. Soon another troop of cavalry charged out of Galeana. The Apache mounted and rode to meet them, but the soldiers dismounted and started digging in. The warriors sat back and enjoyed watching the soldiers covered in sweat furiously throw dirt out of trenches to protect themselves. 2 Soon, the sun not far above the western mountains, began casting long shadows across the *llano* creeping over the Apache and Mexican soldiers eyeing each other. As darkness filled the *llano*, the Apache decided to leave off attacking before returning to their women and children.

THAT NIGHT THERE was no victory dance because the Apache had lost two warriors, but according to Betzinez the original attack had gone according to plan, its faultless execution a clear demonstration of the fighting discipline under the leadership of Juh and Geronimo. Word came that a large group of Mexican soldiers from Casas Grandes was on the way to attack them. The Apache disappeared deep into the mountains and after camping safe together for several days, the band divided again, Juh returning to his stronghold, and Geronimo and Chihuahua establishing a base camp high in the Sierra Madre near the headwaters of the Río Bavispe, an area the Apache called "Bugatseka" (On Top Rocks White), the Mexicans called it "Mesa Tres Rios."

The base camp of Geronimo and Chihuahua had good water, plenty of firewood, and an abundance of game. They lived there comfortably for a while and then decided on another raid in Sonora. They left the women and children in camp and led the warriors and novitiates west across the Bavispe to the roads used by the pack trains on the way to Ures. They butchered cattle and stole horses as they slipped around towns undetected until they took a heavily loaded pack train of dry goods and other supplies. Upon returning to the camp at the head waters of the Bavispe, they stayed several months before returning to camp on the edge of the great canyon.

SEVENTEEN

The Spring Raids of 1883

THROUGH THE GHOST Face time (winter) of 1882/1883 the Chiricahua who had escaped from San Carlos Reservation camped on the edge of the "great canyon." The great chief Juh rejoined them after suffering a major attack on his camp by Mexican Tarahumara soldiers. In the attack, he lost his wife Ishton, Geronimo's beloved "sister," two daughters, and a third daughter who was shot in the leg and crippled for life. Many of the women and children in Juh's band were captured and sold into slavery, including Chato's wife and two children. The remnants of Victorio's band had also been with Juh. Among them was Kaytennae, his wife Guyan, and young son Kaywaykla who all managed to escape. The Juh band had become demoralized by their misfortunes and groups were leaving with mutual bad feelings. Juh, his three sons (including the future famous Daklugie who was then about twelve years old) and a few followers left to wander and raid on their own. Juh left Jacali, his wounded daughter, in the care of those in the main band. Warriors in the main band had spent the Ghost Face sharpening their knives, oiling their rifles, making arrows with wicked multi-barbed arrowheads filed out of barrel band iron, plaiting good rawhide ropes, and planning two major raids for the time of Little Eagles (early spring). One raid was to be on pack trains in Sonora, and the other for ammunition across the border in Arizona and New Mexico.[1]

When the time of Little Eagles came, the Chiricahua sans Juh's little band settled their families back in their Bugatseka base camp area at the head waters of the Río Bavispe. Their camp was in a natural amphitheater surrounded by great mountains with a sparkling, clear stream of water running through it. The warriors rode down out of the mountains to take their familiar raiding trail into

Sonora. They camped together their first night away from their base camp and then split the next day. Chato and Bonito, with Chato in command, left with twenty-six warriors and headed north. Among these warriors were Naiche, Tzoe (who had been part of Loco's band taken from San Carlos by the Apache under Geronimo and had lost two wives and a little daughter at the Aliso Creek fight), and Tzoe's good friend Beneactiney, son-in-law of Chihuahua.

The main raiding party, said to contain about eighty warriors, continuing west went much farther than usual—about one hundred miles southwest of Ures. They plundered towns, took cattle and horses, killed anyone with whom they crossed paths (most Mexicans stayed out of reach), but initially found no pack train. But as they were returning to their base camp, they found and took one. It was loaded with dry goods like blankets and articles needed for camp life, and it had a big load of good Mexican mescal. That night many of the older men got drunk, but the novitiates kept guard and no enemy attacked. Before reaching base camp, two messengers from the northern raiding party found them and gave the news that Beneactiney had been killed. Beneactiney had been Betzinez's cousin and, since Betzinez was not yet recognized as a warrior, was regarded as the head of the family of Betzinez's widowed mother Nah-thle-tla. Beneactiney's death was devastating to his close friend Tzoe and was to play a major role in forcing the Chiricahua back to San Carlos.[2]

A few days after the Sonoran group of raiders returned to their base camp, the band under Chato and Bonito returned from a successful raid in the north that yielded guns, ammunition, and a six-year-old white child they had captured, Charlie McComas. The band had been busy in the north. On March 21, they hit a camp making charcoal near Tombstone and killed three of the four men they found there. They soon hit another camp, killed one man and fired into a tent. When there was no return fire from inside the tent, Tzoe and Beneactiney charged it. A man hidden just outside the tent shot and killed Beneactiney. A little later the raiders killed three miners and raced on killing a man here, a small party there, and stealing horses to replace their worn-out mounts. They were pursued by cavalry units and outraged posses without success.

SAN CARLOS, AFTER being attacked by Victorio looking for revenge three years earlier and the previous year when the Loco Chihenne were taken captive, made ready for another invasion. The control of the reservation after the great breakout and Loco's kidnapping had been transferred from the Bureau of Indian Affairs to the Army. General Crook was busy planning a campaign into the Sierra Madre to bring the Apache back to San Carlos. He placed Captain Emmet Crawford in charge of San Carlos with experienced Second Lieutenant Charles B. Gatewood and an enthusiastic, but inexperienced, Britton Davis in command of the scouts at San Carlos. With the prospect of another kidnapping or voluntary recruits to increase the raider's numbers, Davis saw his scouts guarding their camps and even establishing outposts in the neighboring hills with guns and ammunition that he had no idea from where they came.

Fight for the Waterhole
Painting by Frederic Remington, 1903.

The raiders never reached San Carlos but instead swung north up the San Simon Valley to the Río Gila and then east across the Steins Peak mountains and across the Burro Mountains to the road between Silver City and Lordsburg. On the Silver City to Lordsburg road, they found Federal Judge H. C. McComas on the way to Lordsburg in a buckboard with his wife and son, Charlie. The raiders killed the two adults, stripped them, and took the little boy. Charlie, who had red hair, was thought for many years to have survived and been raised by the Apache hiding in Mexico because of innumerable tales of a red-headed Apache warrior. What actually happened to him was one of the great mysteries of the southwest. There were at least three versions. The chiefs claimed Charlie wandered off in the mountains and was never seen again. Another version claimed he was running free and wild with the Apache in Mexico. However, around 1960, an old woman who saw what happened claimed that the child was sick and being looked after by several women when Crook's scouts raided a camp in the Sierra Madre. During the raid, the scouts killed an old woman whose son saw it happen. Outraged, he took a stone and smashed the child's head in revenge. The women tried to take care of him, but he died and fearful of revenge by the scouts and Crook, hid the body in brush where it wouldn't be found.[3]

Tzoe was deeply grieved by the death of his friend Beneactiney. When Chato's raiders camped on a high mountain near San Carlos, Tzoe, looking west toward the reservation where his mother and other relatives lived, was in tears thinking of his friend. Tzoe, studying the reservation, decided his medicine wanted him to return to the reservation and support what remained of his White Mountain Apache family. Without argument, Chato and the band gave him "a gun, a horse, and a saddle" and some food for him to return to San Carlos and wished him well. Tzoe later told General Crook that he had been taken to Mexico against his will, that both his wives and a child had been killed at Aliso Creek, and that he had taken the opportunity to slip away from the raiding party. Angie Debo points out that both stories might have been true. Tzoe and Chato were brothers-in-law and close friends. Chato might have helped Tzoe leave without knowledge of the rest of the raiders.

EIGHTEEN

Tzoe Meets General Crook
and the Sierra Madre Campaign Begins

AFTER CHATO'S RAIDERS had attacked and killed Judge McComas and his wife and taken their six-year-old son, Charlie, it appeared that they headed west planning soon to attack San Carlos. The kidnapping of Loco's band was still fresh in the minds of army commanders at San Carlos and there was even the possibility of a massacre of White Eyes. Captain Emmet Crawford commander at San Carlos had been called away to help General Crook prepare for his campaign against the Apache in the Sierra Madre. Lieutenant Britton Davis was in charge of the scouts. The scouts realizing what could happen after the Loco band kidnapping had spread out across the eastern edge of San Carlos, even establishing watch posts in the eastern hills close to the reservation boundary.

DAVIS HAD AT his disposal five highly trusted Apache enlisted as "secret scouts" (also known as "spies") to report to him any signs of unrest or potential disturbances. Close to midnight on March 30, Davis had just gone to bed when he heard the hinges on his bedroom door creak and outlined against the moonlit window was an Apache with a gun in his hand. Davis cocked the revolver on the bed beside him and asked who it was. It was Tar-gar-de-chuse, one of his trusted informants. He said, "Chiricahua come," and reported that they were already in the camp of Nodiskey, a White Mountain Apache leader twelve miles up the San Carlos River from the main agency.

Davis assembled the thirty scouts scattered in camps near the agency, and they were joined by Tonto volunteers who had some special grudge against the

Tzoe Also Known As "Peaches," by Army Photographer, 1885.
Courtesy of the National Archives

Chiricahua. Within an hour, Davis and nearly a hundred scouts, volunteers, and tribal police were marching upriver to Nodiskey's camp. They arrived within half a mile of the camp about 3:00 a.m. and near daylight had made a half circle hiding behind scrubby trees and dirt mounds around the little camp (four or five families lived there). As the light came, Davis's first sergeant called to the camp but no one there was visible. A man's voice answered the first sergeant and the scouts immediately moved forward, surrounded the camp and captured a single Chiricahua—Tzoe. Davis described Tzoe as a handsome young man, about twenty-three or twenty-four, who was called "Peaches" by Crook's campaign soldiers because of his smooth, peach-like complexion.[1]

Tzoe told Lieutenant Davis that he had left the band of raiders near the eastern edge of the Reservation and had come to Nodiskey's camp to get news of his family. He didn't seem too disturbed by his capture and even smiled faintly when Davis took his knife and cartridge belt; the scouts had already taken his rifle. From Tzoe, Davis learned there had been twenty-six raiders, now twenty-four under the command of Chato and Bonito. A year later, after the raiders had surrendered and returned to San Carlos, Davis learned that during the six days they were in the United States they had traveled 400-450 miles on horseback, riding their horses to exhaustion and then stealing new ones as needed, and that Chato didn't sleep except when he could while they were riding. When the party stopped for a short rest, Chato, alert and wide-eyed, kept watch. They were armed with the latest model Winchesters, a better arm for close-in fights requiring rapid fire, than the single shot, trapdoor Springfield rifles used by the soldiers and scouts.

Lieutenant Davis took Tzoe to headquarters and wired General Crook in Willcox, Arizona, of his capture. Crook, preparing his campaign to enter the Sierra Madre and bring the Chiricahua back to San Carlos, had only a vague idea where their camps were. Crook wired Davis to ask Tzoe if he would act as a guide for his campaign against the Chiricahua in Mexico. Tzoe readily agreed and Davis put him on the train to Willcox for General Crook to interview. Tzoe, who arrived under guard and in chains, told General Crook that most of the Apache who were in Mexico wanted to surrender, but their leaders wouldn't let them. Tzoe said he would guide Crook in Mexico and that he was willing to wear the chains until he proved trustworthy. Crook, impressed by the forthrightness of the young man, removed the chains and decided to use him.

There was some concern that Tzoe might be assassinated if a scout with relatives in Mexico realized he was their primary guide to the camps. Al Sieber, who was chief of scouts for the campaign, thus made Tzoe a first sergeant in the scouts so there was no question of why he would be in the lead. General Crook had also gone to Mexico by train that spring and personally obtained permission from civilian and military authorities in Sonora and Chihuahua to pursue the Apache in Mexico. While there wasn't a formal signed agreement to this effect, the authorities in Mexico assured Crook they would not interfere as long as his business was to return the Apache to the United States.

GENERAL CROOK USED Willcox as his main supply depot because it was accessible by train, and it was here that he chose who was to go on the campaign. By the last week in April, he was ready to move his supplies to the border at San Bernardino Springs where he established another supply depot much more convenient to Mexico than Willcox. Crook was joined at San Bernardino Springs by Captain Crawford with one hundred more scouts. Each man would be allowed to take one blanket, forty rounds of ammunition, and the clothes he wore. There would be five pack trains of 266 mules and seventy-six civilian packers (one was eighteen-year-old George Wratten, the interpreter trusted by Geronimo's band when they talked with Lieutenant Gatewood and agreed to surrender in August 1886). The mules carried an additional 160 rounds of ammunition per man was well as hard tack, bacon, and coffee for two months. In all, there were six officers and forty-two men of Company I, Sixth Cavalry, and 193 scouts (all on foot) under Captain Crawford and Lieutenants Gatewood and Mackay. Chief of Scouts and interpreters were Al Sieber, Archie McIntosh, Severino, and Mickey Free. The scouts were a mix of White Mountains, Tonto, and Chiricahua Apache augmented by Mojave and Yuma. Also accompanying them was the famous photographer, Frank Randall, whose Apache photographs are now widely admired. The night before they crossed the border, the Chiricahua scouts had a big war dance, and their medicine man said he saw them having great success.[2]

General Crook and his men, the scouts all wearing red headbands to distinguish them from the people they were after, disappeared into Mexico on May 1, 1883, and for six weeks nothing more was heard from them.

NINETEEN

★ ★ ★

Face-to-Face with the Chiricahua
in the Sierra Madre

WITHOUT KNOWING WHERE the Apache camps were in the Sierra Madre, Crook's campaign, in all likelihood, would have been wasted effort. However, in a stroke of great luck, the White Mountain Apache, Tzoe, who knew where the Apache camps in the Sierra Madre were, had agreed to guide Crook to them.[1]

The Crook expedition followed the Río San Bernardino to the Río Bavispe where it made a great turn from flowing north to south. Tracking along the eastern branch of the north-flowing Río Bavispe, Tzoe turned east near Huachinera toward the tall mountains. They had to go up a long narrow ridge, the only way to get to the top of the mountains. The trail was so narrow that on the way a mule fell over the edge, pack and all, and fell so far down that no attempt was made to recover the pack. When they got to the top of the ridge, they found three cattle in very poor shape that had probably escaped from a herd the Chiricahua had stolen. They camped that night near some springs that Tzoe knew and spent the next four days cooking bread and other food for future use. With food preparations done, fifty scouts and a mule pack train led by the Chief of Scouts, Al Sieber, went ahead. The rest of the expedition followed some distance behind. The lead group of scouts went in single file, ten scouts and then a mule, ten scouts and then a mule.

They found old tracks, followed them to a place near the headwaters of the Río Bavispe where there had been a war dance, and then the tracks scattered in different directions. They climbed over mountains looking for tracks until they found another Chiricahua camp that had been abandoned two days earlier. Sieber and the scouts stayed on that mountainside searching for tracks until the

[fol]lowing afternoon. While some scouts [...]d, others with field glasses scanned [ri]dge across the valley to an adjoin[ing mo]untain and saw a Chiricahua camp [t]op of the ridge. They saw numer[ous ho]rses grazing in a nearby flat meadow [and] Chiricahua in the camp. Sieber [sent] word back to those following to hurry [c]ome up that night, and they [attack]ed early the next morning, May 15, 1883.

★ ★

SIEBER DIVIDED THE scouts into three groups. One group crossed the valley and went up the far ridge to the right, one group went to the left, and one group up the middle directly toward the camp. Some of the scouts, who were afraid, started to say their knees hurt them as an excuse to stay in the rear. Chihuahua and his brother, probably Ulzana, had just returned to the camp with a good herd of cattle from a raid. The scouts attacked the camp, but some firing too early, provided warning to many who escaped. Nine of the camp members were killed (John Black Rope, aka John Rope, who was a scout, says four were killed) and three girls and two boys captured. The Chiricahua had been butchering the stolen cattle and meat was spread out everywhere on bushes to dry. Freshly cooked mescal was also drying. There were also large quantities of juniper berries and nuts in baskets. This food would be cached for carrying the camp through the cold days of the Ghost Face. The scouts took everything they wanted and set the camp on fire.[2]

A courier from Captain Crawford, who was in charge of one group of scouts, had reached Crook, who came up quickly, but didn't arrive until the camp had been taken and burned. The scouts went to Crook's camp, their horses loaded with plunder taken from the Chiricahua camp—gold and silver watches, photograph albums, fancy weapons and clothes, food of all kinds, much American and Mexican money—and their captive children. Crook questioned the children who "behaved with great coolness and self-possession, considering their tender years." The oldest, well into her teens, a daughter of Bonito named "Antelopes Approach Her" who later married Alchesay's (a great White Mountain Apache chief and one of Crook's favorite scouts) brother, said that her people had been dismayed to find their stronghold discovered and would be even more upset when they learned that Tzoe, who knew their secret places, had led Crook there. She told Crook that most of the warriors were out on raids—some had left early that day—but she was sure Loco and Chihuahua would be glad to return to the reservation, but not so sure about Geronimo and Chato, and

Chihuahua, ca. 1884.
Photograph courtesy of the Library of Congress.

that Juh was still out even though most of his band had been destroyed by the Mexicans. Very important to Crook was her news that a small white boy named Charlie, captured by Chato on a recent raid, had been in the camp and had run off with the women. She believed that if she could contact them, she could bring in the entire band including Charlie. Crook sent her and next oldest girl captive on the best captured horse to find the band and carry a message to Chihuahua that Americans had only come to take the people back to San Carlos and not to make war, and that the attack on his camp was an accident and had not meant war.

THE NEXT DAY women carrying white rags on sticks began coming into the camp. Among them was a sister of Geronimo, probably the mother of Jason Betzinez, Nah-thle-tla. She told Crook that Chihuahua wanted to come in and was trying to gather up his people who had been scattered by the attack. She said that the scouts had taken a white horse with a Mexican saddle that had a pair of black saddle bags and a silver bit and bridle. If Crook wanted to be friends with Chihuahua, then he had to give it to her to return to Chihuahua. Crook found the horse, saddle and silver bit and bridle among the scouts, took them, and gave them to her. She took the horse and trappings back up the mountain to the hidden Chiricahua. The next day, Chihuahua rode the white horse fast into Crook's camp. On the end of the horse's tail was a strip of red cloth; another strip hung from the bridle, and he carried a lance with a red strip tied at its end. The horse slid to a stop at a group of scouts who scattered out of the way. Chihuahua asked for the head officer, and they pointed toward Crook's tent.

Chihuahua rode the horse through scattering soldiers and officers to the tent where Mickey Free had run to act as interpreter. Crook came out of his tent, Chihuahua dismounted, and they shook hands. Chihuahua wanted to know why the scouts had killed an old woman, who was his aunt, when they attacked the camp. It seemed to him that if Crook wanted to be friends, then he wouldn't have done something like that. Crook assured him it was an accident, that he wanted the people to return to San Carlos, and he gave Chihuahua some food and tobacco to take back to his camp. Chihuahua sent runners to the bands out raiding to tell them to come in, while in the meantime, despite the wishes of his women who wanted to surrender, he moved his camp to make it harder to find and attack.[3]

By nightfall of that day (May 18), forty-five Chiricahua men, women, and children had come into Crook's camp, and they were given rations. By the next day, the number who had surrendered was an even one hundred. Crook moved his camp to place near a steep ridge. It was near water and had a large open area where the people could camp without crowding together. The women tore up flour sacks and tied them to poles to signal to the returning warriors that all was for peace. There were signs that Chihuahua was not entirely ready to surrender and might join forces with the returning warriors to attack Crook's camp. The scouts piled up rocks and pine logs to lie behind and kept their arms in readiness. Geronimo and his warriors returned that night.

TWENTY

General Crook Meets with the Chiefs
and Geronimo To Talk Peace

MOST OF THE men in Crook's Sierra Madre expedition were Apache scouts who had signed up to scout for the army. Their attack on the first inhabited camp they found quickly convinced the Chiricahua that there was no place left to hide in Mexico. Most wanted to return to the reservation anyway, but their leaders had said no. Now a major chief, Chihuahua was ready to return. Only Geronimo and those riding with him like Naiche and Chato, who had been in eastern Chihuahua looking for persons to capture and swapping back to the Chihuahua for his wife, Chee-hash-kish, and for others released from Mexican slavery, had not returned to the camp.

Geronimo and his thirty-six raiders arrived that night and had taken positions in the rocks on the high ridge a thousand feet above the camp. In the morning light, they looked like great ominous black birds watching and waiting to swoop down on the camp. The women called up to them saying not to shoot, that they (the Blue Coats) didn't want any fighting but only to make friends. Geronimo sent down two messengers (Betzinez says old women, Crook's Executive Officer, Captain Bourke, says old men) to learn General Crook's intentions. If they failed to return, Geronimo planned to attack. Other communications went back and forth. Geronimo's sister climbed up to the raiders and was sent back with a request that some of the scouts climb up and meet with them. Relatives of those in the raiding party went to meet them including Dastine ("Crouched and Ready") a Cibecue scout and relative of Geronimo's father-in-law Jelikine and Haskehagola ("Angry, He Starts Fights") also a Cibecue scout. After the talks (the raiders wanted to learn firsthand why Crook had come and the scouts were helping him) the scouts climbed back down to the camp.[1]

Soon after the scouts returned from talks on the ridge, the brother of Tulan
(Tulan meaning "Much Water,") and one of the scouts in the camp, who had
been holding out with other Geronimo warriors, yelled and started to run into
the camp. Many rifles pointed at him, but he threw his gun and cartridge belt on
the ground and said to Tulan, "My brother, you have been looking for me, and I
am with you again as if I belonged to you." The brothers embraced. This was the
first warrior to come into the camp, and he was soon followed by all the others
except the chiefs who stayed apart by themselves, refusing to come in.[2]

GENERAL CROOK'S CAMP was on a little knoll with its sides covered with
high yellow grass. That afternoon Crook went off by himself hunting birds
with a shotgun. The Chiricahua chiefs and leaders suddenly rose up out of the
grass, grabbed his shotgun, and snatched away his sack of birds. They said he
was shooting at them. The interpreter, Mickey Free, seeing what was happening, ran down to them, yelling for them to wait. After a brief discussion, Crook
and the Chiricahua chiefs and leaders agreed to find a shady place where they
could sit and talk. Two hours later General Crook returned to camp with all the
Chiricahua chiefs. [This was probably Crook's most courageous act in his long
military career. He suppressed the story and so did his officers; it wasn't known
until 1936 when John Black Rope's reminiscences were published in Grenville
Goodwin's, *Western Apache Raiding and Warfare 2*].

Sometime after the chiefs came in, three Mexican women and a baby came
into the camp. They had been captured by the Chiricahua on their raid. Geronimo
had taken them in the hope that he could trade them for his wife Chee-hash-kish,
Chato's family, and others who had been taken into slavery by Mexican soldiers
during a trading trip to Casas Grandes in 1882. But neither Geronimo nor Chato
ever saw their loved ones again. A Spanish speaking Blue Coat officer went to
the Mexican women and asked them where they came from. They told him their
story, which he wrote down. They were in bad shape, exhausted, scratched and
torn by the brush, their clothes in rags and sandals worn down to nothing as they
ran through the brush to keep up with the raiders. They were taken to a fire, fed,
and given new clothes and tall army boots to wear. When the expedition returned
to Arizona they were sent back to their people in Mexico.

Crook and Geronimo spoke together several times. Crook was well aware that
he was balanced on the sharp edge of a probable disaster, but he told Geronimo

Apache Scouts Listening
Painting by Frederic Remington, 1908. Courtesy of the Sid Richardson Museum.

he didn't care whether he surrendered or fought it out. He reminded Geronimo that the Chiricahua camps in the mountains were no longer impregnable and the Mexican military would also be coming to invade them. Geronimo replied that he always wanted to be at peace, but his people had suffered bad treatment at San Carlos, which agreed with Crook's own assessment of the situation, and that he had been driven away, which even Clum had said happened. The Mexicans, Geronimo said, were treacherous, made war on his women and children, and ran like coyotes from his warriors. He told Crook that he had been trying to arrange an exchange of prisoners using the Mexican women who had come into the camp. He said he couldn't cope with both Mexican and American soldiers assisted by scouts, and if he couldn't make peace, then he and his warriors would die in the mountains fighting to the last man. Crook stayed aloof and apparently unconcerned.[3]

On the morning of May 21, Geronimo, Naiche, Chato, and a leading warrior, Tcha-nol-haye, sat and ate with Crook. They all seemed in good humor and ate with gusto the bread, beans, and coffee they were served, but wouldn't touch the bacon. (Eating pork was taboo to the Apache. Pigs ate anything, including snakes, which they considered nasty.) Geronimo said he had sent some of his young men out to collect his scattered people, and Chihuahua's calls for his people to come in were producing results as increasing numbers of all ages and sexes began appearing on good ponies and driving pack and loose animals. Kaytennae came in with his band of thirty-eight, who according to Bourke were "mostly young warriors… driving steers and work animals and riding ponies and burros. All were armed with Winchester and Springfield breech-loaders, revolvers and lances tipped with old cavalry sabers. The little boys carried revolvers, lances, and bows and arrows."

This growing assembly of Apache was making a serious dent on Crook's supplies. He told the Apache to help out by slaughtering their own cattle, and the young men went to work. On May 23, rations were issued to 220 Apache who had come into Crook's camp. That day Nana appeared with seventeen of his people. The next day, May 24, the expedition with the surrendered Apache started back but went only a short distance and stopped at pleasant place on the Río Bavispe where they spent a few days while the women gathered and cooked mescal for food on the return trip. It was during this time that Loco appeared with a few of his people and told Crook that some who had been separated during the fight at Aliso Creek had returned to the reservation and that he had started back before Crook had entered the mountains. Geronimo asked Crook to remain in the mountains a week longer so he could finish collecting his people (even though he had not actually surrendered he was practically begging to do so). Crook's posed indifference may have aroused the fears of the warriors that they were to be punished when they returned to San Carlos, and they developed a desperate plan to attack the expedition.

TWENTY-ONE

Geronimo's Vision and the Plot
to Assassinate the White Mountain Scouts

AT NEARLY THE same time General Crook entered Mexico, the Chiricahua leaders held a council and decided to send out two raiding parties. The first group under Chihuahua and his brother Ulzana planned to raid in Sonora on the western side of the Sierra Madre for livestock; the second group under Geronimo included Chato, Bonito, Naiche, Kaytennae, Zele, and Jelikine. Geronimo planned on taking captives in Chihuahua to exchange for their people enslaved there. Among the slaves were Geronimo's wife, Chee-hash-kish, mother of Chappo and Dohn-say, and members of Naiche's and Chato's families. The Sonoran raiders left about May 3 and those for Chihuahua about May 6.

The warriors led by Geronimo came out of the mountains and crossed the main road south of Galeana. They walked on their heels in the dust to leave tracks that looked like small diameter round holes consistent with the tracks of their horses wearing rawhide over their hooves. The raiders continued east and then turned north taking cattle for food while watching the roads for potential captives. Near the village of Carmen, not far from the Mexican Central Railroad, they sighted a party of two men and six women, one nursing a baby. They killed the men and captured the women who were wives of soldiers stationed at nearby towns. Geronimo told the women not to be afraid, that they wouldn't be harmed, but in fact, they were understandably terrified. He sent the oldest woman to the officials to explain that he had taken them with the intent of an exchange of prisoners. The Chiricahua continued north watching for other travelers.[1]

One evening a day or two later, they were gathered around a fire eating. Betzinez, Geronimo's cousin and warrior acolyte, had cooked him piece of beef which he was eating with his knife. Suddenly, as if in a trance, Geronimo dropped

Lieutenant Gatewood's White Mountain Apache Scouts, ca. 1880.
Photograph courtesy of the National Archives.

the knife and said, "Brothers! Our people we left in camp are in the hands of the Blue Coats! What shall we do?" Betzinez, years later, telling of his experiences riding with Geronimo, said this was a startling example of Geronimo's mysterious supernatural power to tell what was happening at a distance and that he couldn't explain it to that day. "I was there and saw it. No. He didn't get the word by some messenger. And no smoke signals had been made." In response to Geronimo's question, every man said they should return to their camp in the mountains immediately. They were at least a hundred and twenty miles away and completely out of touch with it. They started their return trip that evening and traveled all night. Their captives slowed them down. Betzinez said, "We tried to help the women and get them to walk faster, but we really didn't expect Mexican women to walk as far and as fast as Apache women."

Before the Geronimo band reached the road south of Galena, the men took some cattle to take back. The night before they returned to their main camp, Geronimo made another prophecy. He said that during the next day's travel, a man standing on a hill to their left would report the capture of their camp, and it happened exactly as he predicted. In the middle of the next afternoon, a man called to them from a hilltop and then came down the rocks to report that Crook had captured their camp and taken their people into custody. They held another council and decided to investigate. Abandoning their captives and cattle, they made their way to a high ridge above Crook's camp during the night and dawn. Geronimo put them in firing positions among the cliff's crags a thousand feet above the camp. There they saw white strips of cloth on sticks near Crook's camp and women calling up to Geronimo and Kaytennae that Crook only wanted peace. The chiefs asked four scouts to come up and parley.

After the parley, tension between the Chiricahua and the Blue Coats relaxed during the day and after Crook met and talked in the afternoon with Geronimo and the chiefs. Geronimo later admitted he "was astonished to see General Crook there." He believed Crook had been blessed with supernatural powers because no mere mortal, especially a White Eye could have invaded their sanctuary, and he thought Crook "was so powerful that he could command the sun, the moon, and everything." The next day, Crook told Geronimo to surrender or fight it out and astonished all the leaders by saying, "I'm not going to take your arms from you because I'm not afraid of you." After this Crook claimed that Geronimo begged to return to the reservation.[2]

Crook had told the leaders that he had just come to look for them, and to take them back to the reservation in a good way, not to fight, but to join with them as friends. Some leaders said all right, others said nothing. Most of the chiefs, including Geronimo, were angry at the scouts who had invaded their mountains and wanted vengeance. Most of the White Mountain scouts were enjoying themselves at dances every night with the Chiricahua women, but a few sensed uneasiness after the first day's short move. The socializing soon stopped and the women started baking mescal and drying meat in preparation for the long march back to San Carlos.

THE CHIRICAHUA CHIEFs and war leaders met in council the next day after the food preparation work began. Their thirst for revenge against the western Apache scouts for betraying them to the Blue Coats drove them to a plan for revenge. They would hold a dance again that evening, use the young Chiricahua women to lure the scouts to attend it, as they had in the past, but at a prearranged signal, the women would fall back and the Chiricahua men would slaughter the scouts who had betrayed them.

First, they called Kaytennae, one of their best young warriors, to come to their council. He knew many of the White Mountain scouts who would be attacked. They asked him if he would join them in their treachery, and he agreed. Then they called Jelikine to come to the council. Jelikine was not a chief, but he was indisputably one of their bravest and best fighters. After Geronimo, who was his son-in-law (Geronimo had recently married a young woman, Zi-yeh, Jelikine's daughter), explained the plan to him, Jelikine was amazed and angry at the treachery being planned. He wanted nothing to do with the plan because the Cibecue people had raised him. He said, "[These] White Mountain people are like relatives to me," and left the council. Jelikine gave those like Naiche, Chato, and Bonito who each had friends or relatives with the White Mountains, second thoughts.

Geronimo could tell the plan might be losing support so he sent for Jelikine again. According to John Black Rope, one of the scouts who might have been killed, Geronimo said to Jelikine, "My father-in-law, tonight we mean to do as we told you. Whenever we have gone to war before you have gone with us. But now you won't make up your mind to say yes or no." Jelikine answered, "I told you already that I would not help you do this." He was mad and started to walk away. In a little bit he turned back and came to the council again. He said, "You chiefs don't mean anything to me. I have been with you many times and helped you kill many Mexicans and Whites… and that is the way you got the clothes you are wearing now. I am the one who has killed these people for you, and you have just followed behind me. I don't want to hear you talking this way to me again." [3]

The dance was held that night, but an old scout had just died from a snake bite and Al Sieber cut it short. John Black Rope says one of the scouts had learned of the plan and told Sieber, who looked for and found the death of the old scout as an excuse to stop it. If the Chiricahua had intended to carry out their plan, they never had another opportunity to put it in motion.

TWENTY-TWO

The Long Walk Back to San Carlos

ON MAY 24, 1883, General George Crook with fifty mounted troopers and nearly two hundred Apache scouts on foot, began leading their Apache "friends" who had left San Carlos Reservation for Mexico and the Sierra Madre in 1881 and 1882 back to San Carlos. They traveled a short distance and then stopped at mid-day so the women could spend a few days roasting mescal to augment General Crook's fast dwindling supplies.[1]

Geronimo, looking for his people, sent a messenger asking that the group stay where they were for a week, making the argument to Crook that more time was needed to collect and bring in his people. It was a reasonable request, but Crook told him that supplies were so short they couldn't stay more than the three or four days needed to cook the mescal. While the chiefs were still out collecting their people, Crook resumed his long walk out of the mountains on May 28, 1883. Late that night Geronimo, Chato, Kaytennae, and Chihuahua came to the camp with 116 of their people. Again, Geronimo asked Crook for a few more days delay and again Crook had to tell the chiefs that there were not enough supplies to delay the trip any longer. Geronimo told Crook that if he would travel slowly, then his people would try to catch up with him by the time he reached the border; if they couldn't catch Crook by the time he reached the border, then they would move through the mountains to San Carlos without any cavalry guards. Crook agreed to let Geronimo stay out to continue gathering his people, but he made sure Geronimo and others understood that if they traveled to San Carlos without him, they would have to take their chances fighting against Mexicans or Americans they might encounter. The three hundred and twenty-five Apache, mostly Chihenne people under Loco, Nana, Kaytennae, and Bonito went on with Crook while the others turned back.

Geronimo and the others were sincere in asking for more time to gather their people and not just looking for an excuse to do more raiding. However, after the leaders stayed behind and were free once more, there were opportunities for raiding, and they took them. Those returning with Crook, most of whom had survived their abduction from San Carlos the year before, were glad to be returning to the reservation since they had been prevented from returning on their own by Geronimo. The women, apparently tired of their rugged lives in the mountains, had been the first to surrender to General Crook's scouts. Betzinez said they had a "great relief.... No more worries, no more sleepless nights, fearing attacks by an enemy." [2]

GENERAL CROOK HAD hoped the campaign would find the little six-year-old boy, Charlie McComas, who Chato and his raiders had taken roughly two months earlier in March of that year after killing the boy's mother and father on the road to Lordsburg. The Apache told Crook that they could not find the boy after he had disappeared into the brush when the scouts attacked their camp. What happened to Charlie McComas had been debated and was a mystery for years. As late as 1938, there were archaeological expedition claims of finding a lost tribe of Apache in the Sierra Madre who were led by a red-haired, blue-eyed man believed to be Charlie McComas.

There were Apache who knew what had happened to Charlie McComas. Jason Betzinez got the story from a fellow student when he was at Carlisle. When the scouts attacked the Apache camp in the Sierra Madre, an old woman threw up her hands and begged to be taken prisoner. One of the scouts killed her anyway. Her son, seeing her killed, picked up a rock in uncontrolled rage and revenge smashed Charlie in the head. But the child didn't die. Sam Haozous claimed that the following day his mother and aunt were making their way through the brush and rocks on the mountain side down to Crook's camp and found the child still living. His aunt who was strongly attached to the boy said, "Poor little fellow. We can't let him die here. Let's take him along." But Haozous mother said, "If we bring him in, the soldiers will blame us." So, they left him. Nobody else was on their path, and there is little doubt the child died there. [3]

Apache Women Cooking Mescal, Photograph by Edward Curtis, 1903,
courtesy of the National Anthropological Archives

CROOK DID NOT return the way he had come following the Río Bavispe and then up the mountains in Sonora from near the village of Huachinera. It's likely that he believed he was much more likely to clash with the Mexican military on the Sonora side of the mountains where Geronimo often raided, and that the Mexicans having seen the Apache scouts and American troopers moving down the Río Bavispe would be ready and waiting for them to return.

Crook had a large number of Apache he needed to protect and keep together in order to get them back to the reservation, but with limited supplies. The scouts and the Chihenne warriors returning to San Carlos had to hunt every day to keep the people fed. The expedition came down out of the mountains near Carretas in Chihuahua and stayed on the eastern edge of the *llano* close to the trail the Chiricahua had followed when they were headed for Juh's stronghold with Loco's people they had abducted the year before. Some of the scouts ignored the Apache custom of avoiding anything to do with the dead and looked at the site of the Aliso Creek ambush led by Colonel Garcia where nearly half of the women and children had been killed. It was terrible to see. Crook's Executive Officer, Captain John G. Bourke, reported seeing human bones, picked white and clean by coyotes. Scout John Black Rope said he and others shouldn't have gone to see the place but did it anyway. They saw many bleached out bones, pieces of women's dresses, and lots of beads scattered on the ground.[4]

The expedition moved on up the valley and around the Sierra Espuela before heading west toward Crook's San Bernardino base camp near the border at Silver Springs. They crossed the border on June 10, 1883. The soldiers had seen them coming and made great pots of food which the weary people and scouts lined up for serving and then devoured. General Crook's expedition had been out nearly six weeks, and out of communication with the rest of the world for over three weeks. When word was received Crook had returned safe with the Apache, the newspapers were full of angry telegrams saying the government should hang all the men and spread the women and children among the tribes of the Indian Territory (i.e. Oklahoma). This "news" got to the Apache. Bourke believed it reached the ears of Geronimo and others who had stayed back to collect their people and drove them back into the mountains until they saw it was safe to return the following year.[5]

The newspaper rants became so serious that Crook issued a warning against it in his official report. "The glibness with which people generally speak of moving them would indicate that all we have to do is to take them from their camps, as you would chickens from a roost, without reflecting that to attempt their removal would bring on the bloodiest Indian war this country has ever experienced."

Crook took no chances that the Apache would change their minds about returning to San Carlos. The scouts and returning Apache were escorted back to San Carlos by Captain Crawford and four companies of cavalry that had waited at the border. They arrived back at the reservation on June 23. The Indians on the reservation knew they were coming and gathered to greet them. For most it was a home coming. If Crook had any misgivings about the leaders still out, he didn't say so. His final report on the campaign dated July 23, closed with him stating that the leaders who had stayed out and still not arrived was "of no significance. Indians have no idea of the value of time." He settled the ones he had and waited for the others. Most of the leaders returned near the end of the year. Geronimo returned in February of the next year with a large herd of cattle he planned for the Chiricahua to develop as their own. The times were to be ones of great change for many of the Chiricahua leaders.[6]

TWENTY-THREE

Apache Women Escape Slavery In Mexico

THE APACHE WITH whom General Crook returned to San Carlos in June 1883 were the first to arrive. The chiefs who had stayed back to collect their followers began coming in late October of 1883. Among the last to arrive with their followers were Chato who arrived in early February 1884, and Geronimo appeared in late February. The last group to return had not been with any Apache associated with General Crook's return, rather it was five women who had escaped five years of Mexican slavery and walked back to their people in 1884. This is their story.[1]

MEXICAN TROOPS UNDER Colonel Joaquin Terrazas, attacked Victorio and his warriors, who low on ammunition, were easily defeated at Tres Castillos in October of 1880. Victorio and three others used their knives to stab themselves in the heart after they had fired their last bullet. After finishing off Victorio and his warriors, the Mexican troops began collecting women and children and killing those wounded or too young or too old to work. There were about a hundred in the initial group of survivors, but the Mexicans executed fifteen boys out of that group they believed were too old to train as slaves. Orders came from Ciudad Chihuahua that no prisoners were to be killed and the executions stopped. However, on the ninety-mile march south to Ciudad Chihuahua, the prisoners herded along like cattle, another fifteen or sixteen were shot who were too weak to continue. When the prisoners reached Ciudad Chihuahua they were jailed and looked over by slavers.

*Two Apache women, Siki and Huera, who escaped slavery in Mexico and walked
over 1,200 miles to return to their people at Fort Apache in 1884.
Photograph of Siki by F.A. Rinehart, 1898 Omaha Exposition, National Archives.
Huera Photograph courtesy of the Arizona Historical Society.*

In Mexican jails, prisoners depended on relatives and friends to bring them
food. The Mexican army that wiped out Victorio had two Lipan Apache scouts
they had forced to help them. One of these was named Big Water. After the prisoners were jailed, Big Water supplied them food until they were shipped about
750 miles southeast to Mexico City by train. In Mexico City, one man bought four
including a young woman named Siki, Huera, and two other unnamed women.
Huera was to become a famous maker of *tulapai* and a wife of Mangas who had
been out with Nana looking for supplies when the attack came. (She was the
woman whose stories about him about to be put in the guardhouse convinced
Geronimo he needed to escape the Fort Apache reservation in 1885.)

The buyer didn't take the grandmother, who was named Nah-dos-te. When
they started to leave, Siki ran back and put her arms around her grandmother so
the purchaser took her too, and being the oldest of the five became their natural
leader. They were herded through the Mexico City streets after dark, but Nah-
dos-te could tell by the stars that they were moving north. They were taken to a
hacienda on the outskirts of the city where maguey was grown, given food and
water, and allowed to bathe.

A Mexican woman about the age of Nah-dos-te put them to work carrying wood, drawing well water, scrubbing walks, and other household tasks, which except for being captives, the Apache women thought were easy. Nah-dos-te urged the younger women to work cheerfully and be respectful of their owners. They all already knew a little Spanish and soon became fluent in the language. Three of the women were used to work the maguey fields but Siki and Nah-dos-te were kept from communicating with them. Nah-dos-te was so well liked by the family that bought them she became like a nanny to the children in the household.

Nah-dos-te knew that the fruit of prickly pear (called tuna) ripened that far south in the winter months, but in their homeland at Ojo Caliente in New Mexico during the summer months. She believed if that if they could escape when the tuna were edible they would find ripe ones as they worked their way always north up the Río Grande back to Mexican trading posts at Ojo Caliente. She knew they had to have at least one knife in the group and each had to have a blanket to survive. In the kitchen where she worked, the knives were carefully counted and locked away each night, and the machetes used in the fields were too large to hide in their skirts. Five winters passed before they had their chance to steal a knife and escape.

AFTER FIVE WINTERS, Nah-dos-te had become a trusted household servant and permitted to shop daily in the local market. One day while she was shopping, a boy stole something in the market, and while the butcher watched the chase, she stole one of his long sharp butcher knives and hid it under her skirt and kept it hidden there for some time while the tuna ripened. She managed to leave signs on a rock wall the others passed to work in the fields that told them she would be ready to go in three days.

At sunset on the appointed day, Nah-dos-te sent the overseer on a false errand, and she and Siki climbed the wall around the big house to join the village women going to evening mass. As they passed the next field, Huera and the other two joined them. They were all dressed as peons and nobody paid any attention to them. When they got to the church, they continued on as if on a leisurely evening walk. The night was very dark and hearing horses and wagons pass by, they stayed off, but parallel to, the road. Near daylight they hid under a bridge all day without food or water. When darkness fell they continued on parallel to the road until they came to a shack with no dog on guard, took a water jug hanging near the door, and filled it from a little nearby spring before hiding in the brush and eating tuna. They were so exhausted they slept with no one on guard.

About a week later, they came to a waterhole where they saw cattle tracks. They hid in brush and waited hoping to catch and kill a calf, but they had to be careful to avoid being attacked by its mother. Eventually they were able to cut the throat of a yearling. They skinned it, took the meat and wrapped it in their blanket, took the stomach for a water bag, and wiped out their tracks. They hid in the brush to slice and dry the meat and make foot covering out of the green hide to replace their worn-out huaraches. They traveled at night, avoiding villages, and staying constantly on the lookout for riders. Sometimes they split up to meet later in the evening at some obvious landmark. Only Huera had been able to bring a blanket, wrapping it around her body under her skirt when they escaped. The nights were cold and the clothes covering them during cold windy days poor, but they didn't dare make a fire until they had circled around Ciudad Chihuahua, nearly 750 miles from Mexico City. In Chihuahua, Nah-dos-te knew where she was by the shape of the mountains. There they found another cattle watering hole and killed another yearling, made a fire, and for the first time since they had escaped ate cooked food. They had been working their way north for three months and their clothes were in shreds and their feet bare. They used the meat and hide from the yearling for resupply and moved northwest to avoid El Paso del Norte. They crossed the border south of the Florida Mountains and rested three days at Tres Hermanas where they killed another beef.

They were in familiar country, but their modesty forbade them from going home in the rags they wore. Victorio had stored supplies in a Florida Mountains cave six years before, and they planned to rest there and make dresses of calico that had been taken from a smugglers train. Mice had damaged the calico, but they salvaged what they could and made dresses. The best pieces they took with them to trade for food when they got to Monticello, the Mexican village not far from where their people had once lived. Since they had been gone, their people had returned with Crook from Mexico to San Carlos and then settled along Turkey Creek near Fort Apache. A new trader at Monticello, who didn't know them from the days before they left with Victorio, didn't believe that they had walked there from Mexico City, and thought they had stolen the calico they offered to trade. However, he fed them, furnished them blankets, and let them sleep on the storeroom floor until troops from Fort Wingate carried them in wagons to their people.

Nah-dos-te and her companions, one knife and one blanket between them, had walked over 1200 miles across mountains and deserts, in the cold of night by the light of the moon with only the stars to guide them, and lived off prickly pear fruit. They had waited five years as slaves in Mexico for their opportunity to escape, and their walk had taken six months.

SEVERAL GROUPS OF Apache women were known to have escaped Mexican slavery in addition to the one described here. Apache slaves were taken in 1873 when Mexican soldiers attacked a Geronimo camp. They were made slaves on a maguey plantation for five years. Three women, one included Eugene Chihuahua's "grandmother" (his maternal grandmother's sister), Id-is-tah-nah (Mexican name was Francesca), managed to escape each with a knife and blanket. During the long trek north, Francesca was attacked while they slept, and nearly scalped by a jaguar trying to drag her off before the other women could drive it off. She was no longer an attractive woman and as a widow, no man wanted her. She was a medicine woman who taught Eugene the Dance of the Mountain Spirits, and he did the dances in her honor. Geronimo, greatly admiring her spirit and courage, later married her.[2] Her headstone at the Fort Sill Apache cemetery reads 1861–1901. The last woman Geronimo married, Sunsetso, aka Azul, had also escaped slavery in Mexico as a young woman and made her way back to her people by herself. She was about twenty-five years younger than Geronimo, but they were a happily married couple. When the Chiricahua were at last freed as prisoners of war, she moved to Mescalero with most of the other Chiricahua in 1912. She passed away there in 1934 having never remarried.

PART FOUR:
THE SECOND PEACE

After the Apache chiefs and Geronimo returned to San Carlos with their people, General Crook let them pick the place on the reservation where they wanted to live. Geronimo wanted to do away with the reservation boundaries and settle on Eagle Creek where ranches of white settlers had been established. Crook refused Geronimo's demand and told the Chiricahua to look for a place on reservation land. They chose to live on Turkey Creek near Fort Apache. Crook placed Captain Emmett Crawford as the agent in charge of the reservations to ensure the Apache received their full ration allotments and were treated fairly. He made Lieutenant Britton Davis the subagent in charge of the Chiricahua at Turkey Creek and Fort Apache. Both Crawford and Davis were exemplary officers who did the best they could with what they had for the Apache.

General Crook's rules for reservations where he was responsible sowed seeds of discontent among the Chiricahua. Lieutenant Davis called the Apache leaders together and made sure they understood General Crook's rules, which among others forbade the making and consumption of tulapai *and forbade men beating their wives. These rules angered the Chiricahua. The chiefs said that when they surrendered, they had agreed to be peaceful and to live peacefully with each other, which they were doing. However, nothing had been said about agreeing to having their lifeways controlled.*

They ignored the rules and continued to make tulapai, *which Davis' Apache policemen ignored. However, a young wife, badly beaten by her drunk husband, came to Davis for medical help. Davis had her driven to the post surgeon, and following the rules, despite her protests, locked her husband in the calaboose for two weeks. This angered the all the Chiricahua and began a slide toward another Geronimo-led escape from the reservation.*

TWENTY-FOUR

Juh and Jelikinne Ride the Ghost Pony

ENERAL CROOK'S SIERRA Madre campaign drew to an end when many of the Apache, who had left San Carlos in 1881 and 1882, returned in late June 1883. It wasn't until mid-October that war leaders who had stayed in Mexico, true to their promise, began to bring in the groups they had promised to roundup and return back across the border. In late October, Naiche and Gil-lee came in with nine warriors and eighteen women and children. In mid-November, Chihuahua and Mangas with ninety of their people came in. Chato with nineteen of his people returned on February 7, 1884. Geronimo appeared in late February 1884 with twenty-six warriors and seventy women and children. They brought with them about 350 head of beef cattle stolen in Mexico that he planned to use for increasing the Chiricahua herd. Unfortunately, Crook wouldn't let him keep the cattle, sold them to the reservation for meat, and returned the sales funds to their owners in Mexico. Geronimo was still complaining twenty years later at Fort Sill about Crook unfairly making them sell the cattle and returning the funds to their Mexican owners.

CROOK HAD NOT found Juh, the great Nednhi war chief, among the Apache leaders with whom he met in May 1883. After the abduction of Loco's people from San Carlos, and the disasters that had followed, Juh had decided to leave the big camp of Chiricahua over friendly disagreements about where to camp and where and when to raid.

Spring Flowers at Peridot, Arizona.
Photograph by John Fowler, courtesy of the National Archives

In late January 1883, four months before Crook arrived in the Sierra Madre, Tarahumara Mexican militia from the town of Temosachic about one hundred miles south of Casas Grandes, surrounded an Apache camp in the Sierra Madre foothills and attacked it without warning early one morning killing and capturing mostly women and children. Juh's wife (Geronimo's "sister" (actually first cousin) Ishton) and two daughters were killed. His daughter Jacali was seriously wounded in the knee (she eventually lost the leg through the services of an army surgeon). His three sons, Daklugie (the youngest, about eleven or twelve), Daklegon, and Delzhinne, (both strong warriors) escaped as did most of the remnants of Victorio's band camping with Juh and who included Kaytennae, his wife Guyan, and adopted son Kaywaykla.[1]

Juh led the survivors back to the big Chiricahua camp on the edge of the great canyon. The Chiricahua planned new raids for the coming Season of Little Eagles, but Juh's people didn't participate in them. Juh's band was breaking up because of mutual finger pointing and ill will resulting from the Mexican raid.

In the Season of Little Eagles before the raids began, Juh, his three sons, and a few followers left the main group to wander the mountains on their own. Juh's daughter, Jacali, stayed with the main band, which left the great canyon and moved north to establish its base camp in the area the Apache called Bugatseka (Tres Ríos Mesa) on the headwaters of the Río Bavispe. It was near there that Crook appeared with his scouts and mounted troopers in May of 1883.

AFTER CROOK LEFT Mexico with most of the Chiricahua, Geronimo and the other war leaders continued to look for their people and to raid Mexican ranchos and haciendas. During fighting in a raid near Nácori Chico, a long range, lucky shot by a soldier hit Jelikine, Geronimo's father-in-law and fierce warrior, in the head and killed him. This demoralized the Apache and most retreated to their base camp. Fifteen warriors left the camp to avenge the loss of Jelikine.[2] After several weeks of raids, they were resting in their camp one day around August 9, when a woman who called herself Mañanita appeared out of the brush. She had no moccasins and her feet and legs were scratched, bruised, and swollen from many miles of walking. Forty-four days earlier she had escaped captivity (she later told Captain Crawford at San Carlos she was a wife of Geronimo who was captured when the Tarahumara attacked and wiped out Juh's camp) in Ciudad Chihuahua and walked through the mountains to find their camp. She told the warriors that thirty-five Apache prisoners were alive in captivity in Ciudad Chihuahua. Among them were Chato's wife and two children, Geronimo's wife, and Chihuahua's brother. This information made the Apache anxious to deal with the Mexicans to get their family members back. They moved their camp east to Piedras Verdes about seventeen miles southwest of Casas Grandes.[3]

Two Chiricahua women entered a Mexican military camp about two miles east of Casas Grandes. They told the *commandante*, Major Oñate, that Geronimo, Naiche, Chato, and Juh were eager to make a treaty. Major Oñate and twenty-five soldiers headed for the Apache rancheria guided by the two women. The *commandante* and four soldiers met with the chiefs. Juh requested that the Apache be given land between Piedras Verde and the Río Casas Grandes, and seeds and training in how to farm so they could become self-sufficient and peaceful. Oñate forwarded the request to Brigadier General Ramon Raguero in Ciudad Chihuahua. Either Raguero or General Carlos Fuero authorized the request in order to draw the Chiricahua into the city where the Mexicans planned to slaughter as many as possible. General Fuero especially wanted to capture and execute Geronimo for wiping out Mata Ortiz near Chocolate Pass.

A FEW DAYS after this meeting Chihuahua and Juh ventured into Ciudad Chihuahua under a flag of truce. Juh sent Avencio Escudero, once a chief politico for the Galeana district, a request for a written pass to trade at Casas Grandes and that he had a boy he would trade for it. The Apache had livestock, plunder, and rifles without bullets they were willing to trade for ammunition and mescal. Chihuahua seemed to be on to the Mexican's game. He knew that if they were going to double-cross the Apache, the attack wouldn't happen on the first trip into the city, and he never returned after the first visit. Juh had a number of Mexican friends in Ciudad Chihuahua and so made several trips. The Mexicans supplied mescal to the Apache camp and gave it to Juh when he went into town. According to a warrior, Zele, who was there after he returned from a raid around September 6, Juh stayed "all the time drunk" from the mescal the Mexicans provided.

On September 12, 1883, the Chiricahua met with Lieutenant Colonel Miguel González a few miles from Casas Grandes. Geronimo did most of the talking and asked about the captives in Ciudad Chihuahua. González answered he would pass the request to his chief. In the meantime, he tried to talk the Apache into moving their camp near his. Naiche refused saying, "You people have always talked nice to us poor people…. We don't believe you anymore." [4] González was playing for time. General Raguero was putting together two hundred cavalry for González's use, but they wouldn't be ready for another two weeks.

González met again with Juh, Naiche, Geronimo, Chato, Kaytennae, Zele, and other warriors on September 20. According to Naiche, González promised to release the captives if the Chiricahua made a treaty and went to work as farmers. He said to prove his good faith that if they came to Ciudad Chihuahua, he would exchange three prisoners for the three children Juh was willing to trade. Geronimo again dominated the conversation.

Juh was so drunk at the second meeting, it took several tries before he mounted his pony to ride away with the others to their camp several miles from Casas Grandes. Many thought Juh was no longer fit to lead. He was drinking whenever he could and his desire for alcohol clouded his judgement leading to unnecessary risks that got warriors killed. He was despondent and probably had no intention of returning to San Carlos.

Several Mexican "friends" rode with him after the second meeting with González. The trail, one he had ridden hundreds of times in his life, passed along a high bluff overlooking the Río Casas Grandes. The Mexicans left for Casas Grandes that evening leaving four bottles of mescal for their friends. Juh continued his drinking binge and was joined by others including Chato. The historically accepted version says the next morning, Juh still drunk, fell off his horse while riding along a high bank overlooking the Río Casas Grandes. He was either killed from the fall or drowned.[5]

However, Juh's youngest son Daklugie tells a much different story. According to Daklugie, Juh knew very well the Mexican trick of getting the Apache so drunk they couldn't defend themselves and then slaughtering them. Juh had a strict rule to avoid this. On any trip into Casas Grandes half the men could drink, but the other half had to remain stone cold sober to keep the Mexicans wary of being attacked themselves if they were planning their old trick. On Juh's last trip into Casas Grandes, most of the men remained sober. Some did trade for mescal, but it was Juh's *segundo* (his number two), Ponce (who had taken Geronimo's place when the Chiricahua split up), turn to drink so Juh remained perfectly sober. He got Ponce and the others drinking out of town first followed by the sober ones. Juh brought up the rear with his sons Delzhinne and Daklugie. The other son, Daklegon, was in the front with Ponce.

They were riding single file up the Río Aros, the bank less than five feet about the river. Juh's mount suddenly shied to the left, the bank crumbled and Juh went into the river. Daklugie and Delzhinne got to him as fast as they could. Daklugie who was eleven or twelve years old says the water was waist deep on him (maybe two and a half feet) and when he reached Delzhinne and Juh, Delzhinne was holding his head out of the water and Juh was unconscious. No one knows if he was injured by the fall or had a heart attack. Water was running out of Juh's mouth, and they turned him so he could expel the water. They pulled him over to the opposite bank which had a sandy beach. Daklugie says he and his brother could have lifted Juh out of the water, but Delzhinne thought leaving him in the shallow water with his face down while Daklugie held his head out of the water might help revive him. Delzhinne charged ahead for help. Daklugie thought Juh tried to speak two or three times, his lips moved with no sound. It seemed to Daklugie to take a long time, but Delzhinne at last returned with Daklegon, Ponce, and the other warriors. Juh was still breathing, but soon stopped. The warriors scraped out a grave on the west side of the Río Aros, wrapped Juh in his blanket and buried him. As Daklugie told Eve Ball, "It was a sober and sorrowing band who rode up the river and made camp that evening." [6]

TWENTY-FIVE

A New Life for the Chiricahua at Fort Apache

WHEN GENERAL CROOK began the long walk back from the Sierra Madre to San Carlos Reservation with 325 Apache, he gave their major leaders like Chihuahua, Naiche, Mangus, Chato, and Geronimo time to stay behind, gather their scattered people, and return later without his protection. But, in September, General Crook sent Lieutenant Britton Davis to the border with a company of soldiers to watch for the returnees and escort them, for their protection, to San Carlos. By the end of November, 423 Chiricahua and Chihenne including about 353 women and children and eighty warriors were on the reservation. In December, a few more came in. Chato appeared with nineteen followers the first week of February 1884, and Geronimo appeared at the border in late February with a long line of his people—26 warriors and 70 women and children (Geronimo later told Captain Crawford at San Carlos there were also 25 men, women, and children still out, but these came in April)—walking and running and behind them 350 head of cattle with which he planned to sell or start a Chiricahua herd at San Carlos.

On the way to San Carlos, returning Apache with Davis stopped, at Geronimo's insistence, to rest the cattle for a day (Geronimo wanted to rest at least three days to keep the cattle from losing too much weight) in the Sulphur Springs valley. That evening a U.S. marshal from the Southern District of Arizona and a Nogales (U.S. Port of Entry for Arizona) customs collector arrived at Davis's camp. The customs collector had come to collect a $1,000 entry fee or confiscate the cattle and the marshal to arrest Geronimo and his warriors for murder and destruction of Arizona citizens' property. Davis managed to talk Geronimo into disappearing silently with his people and the cattle herd during the night while the marshal and customs collector slept off a quart of whiskey Davis's West Point friend, Lieutenant J. Y. F. Blake, had brought with him from Fort Bowie intending to visit and have a drink with Davis.

Davis and Blake delivered Geronimo, his people, and the cattle herd to Captain Emmett Crawford who was then in charge of the reservation. To Geronimo's great disgust, General Crook took his herd of stolen cattle, sold it to San Carlos, and gave the money to Mexican authorities to properly distribute back to their owners.

Before the last few Apache with Geronimo arrived in April, plans were being made for the settlement of all the Chiricahua and Chihenne.[1] Geronimo sent a formal statement to General Crook on March 21, 1884, about what he wanted and expected if they were to stay on the reservation. In the statement, Geronimo told Crook that he was pleased to be at San Carlos (this was obviously before he had his cattle taken away) and not among the rocks and thorns in the Mexican mountains and that he knew that he had nothing to fear on the reservation and could sleep easy. Furthermore, as he later repeated when he surrendered to General Miles, September 4, 1886, he wanted the past to be "blotted out," and he understood his people had much to learn about "civilized" pursuits. He had surrendered entirely without thinking of resisting any orders, but if in the future someone said anything bad about him, he wanted to know right away who was telling bad things about him. His greatest concern was finding a suitable homesite, and he saw no reason for reservation boundaries. Now that there was no more war, the line around the reservation should be taken down. He wanted to know where they were to live and whether they would have enough land to live on. He begged to be settled on Eagle Creek and suggested that land owned by Americans living there be bought and given to the Indians. He said Crook had promised them settlement on Eagle Creek (Geronimo was sincere in his statement, but Crook did not make that promise), but if they could not settle on Eagle Creek, then he wanted to settle at Ash Flat. He argued against being settled at Camp Apache and believed there was not enough land to support the large group of Apache who had all returned from Mexico.[2]

Geronimo's missive also said he was particularly concerned about the Mexican captives including Daklugie's two brothers, his wife Chee-hash-kish, and Chato's family. He had tried to negotiate with the Mexican authorities at Casas Grandes for them before he returned to San Carlos and had no luck, but he was certain the Mexicans still had the captives and that General Crook could get them out. He mentioned that he had heard of the "little white boy" Crook had asked about, but

Apache Rancheria, San Carlos, 1884. Photograph by Frank Randall,
courtesy of the National Archives.

said that he, Geronimo, had never personally seen him. He ended his statement
by saying his band's objective was to choose a place to live apart, away from the
unfriendly tribes on the reservation.

THE PEOPLE WHO had returned with Crook must have suffered through that
summer on the baking flats around the agency with the seemingly interminable
wait for the others to return so it was possible to relocate them all at the same
time. Crook wanted to help them. In January 1884, he talked the people into
letting him send 47 boys and 5 girls to the Carlisle Indian Industrial School recently established by Captain Richard A. Pratt. Among the children were a son
of Loco and two sons of Bonito. After Captain Crawford took over as agent at
San Carlos, he assigned Lieutenant Britton Davis the duty of issuing rations and
the outrageous ration frauds perpetuated against the Indians ended.[3]

When Davis was sent to the border in October 1883 to shepherd the late ar-
rivals back to San Carlos, Archie McIntosh was assigned the rationing. McIntosh,
married to an Apache woman with Chiricahua relatives, had been with General
Crook for twenty years and was unfailingly dependable with strength and courage that often meant the difference between success and failure. On March 28,
1884, Crawford received a tip that McIntosh was stealing supplies for his ranch

on Pinto Creek near Globe. Crawford was shocked and didn't believe it at first, but upon investigation learned it was true.

Confronting McIntosh with what he had learned, Crawford was further shocked when McIntosh shrugged it off and said it was done at every post in the military department. Crawford told the chiefs what he had learned. The chiefs all said they wanted McIntosh kept, that he was a good man, and it made no difference to them if he kept half their rations. (Crawford believed that McIntosh oversupplied the chiefs and principle men and undersupplied the rest). The chiefs told Crawford to telegraph Crook and say they wanted McIntosh kept, but if he, Crook, fired him, that was all right too. Crawford fired McIntosh but told him he could telegraph an appeal to Crook. After the meeting, Geronimo, Chato, and Mangus privately told Crawford he had done the right thing. McIntosh got the chiefs to write a telegram to Crook and appeal that McIntosh stay. The telegraph operator wouldn't send the appeal until Crawford read and approved it. Crawford read the appeal, refused to let it be sent, and ordered McIntosh off the reservation, telling him that if he ever attempted again to breed discontent among the Indians, he would put him in irons.[4]

GERONIMO DIDN'T GET the Eagle Creek location he wanted for the people. In the spring of 1884, Crook did allow them to choose any untaken location on the Fort Apache Reservation. They looked at Ash Flat and apparently turned it down. They selected an area around Turkey Creek about seventeen miles southeast of Fort Apache and close to the settlement of the White Mountain bands to whom some of the Chiricahua had marriage or other connections. It was a fine land with tall pines, clear streams, abundant game, and ideal summer climate for these mountain people, but it couldn't be farmed the way the bureaucracy far away in Washington demanded despite the recommendations of Davis and Crawford to furnish the people with breeding stock for cattle and sheep raising (the same thing Geronimo had asked for). The people were issued a dozen wagons, a dozen plows, and a dozen sets of double harness. Two weeks were spent training the wild Indian ponies and Indians to use the farm "machinery" on the San Carlos River bottom land. There were lots of laughs as the wild ponies too small for the harness that had to be padded or otherwise adapted took off with the plows sailing behind them barely and rarely catching the soil and the Apache running trying to hold on to the plow handles.

IT WAS AT this time that Frank A. Randall brought his photographic equipment from Willcox Arizona, where he had settled, to make the famous portraits of the Chiricahua and Chihenne leaders, including the famous one of Geronimo kneeling with his rifle that was later falsely claimed to have been made by Ben Wittick or attributed to the Army Signal Corp. Then in late May or early June after all the necessary paper work supplies were collected, Lieutenant Davis led the people to what they hoped would be their permanent home on Turkey Creek.

Kaytennae 1884, Photograph by Frank Randall,
courtesy of the National Archives.

TWENTY-SIX

Discontent Begins to Grow

AFTER WAITING THROUGH the burning summer of 1883 and ghost face (winter) of 1883/1884 at the confluence of the San Carlos and Gila rivers, the Chiricahua and Chihenne people moved to their own piece of the Fort Apache Reservation on Turkey Creek in June 1884 after their chiefs and war leaders brought in their people from Mexico. They numbered a total of 521 including 127 men and boys capable of bearing arms. At Turkey Creek they were joined by members of the White Mountain and Coyotero bands, which increased their number to 550.

General Crook put Lieutenant Britton Davis in sole charge. Mickey Free was his interpreter and Sam Bowman, an interpreter the Apache respected, was cook and general helper. Davis established his personal tent and a much larger supply tent in a shady area under some tall pines. To keep order, Davis had a company (about twenty men) of scouts enlisted from the recently returned Chiricahua and Chihenne bands. Chato who had developed great respect for General Crook was made first sergeant. Davis was later to write that Chato was, "One of the finest men, red or white, I have ever known." Geronimo's "brother" (first cousin) Perico became second sergeant, and Geronimo's nearly grown son, Chappo, asked for and received the job of Davis's "striker" (paid servant earning five dollars a month more than an ordinary scout). Davis also brought with him from San Carlos an inconspicuous man and woman who were two "secret scouts." The Apache liked Davis. He was honest, fair, and treated them like individuals.[1]

★ ★ ★

Geronimo, Naiche, and the Chihenne choose their campsites several miles from Davis's tent. Kaytennae a Chihenne who served as Nana's *segundo* and who would one day be a chief, chose to put his camp on a high ridge about Davis's camp where he could keep an eye on its comings and goings. The camps of Chihuahua and Mangus were not far from Davis's camp. The orphaned Daklugie, son of Juh, and Istee, son of Victorio, lived with the Mangus family. Daklugie had wanted to stay with Geronimo, but Geronimo, probably believing Daklugie would have a greater chance of survival staying with easy-going Mangus than himself, insisted the boy stay with Mangus. Kaytennae was in charge of the training for Daklugie, Istee, and Kaywaykla, his step-son.

Each day Davis talked with Chato about camp conditions and the needs of the scouts. Loco, Bonito, and Gil-lee often stopped by Davis's tent to discuss business or just pass the time of day. Mangus and Loco often backed Davis in arguments with the other leaders. Geronimo, Naiche, Chihuahua, Nana, and Kaytennae remained distant from dealings with Davis. Davis being close to many of the Apache and from his daily talks with Chato and others knew there was an undercurrent of discontent growing among the Apache, and he believed it came from Kaytennae.

Kaywaykla described the origins of their discontent from the Apache viewpoint. The Chiricahua and Chihenne leaders didn't trust Davis's helpers to give him the truth. They blamed Mickey Free (after he was kidnapped, probably by Coyotero Apache, as a young boy) for starting the Cochise War, and they believed he didn't correctly translate what they said, often putting their words in a bad light. They trusted Bowman, but Davis usually used Mickey Free. They viewed Chato as a traitor because, failing to become Nana's *segundo* rather than Kaytennae, he had become a scout leader and had developed a bitter rivalry with Kaytennae. They hated Chato's friend and former brother-in-law, Tzoe, who was part of Davis's scout company because Tzoe had guided General Crook to their camps high in the Sierra Madre. Davis often sent Tzoe with messages to Fort Apache about seventeen miles away. The Apache knew about the "secret scouts" and were certain that Chato was one of them.[2]

Although Chato told Davis of things he observed or imagined among the people that were colored by his hate for Kaytennae, he was not a "secret scout." The people, knowing Davis was honest and fair, hoped he would soon discover the double-dealing of his trusted staff while Kaytennae watched his camp from high on a ridge and Perico and Chappo kept their eyes and ears open from within the camp. Kaywaykla believed that Geronimo had encouraged Perico and Chappo to enlist with Davis so he might have a direct ear into what was happening inside

Davis's tent. Apparently, Perico and Chappo didn't understand they were to be Geronimo's de facto spies and had enlisted in good faith.

DESPITE STRONG UNDERCURRENTS of possible betrayals, the forbidding of the making of tizwin (a White Eye term for tulapai) and the control of their families (primarily the authority to beat their wives) soon became a festering wound of discontent. When Crook first came to Arizona and worked to straighten out management and hostility problems on the reservations, he laid down rules regulating tizwin making and how men treated their wives. Soon after their camps were established on Turkey Creek, Davis had a come-to-Jesus meeting with the chiefs, told them Crook's rules and warned that breaking the rules would land them in the calaboose. The Chiricahua and Chihenne chiefs were nearly unanimously opposed to Crook's rules. Chihuahua didn't hesitate to voice strong disapproval; Kaytennae said nothing but was sullen and churlish.[3]

Crook forbade tizwin making and drinking because it nearly always brought disorder and violence to the camps. The Apache logically argued that they had promised Crook they would keep the peace with the White Eyes, Mexicans, and other Indian tribes, and they had been true to their word. All Whites Eyes, Blue Coat officers, and Mexicans drank something to feel good, why would it be denied the Apache? The Apache had always made tizwin, and they didn't want their people thrown in jail for what was a long-held tribal custom.

The crux of the problem with the rules for how men treated their wives has to be seen against the Apache view of marriage. A woman occupied a secure and honored place in Apache society. In very broad terms, it was man's duty to provide food, materials for hearth and home, and family protection. It was a woman's duty to be neat in her home and self, to provide a good and comfortable hearth and home, and to care for their children. Apache society was matriarchal where a man became a member of his wife's family and gave her family the right to intervene and protect her if he abused her. If she was lazy or nagged him, he could do nothing but scold her in private. Apache women were expected to be chaste, and nearly all were. In cases where an Apache wife was adulterous, the husband was obligated to vindicate family honor by cutting off the end of her nose so she would be so ugly no one else would want her. If he failed to do this, he lost status in the band. Crook unequivocally banned this practice on all the reservations he controlled, so the Apache soon substituted a beating for cut-the-nose punishment. In some cases, a man even killed his wife and then himself in his grief and humiliation. No wronged husband ever complained. His shame was too great.

Thus, at Davis's rules meeting the leaders told him that neither family discipline nor tizwin making and drinking had entered into their agreement with Crook, and they didn't accept those rules. Davis didn't waver in his intent to enforce them. Seeds of discontent were soon to sprout.[4]

TWENTY-SEVEN

A Summer of Surprises

NOT LONG AFTER the meeting with the Chiricahua leaders Davis went turkey hunting. Climbing a trail up a mesa he heard a turkey gobble in the creek bottom behind him. He turned back down the trail and near the creek bottom took a turkey. Late that night, his female secret scout tossed a pebble on his tent, her signal that she had information for him. She told him the good spirit of one his ancestors must have been in the turkey he heard. Kaytennae and his followers had been having a tizwin drink on the mesa. When they saw him coming up the trail with a gun, they thought he was coming to arrest them and laid an ambush to kill him when he reached the top. Then they planned to incite as many others as possible and make a break for Mexico.[1]

Davis decided he had to nip this source of potential rebellions in the bud. He sent for four troops of cavalry (about 80 men) from Fort Apache to arrive at sunrise. Then he sent his scouts to summon all the leaders to his tent. Kaytennae had thirty-two followers, all reckless young warriors. Davis knew he could count on Chato, Bonito, Loco, Mangas, and Gil-lee to back him up; Geronimo and Naiche would probably be uncommitted one way or the other, and Davis didn't consider Nana's opinion significant. If the majority wanted peace, he would win, otherwise there would probably be a fight like the disaster when Colonel Carr tried to arrest the prophet, Noch-ay-del-kinne three years before.

The confrontation that morning, June 22, 1884, with the cavalry dismounted and ready and Kaytennae and his warriors sullen and defiant, happened in Davis's tent with twenty of the chiefs and leaders and other warriors surrounding it all armed. There was not a child or woman in sight. (With good reason, Crook refused to disarm the Apache. They were experts at concealing their weapons;

Kaytennae and family 1889, Photograph by Frank and Wallace, Mobile, Alabama, courtesy of the National Archives.

there were plenty of dealers who wouldn't hesitate to sell arms and ammunition to them; and only by being armed could they protect themselves from disreputable White Eyes on the reservation). It was the first time the leaders had come armed to a meeting with Davis.[2]

Kaytennae's followers spread out and cocking their weapons advanced on the tent, but Davis's scouts stood firm. Kaytennae was arrested without incident. Bonito and one of the scouts stood surety for him if he were not disarmed. Traveling with them to San Carlos without trouble he was tried by an Indian jury and convicted of threatening to start an uprising. Captain Crawford sentenced him to three years in irons on Alcatraz Island. Crook saw great leadership potential in Kaytennae and recommended that he be kept in irons at hard labor for a month and then the terms of his confinement relaxed, that he be allowed to move about the island, visit San Francisco, learn how the White Eyes lived, and learn whatever he could to benefit his people when he was released. In fact, Crook offered to have him released after three months of confinement but Geronimo and Chato said no, that he would keep the others stirred up. Crook had him released after about twenty months. Kaytennae had learned to read and write a little and returned willing to cooperate with the military. Within two or three days after his arrival by train at Fort Bowie Station, Crook took Kaytennae with him to discuss surrender with Geronimo and the chiefs in March 1886 at Cañon de los Embudos.

At the time of his sentencing, Kaytennae's family was heartbroken. They believed he would be executed at Alcatraz. Soon after Kaytennae left for Alcatraz, his young adopted son, Kaywaykla, went to pick up the family's ration share. There Chato told him Kaytennae would be "chained on a rock so far from land that no man could swim across the water." When Kaywaykla told that to his grandfather, Nana, the old man replied that he had seen all the rivers in the land and there was no water so wide that Kaytennae could not swim across. Nana also said he had prayed to Ussen and was told that Kaytennae would return. The fear persisted that he was to be executed and that Geronimo, Naiche, Chihuahua, Mangas, and Nana would be the next to go.

General Crook responding, to Geronimo's request to appeal to the Mexican government for the release of his people held in slavery, urged Washington diplomats and pols to get them released. An attempt was made but without success. The Mexicans refused to admit they dealt in Apache slaves and even sent photographs of the captives to Crook to show that they were happy and free and could return to their people if they wished. All knew the Mexicans were in fact still dealing in Apache slaves. In fact, just before the 1885 breakout, five of the captives from the Victorio debacle at Tres Castillos managed to escape and return over twelve hundred miles through Mexico and New Mexico with nothing but a knife and a blanket to the vicinity of Ojo Caliente Reservation.[3] The army took them by wagon to Fort Apache where there was a joyous reunion with their relatives.

BY THE TIME the Chiricahua's were settled at Turkey Creek, it was too late to plant for major crops but the Apache did plant little gardens of corn and vegetables and delighted in the discovery of cultivated potatoes, melons, and pumpkins. The Apache women collected empty ration cans, cut them into strips and wrapped them around the end of a tapered stick to make cone shaped bells they suspended from buckskin thongs for ceremonial garments to jingle when they walked. Davis used a particular brand of chopped ham, and when he gave that can to Kaywaykla to give to his mother, she saw a tall thin man with hooves and a tail on the wrapper and immediately concluded that Davis had been eating man meat—he was a cannibal. No more collecting discarded cans from Davis. Nana made medicine for her and the family suffered no ills.[4]

TWENTY-EIGHT

Wife Beating and Tizwin Drinking
Start a New War

LIEUTENANT BRITTON DAVIS was in sole charge of the Chiricahua and Chihenne people and had done his best to treat them fairly and with respect. Nevertheless, Davis's tenure had encountered a couple of rough spots in the summer of 1884. First, Apache leaders refused to accept General Crook's reservation rules about making a beer from corn, known as tizwin, and for men beating their wives. Second, Kaytennae, Nana's *segundo* (number two), had been sentenced to three years in irons at Alcatraz after he and others had nearly ambushed Davis and planned to afterward lead a breakout back to the Sierra Madre.

With the coming of fall, the Season of Earth is Reddish Brown, the Apache had a big dance and feast and then moved down to a lower altitude to the valley of the White River near Fort Apache where the winters were warmer. Davis established his tent about three miles from Fort Apache. The Apache established their camps along streams or the nearby foothills. As he had done on Turkey Creek, Davis had his large tent from which he continued to distribute dry rations and the meat ration was issued at the slaughterhouse at the fort.

The undercurrents of discontent that had started in the summer continued to flow in the Season of the Ghost Face, but since their return from the Sierra Madre the Apache leaders were doing all in their power to keep the peace promised to General Crook in 1883. There had been no acts of violence, no one had been killed, and not a single horse stolen since the return of the Chiricahua and Chihenne people first to San Carlos and then to Fort Apache. General Crook stated in his 1884 report that "for the first time in the history of that fierce people, every member of the Apache tribe is at peace."

During the winter of 1884/1885, the weeds of suspicion about actual White Eye intent didn't die off but began to flourish at Fort Apache. Apache children at the fort were asked by soldiers to point out the better-known warriors and leaders like Naiche and Geronimo. Then when their officers weren't looking, the soldiers would do a hand slash sign across the throat toward the leaders to tease the Apache. The Apache didn't understand the soldiers were teasing and joking. They thought the soldiers were their friends trying to warn them about their coming executions. Geronimo had always thought executions, at least of the leaders, were imminent.

In the Season of Little Eagles (early spring) when the Apache went back to Turkey Creek in 1885, teasing by the soldiers began to pay an unwanted dividend. The wife of Mangas, Huera, who had escaped Mexican slavery and returned after walking with four other women over twelve hundred miles from Mexico City and who was widely admired for her tizwin, warned Geronimo that he and her husband, Mangas, would be arrested and jailed.

Another Apache, Nodiskey, from the White Mountain part of the reservation, had married a Chiricahua woman and come to live with her and her family. He was active in spreading rumors of impending doom and had a long talk with Geronimo and tried to convince him that he would soon be arrested—Geronimo later claimed he didn't believe him. Davis suspected Nodiskey was a troublemaker and wanted to arrest him, but he never found sufficient evidence to prove it, and Davis was unaware of the fear and discontent being stirred up that winter by the soldiers and their jokes.

The weeds of Apache suspicions had grown to certainties. A song of blood and fire was coming and bureaucratic infighting over how the reservation was managed would provide its prelude.

THE WAR WITH the Apache appeared over. The BIA bureaucrats assumed they could now assert their authority over the army on the reservations and the old feud between the War and Interior Departments broke out once more. The Army had been in control of the reservations since General Crook had returned to Arizona in 1882. Crook had appointed Captain Crawford in charge of San Carlos. In the spring of 1885, Crawford and the BIA agent issued conflicting orders for farming practices, the arrest and punishment of offenders, and the purchase of cattle. Crook tried to quit managing the reservations unless he had undivided control. His request was denied, but a disgusted Crawford requested permission to return to his regiment and Crook granted it. He replaced Crawford with Captain Francis E. Pierce.

Although none of this infighting between agencies and resignations applied to the bands at Turkey Creek, they knew about Crawford leaving and this left them worried. They constantly asked Davis if that meant *Nant'an Lpah* (General Crook) had gone also. Geronimo particularly needed reassurance. The Apache were also probably aware of the arguments and grasping for power going on between the departments and that probably made them bolder in claiming more independence.

In the clear mountain air of the Season of Little Eagles, after the Chiricahua and Chihenne people returned to their camps on Turkey Creek, discontent with Crook's rules began to grow. As early spring turned to blossoms and new growth everywhere in the high country along Turkey Creek, a young woman with her arm broken in two places, her hair matted with blood, and her shoulders covered with welts and bruises went to Davis for medical attention.[1] The post surgeon cleaned her up, put a splint on her arm, and bandaged her welts and bruises. Davis arrested her husband and sentenced him to two weeks in the Fort Apache calaboose.

Apache leaders began appearing at Davis's tent demanding the husband's release. Davis refused. In early May, Davis arrested and jailed an Apache for a tizwin drink. Mangas and Chihuahua were at Davis's tent that afternoon to protest. Davis wasn't surprised that Chihuahua had come, but Mangas rarely voiced an opinion about anything. Davis learned through one of his spies that Huera was telling her husband the same stories she was telling Geronimo, no doubt concerned that if she made her tizwin she would be jailed too.

The leaders held a council and decided they would have a big tizwin party and challenge Davis to arrest them all. Before sunrise the morning of Friday, May 15, after the big tizwin drink they all assembled with about thirty others around Davis's tent. Many were armed and no women and children were there. When Davis came out of his tent, they told him they had come for a talk. All of them, except Chato who stayed with the scouts, entered the tent and squatted in a half circle in front of Davis. Loco, hungover, calmly began to make his case, but Chihuahua who was still clearly drunk jumped up and interrupted Loco to make his own case. He repeated all the old arguments revolving around them never agreeing to rules Crook never mentioned in Mexico and that they were being punished for things they had a right to do as long as they didn't harm others.

Davis tried to explain the rules. When he got to wife beating, Nana stood up, said something with an angry face to the interpreter Mickey Free, and hobbled out of the tent. Free didn't want to translate, but Davis insisted. Nana had said, "Tell the *Nant'an* Enchau (Stout Chief) that he can't advise me how to treat women. He is only a boy. I killed men before he was born."

Chihuahua continued his harangue. "We all drank tizwin last night, all of us here in the tent and those outside, except the scouts: and many more. What are you going to do about it? Are you going to put us all in jail? Your jail is not big enough even if you could put us all in jail."

Davis told them this was too serious for him to decide and that he would use the talking wire to ask *Nant'an Lpah* and let them know the answer. Bonito and Gil-lee started to say something but Chihuahua cut them off. The council was over. No one else had spoken, including Geronimo, and Chihuahua was the only one who seemed drunk.[2]

DAVIS WROTE HIS telegram to Crook. Following army protocol, he first sent it to Captain Pierce at San Carlos to forward to General Crook for response. Pierce, in command of the reservation, but with no knowledge of Apache, relied on advice from the highly experienced Chief of Scouts, Al Sieber. But the same night the Apache were getting drunk, Sieber was gambling and doing his own drinking. When the telegram came in, Sieber was sleeping off the whiskey from the night before. When Pierce woke him up to show him the telegram, Sieber read it with bleary eyes and a fine hangover. He said to Pierce, "It's nothing but a tizwin drunk. Don't pay any attention to it. Davis will handle it." Then he went back to sleep. Pierce went back to his office and pigeonholed the telegram.

Back at Turkey Creek, the rest of Friday passed with no answer. Saturday passed, no answer, and so did most of Sunday. Davis saw the leaders everyday but had nothing to tell them. Rumors began to fly. The leaders were going to be hanged or have their heads taken. The whole band would be arrested and taken to a dark place somewhere. Davis kept in contact with his scouts and waited, never imagining the telegram had not reached Crook. He thought Crook was probably making arrangements to handle the situation and would let him know his plans as soon as they were ready. Both Davis and Crook would later say that had the message gone through, the affair would have been a minor incident.

At Fort Apache on Sunday, May 17, about four o'clock in the afternoon, Chato and Mickey Free came to Davis who was umpiring a baseball game at the fort

Apache!
Painting by Frederic Remington.

while waiting for Crook's reply to his telegram. They told him that a number of Chiricahua and Chihenne had broken out of the reservation and were on their way to Mexico. Davis immediately attempted to telegraph Captain Pierce, but the line was dead. Geronimo's third reservation escape had begun.[3]

PART FIVE:
DECEPTION RENEWS
AND ENDS THE WAR

The end of the Apache Iliad stretched over a period of fifteen months and ended with the surrender of the Naiche-Geronimo band of eighteen men and twenty-two women and children and the shameful exile for twenty-seven years of three hundred fifty Chiricahua and army paid scouts who had never joined those who had escaped the reservation with Geronimo to raid and make war against the Americans and Mexicans. The tragic ending of the Apache Iliad began with failure to communicate between army commanders and between Apache leaders. The end of the Apache Iliad came with the Apache acceptance of army surrender terms that were deceptions resulting from ignorance and false hope that soon became little more than lies.

Geronimo and Naiche surrendered twice, once after ten months of war to General Crook, and again five months later to General Miles. The first surrender occurred when the Apache came to believe, and rightly so, that as long as the American army was supported by Apache scouts, there was no place for them to safely hide in the mountains of Mexico. Geronimo and Naiche agreed to surrender but changed their minds and two days later left the rest who surrendered and were shipped to Fort Marion in San Augustine, Florida. At Fort Marion, they suffered from short food rations because they wouldn't eat fish and died in alarming numbers (three times the national death rate) from mosquito borne diseases and tuberculosis contagion probably left by previous prisoners from the Indian Wars on the northern plains (the Plains Indians had often traded with French traders who had the disease).

Geronimo and Naiche agreed to surrender for the second time in five months after their warriors learned their families, which they badly wanted to see, had been sent to Florida and they no longer had a reservation. One of Geronimo's best warriors, his "brother" Perico said as they discussed what to do, "I'm going to surrender. My wife and children have been captured. I love them and want to be with them." Soon two more voiced the same sentiment and Geronimo, deciding he couldn't continue to fight without them, agreed to surrender too. Soon they were all on a train rolling across West Texas in the heat of mid-September with the windows nailed shut headed for Florida and never to return to the mountains they loved in Arizona and New Mexico.

At the beginning of the end of the Apache Iliad, Chiefs Chihuahua and Naiche left the reservation after hearing from Geronimo that Lieutenant Britton Davis and his First Sergeant of Scouts, Chato had been assassinated. They feared they would be blamed and severely punished along with Geronimo by General Crook. A few days after leaving the reservation, they learned Davis and Chato had not been killed after all. Chihuahua, believing Geronimo had deliberately tricked him into leaving the reservation, too, was furious and went looking for Geronimo intending to kill him. Geronimo learned that Chihuahua was coming after him and quickly disappeared east into the Black Range of New Mexico. Chihuahua turned north and hoped circle back to the reservation, but too many troopers and Apache scouts were covering the countryside requiring him to also turn south toward Mexico.

Within a month, all the Apache were across the border and believed they were finally safe from soldiers in their Sierra Madre camps. Two columns of American soldiers (Apache scouts) lead by Captains Emmett Crawford and Wirt Davis and guided by first sergeants of scouts Chato and Bylas found the camps, attacked and captured most of the women and children of the "renegade" Apache led by Geronimo and Chihuahua.

In late September, Geronimo led four men back across the border to reclaim their family members they believed held at Fort Apache. General Crook, expecting this response, was one step ahead of them and had secretly sequestered their families at Fort Bowie. Entering Fort Apache under cover of darkness, they were able to find one wife of Geronimo (She-gha) and a woman who Perico took for a wife. On the way back to Mexico the Geronimo raiders captured three Mescalero women one with a young boy (famous Charlie Smith), one with a baby, and a young woman not yet married, gathering piñon nuts on a reservation pass. Geronimo married the youngest one, Ih-tedda, and had two children with her before divorcing her so she could return to Mescalero and escape the prisoner of war camps.

In January 1886, the Apache wintered in a place they believed was the best hidden and most defensible in Mexico. Captain Crawford's scouts found it and in doing so convinced the Apache that it was time to surrender to General Crook at a prearranged time (mid-March 1886) and place near the border (Cañon de los Embudos). Even though Geronimo and Naiche did surrender at this time, a whiskey peddler convinced them that Crook planned to turn them over to civilian authorities for hanging as soon they crossed border. Within two days after agreeing to surrender, Geronimo and Naiche with their followers left the main group and refused to surrender.

General Sheridan blamed General Crook for Geronimo's breakaway. Crook resigned and Sheridan moved him to manage the plains tribes. General Nelson Miles who never agreed with Crook about anything was brought in to "capture" Geronimo and manage the Apache. Miles had thirty heliostats (an optical telegraphy system that used reflective sunlight) mounted on the tops of mountains along the border for "ultrafast" communications to companies of soldiers when the Apache tried to cross the border. Unfortunately, the Apache only crossed the border once while they were out and that was at night.

General Miles brought in 5,000 soldiers (one quarter of the American Army), the Mexicans had 3,000 soldiers, and there were literally hundreds of civilian posse members all attempting to contain and catch Geronimo and Naiche's band. In the five months that followed, the band didn't lose a single man killed, wounded, or captured. Listening to the terms of surrender brought to them by two scouts with relatives in the band and Lieutenant Charles B. Gatewood, the Geronimo-Naiche band decided to surrender and see their families rather than continue to fight. Not long after their surrender, they learned that the surrender terms were lies and they had been deceived into giving up their Sierra Madre fortress in much the same way the Trojan Horse had deceived the Trojans and led them to open the gates of Troy.

TWENTY-NINE

The 1885 Renegade Chiefs: Naiche, Chihuahua, Nana, Mangas

O N MAY 17, 1885,thirty-five men, eight boys old enough to bear arms, and one hundred and one women and children, Chiricahua Apache living along Turkey Creek seventeen miles from Fort Apache, left the reservation headed for the Sierra Madre in Mexico. They feared General Crook was coming to take them someplace far from the reservation for making and drinking tizwin. They were led by their great and feared *di-yen* and war leader, Geronimo. The majority of the Chiricahua, about seventy percent, never left the reservation and continued to peacefully mind their own business and tend their farms. Chiricahua scouts, in the group who stayed behind and helped the army track and attack the camps of the escapees, were serving as tribal police led by First Sergeant Chato.

The leaders who rode with Geronimo included Naiche, Chihuahua, Nana, and Mangas. The relationships and backgrounds of these leaders are reviewed and described here to provide insight into why they chose to leave with Geronimo when the majority stayed on the reservation.

Naiche[1]

Naiche was the youngest son of the great chief Cochise, and of the leaders described here, he was by far the youngest at about twenty-eight years old. Cochise had groomed his first son, Taza, to be chief of the Chokonen Apache leaving Naiche with no training in tribal leadership. Cochise died in 1874, with Naiche and Taza promising their father to avoid, if at all possible, conflicts with

Frank Randall Photographs of Chiricahua Leaders 1884.
Courtesy of the Library of Congress

the White Eyes. Attempting to keep their promise to their father, Naiche and Taza agreed to Agent John Clum's request and implied demand that they move the Chokonen Chiricahua from the reservation Cochise had wanted, to the San Carlos Reservation in 1876. Later that year, Taza died on a visit east with Clum. Thus, at age nineteen, Naiche, who loved dancing, fighting, drinking, and chasing women, but knew nothing of tribal leadership, was chosen chief of the Chokonen.

Naiche, who had no supernatural power and knowing he was not prepared to be a chief, was not hesitant to ask for help and guidance when he thought he needed it, and he made Geronimo, feared *di-yen* (medicine man) with great supernatural gifts, his counselor and gave him some of his prerogatives as chief, like making war.[2] This agreement happened after Naiche agreed that Geronimo and his band could camp with his people at San Carlos. Naiche did not follow Geronimo off the reservation the first time he left in 1878, but the second time, in 1881, he followed him into the Sierra Madre and was among the warriors who returned to San Carlos in 1882 to abduct Loco and his people. In May 1883, Naiche agreed to surrender to General Crook, but like the other leaders stayed behind in Mexico to "gather his people," and like the others spent most of the summer raiding in Mexico before going north. More than half of the Chiricahua (about 325) returned to San Carlos in June 1883 with General Crook. Naiche returned with Gil-lee and nine other warriors and about eighteen women and children in late October 1883. Happy to move from San Carlos the following spring, Naiche was among those who argued against General Crook's reservation rules against tizwin making and wife beating. Nevertheless, he was reluctant to leave the reservation until Geronimo tricked him and Chihuahua by claiming that Lieutenant Britton Davis had been assassinated (he had not been killed, but Geronimo believed that he had) and they had to run to avoid hanging.

Chihuahua[3]

Born about 1822, and thus about the same age as Geronimo, Chihuahua was a Chokonen sub-chief under Cochise and had the second largest following after Cochise. He believed Naiche was too inexperienced to be chief, and so kept his distance from the main body of Chokonen when all were moved to San Carlos. Chihuahua was a powerful warrior and leader, but he seems to have gotten along well with Naiche who probably often asked him for advice. He was a major leader during Geronimo's second breakout when nearly all the Chiricahua escaped and followed Geronimo when the Apache in Mexico abducted Loco and his people at San Carlos. He went on numerous raids with Geronimo across Sonora in 1882/1883.

Chihuahua was a scout under Lieutenant Britton Davis until he discovered Davis had spies among the people and quit in disgust even though there was time remaining on his enlistment. The Blue Coats knew Chihuahua to be an honorable man and man of his word. However, at Turkey Creek he was outraged to learn Crook's rules about tizwin making and wife beating and was one of the instigators for getting everyone drunk to show Davis he couldn't put them in jail and thus had to change the rule. He was reluctant to go out with Geronimo in 1885 and was tricked into leaving in the same way Naiche was deceived.

Nana[4]

Nana, born about 1800, was the oldest of the leaders to escape in May 1885. He was married to Geronimo's full sister, Nah-dos-te. They had a son who many believe killed himself after Geronimo in a tizwin drunk berated him for "no reason at all." The death of the boy was a major reason for Geronimo's first San Carlos escape. A Chihenne Apache and Victorio's *segundo*, Nana is said to have had a broken foot that didn't heal well and arthritis in his knees that made him appear slow, tottering, and frail. However, the summer after Victorio was wiped out at Tres Castillos, Nana led a group of Chihenne and Mescalero warriors raiding, sometimes covering seventy miles a day in the saddle for over a thousand miles and wiping out everyone (by some estimates fifty people) they came across and taking hundreds of horses and mules and other supplies before disappearing into the Sierra Madre. Like Geronimo, Nana joined forces with Juh in 1881, and after Juh left the main band, remained with Geronimo and other war leaders who surrendered to General Crook in 1883. He was a powerful voice, along with Chihuahua, for rejecting Crook's reservation rules about making tizwin and wife beating. He left the meeting where the chiefs were arguing with Lieutenant Britton Davis over tizwin making and other rules by saying, "Tell the *Nant'an* Stout Chief (Davis was stocky but not fat) that he can't advise me how to treat women. He is only a boy. I killed men before he was born." [5] When Geronimo broke out of San Carlos the third time, Nana didn't hesitate to go with him.

Mangas[6]

Mangas, the son of Mangas Coloradas, was born about 1840 and was about seventeen years older than Naiche. He married a daughter of Victorio, Dilth-Clay-ih, and stayed with Victorio's band until it was wiped out in late 1880. He then rode with Nana from 1881 to 1883 before surrendering to General Crook. He had his own band of Chihenne Apache by 1884.

The similarities between Mangas and Naiche are striking. Among the most important parallels in their lives were they both were the sons of highly regarded chiefs who were betrayed by the American military, and they married women who were daughters of important chiefs. For a while, Mangas was married to Huera, the master tizwin maker, who with four other women had escaped Mexican slavery and returned to San Carlos in 1884. Huera liked to make tizwin and spread tales. She told Mangas and Geronimo she had learned that the Blue Coats would arrest them and put them in the guardhouse. It was no accident that the third breakout was led by Geronimo and Mangas. After the breakout, Mangas separated his small group from the one led by Geronimo that eventually included Chihuahua and Naiche. He managed to avoid surrendering for nearly two months after Geronimo surrendered and was the last Apache to surrender and sent into exile in Florida in late October 1886.

THIRTY

First Sergeant of Scouts: Chato

CHATO WAS ONE of the most paradoxical leaders the Apache had in the ten years before Geronimo surrendered in 1886. James Kaywaykla, a Chihenne Apache, who was a young boy with a near photographic memory for personalities says in Victorio, Recollections of a Warm Springs Apache, that the White Eyes, who killed Chato's brother and father had no more implacable enemy.[1] Chato arrived with nine warriors and nine women and children in early February 1884, nearly eight months after most of the Chiricahua had returned to San Carlos Reservation and became first sergeant of Lieutenant Britton Davis's tribal police at Turkey Creek on the Fort Apache Reservation. Davis held Chato in the highest regard and in 1929 was to write, "[Chato was] One of the finest men, red or white, I have ever known."

The way the Chiricahua disliked, in some cases even despised, Chato because he was a scout is a paradox. Nearly seventy percent of the Chiricahua and Chihenne men were at one time or the other on the army payroll as a scout and few of them were held in contempt by others in the bands. Yet, Chato seems to be the one most considered a traitor because he was a scout. To understand the role Chato played in Geronimo's last escape from the Fort Apache Reservation and why his own people wanted nothing to do with him, a brief review of his background is informative.

JAMES KAYWAYKLA REMEMBERED Chato as an "insolent" young man in Geronimo's band. He often appeared at councils where he wasn't invited as a

Colorized 1886 Photograph of Chato.
Courtesy of the National Anthropological Archives.

participant, interrupted the elders when they spoke, and was seen as a greedy opportunist who schemed for position.[2] Kaywaykla viewed him as treacherous, and unreliable, but perhaps that view was shaded by the fact that Chato and Kaywaykla's stepfather, Kaytennae, often locked horns and Chato went out of his way to make life hard for Kaytennae. Kaytennae believed, and it is probably true, that Chato told tales out of school to try to get Kaytennae in trouble, and as a first sergeant of police convinced Lieutenant Britton Davis that Kaytennae was stirring up trouble among the Chiricahua and Chihenne and had intended to kill him. As a result, Kaytennae was arrested and sentenced to spend three years in chains at Alcatraz (actual time served was twenty months and the chains were gone in less than a month thanks to General Crook). After Kaytennae was released from Alcatraz where he had learned to speak English and to read and write a little, he kept close to Chato ready to dispute at any time, anything Chato told a White Eye that wasn't quite correct. Every group picture where Chato and Kaytennae both appear, shows Kaytennae next to Chato.

Apparently, Chato developed his extreme dislike for Kaytennae after the death of Victorio. Old Nana, then about eighty years-old, had been Victorio's *segundo*. Through a fortunate set of circumstances, Nana, Kaytennae, and a few others were away from Victorio's camp at Tres Castillos looking for ammunition or hunting when the Mexicans attacked. The attack wiped out Victorio and his warriors. After the battle, the Mexicans killed many young boys they thought too old to accept slavery, and took many women and children as slaves. The next year, Nana led nearly a six-weeks-long raid across southern Arizona and New Mexico to avenge Victorio and then disappeared into the Sierra Madre. Nana became the leader of what was left of Victorio's people. Chato probably thought that as old and slow as Nana was, it wouldn't be long before he was gone. He joined Nana's band for a while, and as a well-known and powerful warrior, expected Nana to soon ask him to become his *segundo*. It didn't happen. Nana chose Kaytennae as his *segundo*, and Chato left the band.

CHIHUAHUA, GORDO, CHATO, and Naiche were heads of villages at San Carlos. After Geronimo was released from the guardhouse, he lived in Naiche's village where his family probably stayed while he was locked up. Geronimo, with the help of the great Nednhi chief Juh, left San Carlos in early April 1878 while Naiche and the other village chiefs stayed put. Geronimo and Juh returned about eighteen months later after reaching an accommodation with General Willcox's representatives nearly a year before Victorio was killed.

In late September 1881, frightened by all the military activity at San Carlos resulting from the killing of the prophet, Noch-ay-del-klinne, Geronimo and all the major Chiricahua leaders including, Naiche, Chihuahua, Gordo, and Chato, escaped the reservation to join Juh in the Sierra Madre. With them were over two hundred seventy women and children, seventy-four men and twenty-two older boys capable of using weapons. Chased by cavalry and Apache scouts, the Apache lost one or two warriors killed, one woman killed, and one woman and three children captured. Their escape into Mexico with so few casualties was a monument to their capability.

FOR A WHILE in the Sierra Madre, Geronimo was Juh's *segundo*. It was not unusual for groups to separate from the main band over friendly disagreements. Geronimo leading one group, Juh the other much larger group. During these separations, Chato was often Geronimo's *segundo*. Chato was with the group of over seventy men who returned to San Carlos with Geronimo in the spring of 1882 to abduct Loco and his Chihenne people. They had good luck and made it back across the border with over 320 Chihenne Apache and suffered very minor losses.

Disaster struck the escapees in Mexico when American cavalry illegally crossed the border and attacked their camp at Sierra Enmedio and the Mexican army attacked them the next morning while they were on the way to a rendezvous point. The Mexicans attacked at Aliso Creek in an ambush that let fifteen lead warriors, including Naiche, Chato, and Kaytennae, pass in order to attack the much larger group of women and children.

The ambush took a heavy toll of casualties. Geronimo, Chihuahua and other warriors fought off the Mexicans all day and then escaped with the survivors. The first group of warriors who the Mexicans let pass never returned that day to help the others and no one knows why.

DURING THE SUMMER of 1882, Chato served as Geronimo's *segundo* often because a group of about fifty under Geronimo split with Juh to raid in Sonora while Juh went east with most of the band. Late in the fall of that year, the bands reunited at a camp on the edge of the great Copper Canyon chasm. The Apache spent the winter making plans for two major raids during the coming spring. Geronimo and Chihuahua would lead one group with about seventy warriors and novitiates into Sonora around the town of Ures. Chato and Bonito would lead a lightning raid with twenty-six of the best warriors across the border for horses and ammunition and intelligence about what was happening at San Carlos.

The Chato raid covered between 400 and 450 miles in six days and killed every White Eye in its path. It is said that Chato only slept while riding on his horse. It was on this raid that Chato and his warriors killed Judge and Mrs. H.C. McComas on their way to Lordsburg and took their six-year-old son, Charlie. The raid lost two men. Beneactiney, was killed in a raid on a charcoal camp. Beneactiney's death led his best friend Tzoe to decide that he must return to San Carlos to help his People. Chato and the others let him go and gave him enough provisions to get back to San Carlos.

Soon after sneaking into San Carlos, Tzoe was caught by Lieutenant Britton Davis and his Apache scouts in the village of Nodiskey, and after questioning, Tzoe agreed to lead General Crook to the Apache camps in the Sierra Madre. In the Sierra Madre, near a place the Apache called Bugatseka (Mesa Tres Ríos), Crook's scouts surprised the Apache and attacked only one camp—Chato and Bonito's—Crook later told the chiefs that the attack was an accident and if possible, wanted to negotiate the Apache peaceful return. The Chiricahua were surprised and disheartened that the army had found them and destroyed a large part of their winter food supply, and that one of their own people had shown the army where their camps were. Chato talked with General Crook several times during the meetings with the chiefs and came to the conclusion that he needed to be a follower of General Crook's way and not Geronimo's.

AFTER RETURNING TO San Carlos in early February 1884, Chato joined the scouts supporting Lieutenant Davis, who was solely in charge of the Chiricahua at Fort Apache. In July 1884, Davis made Chato first sergeant, highest Apache rank in the scouts, and he gave Davis his undivided loyalty. Unlike many of the scouts, Chato abided strictly by the White Eye rules, not letting the Apache get away with even a minor infraction that other scouts often overlooked. Thus, if Chato didn't cut his people any slack they didn't cut him any either.

After Geronimo left the reservation for the third time in 1885, General

Crook placed Chato in charge of more scouts and was their primary leader. He supported both Captains Crawford and Wirt Davis whose attacks on the camps of Chihuahua and Geronimo were devastating and ultimately led them and their cohorts to surrender. Chato's loyalty to General Crook and his help in running to earth his former brothers in arms after the May 1885 breakout undoubtedly saved many American, Mexican, and Apache lives, but estranged him from his people for the rest of his life.

THIRTY-ONE

Geronimo Deceives Naiche and Chihuahua

CHIRICAHUA APACHE LEADERS in camps along Turkey Creek at Fort Apache Reservation under the sole supervision of Lieutenant Britton Davis were angry that Davis had enforced General Crook's rules against tizwin making and wife beating. The Apache believed that tizwin making and wife beating were their fundamental rights. To prove their point, they all drank tizwin one night, and the next morning, some still drunk and others with bad hangovers, came to Davis's tent early the next morning to make their case and challenge him to put them all in the calaboose. Davis told them the matter was too important for him to decide and promised to immediately wire General Crook to get an answer. The Apache agreed to wait for General Crook's instructions.

Following army protocol, Davis sent his telegram to General Crook through his commander, Captain Pierce, who had replaced Captain Crawford as the reservation agent in charge of San Carlos and Fort Apache Reservation. Agency headquarters where Captain Pierce was stationed was sixty miles south of Fort Apache. Davis's telegram never left the commander's desk at San Carlos (a case of mistaken situational interpretation by Chief of Scouts, Al Sieber, who was sleeping off a hangover and thought Davis was just reporting a tizwin drunk he would easily handle) to reach General Crook.

Three days went by without an answer. The Apache, especially Geronimo, were becoming more anxious by the day about what Crook would do.

In 1877, Geronimo, who after being tricked into coming to a meeting with the agent at Ojo Caliente Reservation and then captured by San Carlos Agent John Clum, served more than three months shackled in the San Carlos guardhouse expecting to be hung any day. Fortunate circumstances released him, but for the rest of his life he was exceptionally paranoid about what the army might do to chain him again in the guardhouse. Through the 1885 Seasons of the Ghost Face and Little Eagles, he had been told by Huera, a wife of Mangas, and an expert tizwin maker, that the army planned to throw him and Mangas back in the guardhouse. A village chief, Nodiskey, had also told Geronimo that the army was going to arrest him. Geronimo had vowed that he would never return to the guardhouse. The previous summer, First Sergeant Chato had told Lieutenant Davis that Kaytennae had planned to kill him (Davis), which led to Kaytennae's arrest, trial, and sentencing to serve time at Alcatraz in chains. There were also stories that Chato was also telling Davis that Geronimo planned to breakout. In later years, Geronimo would claim that he believed neither Huera nor Nodiskey because he had perfectly behaved at Turkey Creek. However, as the hours dragged by while the Apache waited for word from General Crook, rumors began to fly that Crook was on the way to carry all the Apache off to exile in some dark place, that the leaders would be hanged or have their heads cut off, and that had actually happened to Kaytennae. Few Chiricahua actually believed this, but it's apparent Geronimo did.

AS THE HOURS slid by waiting for Crook's answer to Davis's telegram, Geronimo held councils with the Chiricahua and Chihenne leaders urging them to leave the reservation for Mexico. The only leaders who wanted to go with him were Mangas and Nana. Geronimo, Mangas, and Nana planned to leave the reservation on Sunday, May 17, if no word had come from General Crook.

According to Sweeney, early that afternoon Geronimo met with and ordered his "brothers" Fun and Tisna to return to their normal duties with Lieutenant Davis, assassinate Davis and Chato, take the ammunition Davis had and then rejoin him.[1] Sometime that afternoon while the followers of Mangas, Geronimo, and Nana made ready to leave the reservation, Geronimo told Naiche and Chihuahua that his brothers had by then killed Davis and Chato and that once that was accomplished, the scouts would desert and join them. Chihuahua and Naiche immediately assumed they would be judged guilty by association and believed arrests of all remaining Chiricahua leaders would follow. Chihuahua believed Crook would send him to Alcatraz with Kaytennae. He and Naiche, decided to leave at sundown, following Geronimo out of the reservation.

Apache on Horseback
Painting by Herman Hansen, ca. 1910.

ON SUNDAY AFTERNOON, Davis was umpiring a baseball game at Fort Apache while waiting for Crook's answer to his telegram. About four o'clock, Mickey Free and Chato arrived with the news that Geronimo and unknown number of Chiricahua and Chihenne had left the reservation for Mexico. Davis tried to telegraph the news to his commander at San Carlos but the escaping Apache had cut the line in several places when it passed through tree forks and tied it back together with rawhide whangs (Nana's idea so said James Kaywaykla in later years). The breaks in the line weren't found and the line put back in service until the next day.

The commander at Fort Apache, Colonel Frank Wade readied his troops to take the field that evening while Davis hurried to his camp to call his scouts to accompany the troops. Davis formed his scouts in front of his tent and prepared to issue ammunition (normally the scouts only had four or five cartridges because they could be used like money and gambled away) but fearing some of his scouts would be loyal to the escapees, he first ordered them to ground arms (put the rifle butts on the ground), i.e. to stand at attention, while first sergeant Chato and two others stood ready to shoot any man who raised his gun. Of his twenty scouts, Davis thought as many as half might desert. Perico, Chappo (Davis's "striker," his servant), had already slipped away and were not present at roll call.

When Davis went into his tent for the ammunition, Fun, Tisna, and Cathla and Atelnietze, who also had decided to desert slipped out of ranks and disappeared into the brush (it was near dark) and ran to join the other escapees. That night thirty-four men including the scout deserters, eight boys capable of using firearms, and ninety-two women and children making a total of one hundred thirty-four left Fort Apache. Ten days later, ten women and children in Naiche's band left bringing the total to one hundred forty-four. About 400 Chiricahua stayed at Turkey Creek peacefully minding their business.

THE ESCAPEES HEADED east for Eagle Creek and there the women and children scattered to meet later at a rendezvous point while the warriors laid a dim trail through hard, rough terrain of steep canyons to deliberately slow the cavalry and their scouts to a crawl trying to follow it. The escaping warriors wiped out everyone in their path and took what they needed from ranches and homesteads before leaving them in flames. Four days later they were traveling up the San Francisco River when they stopped to rest. Chihuahua and Naiche's people in one group, Mangas and Geronimo's in the other. It was there that Atelnietze, one of the scouts who had deserted, told Chihuahua that Lieutenant Davis and Chato had not been killed as Geronimo had told him.

Chihuahua was enraged at the news. He, his brother, Ulzana, and Atelnietze, with rifles in hand, headed for Geronimo's camp. Chihuahua vowed he was going to kill Geronimo for the lie that had made him leave Turkey Creek under false pretenses and gotten him in a world of trouble. Roaring rage and idle threats were not Chihuahua's style. If he had found Geronimo then, he would have killed him. But Geronimo learned Chihuahua was headed his way with blood in his eye and knew that he couldn't reason or lie his way out of the situation so he and Mangas broke camp and headed east. Naiche had been in camp with Mangas and went with Mangas's camp as it rushed to get out of Chihuahua's way. Missing a chance to kill Geronimo, Chihuahua hoped to slip back on to Turkey Creek and make amends. He turned north into the Mogollon Mountains but the country was covered by cavalry and scouts ultimately forcing him to turn south toward Mexico.

By June 10, all the Apache had crossed the border into Mexico. Within a couple of months they had, with the exception of the Mangas band, reunited without any apparent ill will. Mangas and his little band, which included Geronimo's nephew, Daklugie and Istee, a son of Victorio, decided to keep their distance from the other bands under Geronimo, Naiche, and Chihuahua who were likely to be attacked by pursuing Army scouts.

When the Chiricahua were ready to talk peace with General Crook in late March of the following year at Cañon de Embudos, part of the discussion was Crook claiming that Geronimo had planned the killing of Lieutenant Davis. Geronimo steadfastly denied it and called on Crook to question the other chiefs, Chihuahua, Naiche, and Kutli, who were at the council when the decision was made to leave. When Crook claimed Geronimo lied to Chihuahua and Naiche about Davis being killed to get them to out with him, Geronimo told him to question the White Mountain scouts, who had no love lost for the Chiricahua, and who would prove his innocence. Crook ignored Geronimo's prospective witnesses. Crook and Davis had gotten the story from members of the band at Fort Apache and were convinced they knew the truth. Thereafter, Crook called Geronimo a liar and even six years later, after Geronimo had surrendered, wouldn't talk to him at Mount Vernon Barracks, Alabama, about what had happened during the last breakout, but questioned Naiche instead.[2]

THIRTY-TWO

The Chase Is On

GENERAL CROOK LEARNED of the Geronimo and Chiricahua breakout at his headquarters in Prescott, Arizona, the afternoon of May 18. Soldiers from Fort Apache were already in pursuit. Crook ordered troops from other forts in Arizona into the field, sent warnings to newspapers and settlements to the east that there had been a Chiricahua breakout, and contacted Colonel Luther Bradley who commanded the District of New Mexico.

After the Apache entered New Mexico and headed for the Black Range, Crook moved his headquarters to Fort Bayard, New Mexico, the better to position his troops and coordinate with Colonel Bradley. During the early days of the breakout, the Apache reinforced what he had emphasized to army management during earlier breakouts—regular soldiers were no match for Apache. He later wrote in his annual report to AG MDP, Fort Bowie, in April 1886:

> *"...but with the exception of the capture of a few animals by the Indian scouts under Chato, and a slight skirmish with their rear guard by the troops from Apache under Captain Smith on May 22, in which three of his command were wounded, the Indians were not even caught sight of by the troops, and finally crossed into Mexico about June 10.... In the twenty-three days from the outbreak until the Indians crossed into Mexico, every possible effort was made by the troops, which were pushed to the limits of endurance of men and animals, but without result other than to drive the Indians out of the Black Range and Mogollons [mountains], and also to save the lives, probably, of many ranchmen and prospectors."*

Surveying the situation, General Crook realized that another campaign into

The Indian Raid
Painting by Herman Hansen, ca 1910.

Mexico like the one with the Apache Scouts invading the Chiricahua camps in the high Sierra Madre would be necessary, but he would have to use a different tactical approach since the camp locations were more diverse and fluid and there were many more ranchers and miners in the southwest with newspapers screaming for protection. In the presidential election of 1884, Grover Cleveland had been elected President, General Sherman had retired as head of the army and been replaced by General Sheridan, and William C. Endicott had become Secretary of War. Neither Endicott nor Cleveland knew anything about Indians and Sheridan knew nothing about Apache and relied heavily on Crook for guidance, although he was skeptical of the value of using Apache scouts.

Crook moved his headquarters from Fort Bayard forty miles southeast to Deming, New Mexico, where he had the most advanced communication and transportation technology of the day—the telegraph and railroads—to organize, assemble, and direct the troops and scouts. Crook's tactical strategy was to organize his forces into two units while he stayed in place in Deming to coordinate their movements and collect, organize, and use information they sent him.

The first unit, consisting of thirty scouts and a troop of cavalry, was placed under the command of Captain Emmett Crawford with Lieutenant Marion P. Maus his second in command. Crook sent Crawford by rail west and then to move south by horse and foot to join forces with Lieutenant Britton Davis trying to drive the Chiricahua out of the western New Mexico mountains. Crawford and Davis united their commands and with their scouts, a cavalry troop and two pack trains crossed the border into Mexico on June 11 heading for the Sierra Madre.

The second unit, under Captain Wirt Davis, didn't leave Fort Bowie until July 7 because he had to wait for Lieutenant Gatewood to finish a sweep of the New Mexico mountains to ensure all the Chiricahua had left. Arriving at Fort Bowie, Gatewood's scouts were added to Captain Davis's command because they knew the Sierra Madre. When Davis left for the Sierra Madre, he had one hundred scouts, his troop of cavalry, and a pack train. As in the 1883 Sierra Madre campaign, Crook planned to rely almost exclusively on the Apache scouts. He had no confidence regular cavalry would be effective against Apache in the Sierra Madre, but he let Crawford and Davis use the regular cavalry as they chose. For the most part they used cavalry to provide protection for the pack trains providing supplies from a base on Lang's Ranch near the Animas Valley border in the New Mexico Boot Heel. In fact, Crawford dispensed with his cavalry altogether and entrusted Chato to use the scouts as he saw fit. Crook used the troopers in three lines along the border to prevent the Apache from coming out of Mexico to raid in the United States.

GERONIMO AND MANGAS crossed the New Mexico border into Mexico at Lake Palomas about fourteen miles southwest of present-day Columbus. Chihuahua crossed at Guadalupe Canyon and went down the San Bernardino River to the Bavispe River where Naiche followed and joined him to camp on a ridge at the junction of several deep canyons northeast of Oputo. Geronimo and Mangas were farther south, northeast of Nácori Chicho, near their old camp on the headwaters of the Bavispe River in Sonora at a place they called Bugatseka on the western slopes of the Sierra Madre. By mid-June of 1885, all the escapees from Fort Apache were hidden in their favorite camps in the Sierra Madre.

The Apache leaders all knew Crook would be after them again and soon with White Mountain, maybe even Chiricahua Apache scouts. They knew from past experience that he would be unrelentingly on their trail. Yet, the leaders were careless and let themselves be surprised twice that summer by Crook's scouts and soldiers in the Sierra Madre.

ON JUNE 23, Chihuahua and his people were going about their morning business in a fog laden camp after a heavy rain the night before. About 9:00 a.m., as the sun was coming out, Captain Crawford's Apache scouts led by Chato fired into the camp from two sides. The Apache scattered leaving behind horses, guns, and ammunition Chihuahua had taken earlier from a cavalry supply camp in Guadalupe Canyon, and cattle they had taken on the Yaqui River. The scouts found the cave where fifteen women and children had been hidden during the initial attack. Among them were Chihuahua's entire family including his daughter Ramona and son Eugene who were well known in their prisoner of war years and his brother Ulzana's wife and two children.[1]

Early in the afternoon of August 7 at Geronimo's Bugatseka camp, a mule brayed a warning but too late, as scouts from Captain Wirt Davis's command poured rifle fire into the camp killing three men, a woman, and a boy about thirteen. Geronimo scooped up his little son, Fenton, and ran into the brush, but the scouts recognizing him poured heavy fire toward his hiding place making him drop the child to escape. Again, fifteen women and children were captured. Among them were Geronimo's wives Zi-yeh, She-gha, and Shtsha-she, a grown daughter, Dohn-say, an infant son of Zi-yeh's, Fenton, Nana's wife and Geronimo's sister, Nah-dos-te, and Mangas's wife, Huera, the expert tizwin maker who the year before had escaped Mexican slavery. Geronimo also lost supplies including cattle, rifles, and ammunition. 2

The loss of supplies and cattle counted for little to Chihuahua and Geronimo—they could always steal more, but the loss of their families was a hard blow and affected how they would choose to surrender when they came face-to-face with General Mile's representative, Lieutenant Gatewood, who brought them surrender terms.

THIRTY-THREE

"Run, Ride, Fight, Hide, Then Ride and Fight Again"

BY MID-JUNE 1885, the Chiricahua were safely in their camps in Mexico. There were four groups of Chiricahua in Mexico. The most eastern was the Geronimo and Mangas group. They had stopped to trade at Casas Grandes, stayed a few days (probably drinking as much mescal as they could) became worried about the Mexicans attacking them when they were drunk, and after a few days went south into their old stronghold camps at Bugatseka. There they joined the group led by Nat-cul-bay-e who was the leader of the first group to cross the border. Nat-cul-bay-e (also known as José Maria Elias) was to play a significant role in the future of the Apache hidden in the Sierra Madre. When Geronimo surrendered in 1886, Nat-cul-bay-e and Atelnietze decided they would be better off in Mexico than in a White Eye prison and never surrendered. They were leaders of the legendary Sierra Madre Apache who raided in Mexico and southern New Mexico and Arizona well into the twentieth century long after Geronimo surrendered.

Chihuahua, whose group consisted of twelve men and at least twenty women and children, crossed the Río Bavispe and reached a place the Chiricahua called Djic-lic (Big Juniper Berries) in the Teras Mountains inside the loop made by the Río Bavispe as it turned from running north to south. Naiche joined Chihuahua around June 14, rested a few days, and then rode to join Geronimo and Mangas in Bugatseka. Chihuahua sent some of his warriors on a raid toward Moctezuma, where on June 17 and 18 they stole livestock. Chihuahua then went southeast and camped about fifteen miles north of Oputo on the south-flowing leg of the Río Bavispe.

On June 8 and 9, Captain Crawford with a troop of cavalry and a fifty-mule pack train met Lieutenant Britton Davis with fifty-eight scouts (including twenty-two under Chato) from Fort Bowie and soon thereafter Al Sieber with another pack train of fifty mules and thirty-four scouts. From then on, Captain Crawford relied on Chato's advice.[1] Chato believed Chihuahua and Naiche planned to meet in the Teras Mountains northeast of Oputo and decided to come up from south of the assembly point where they wouldn't be expected. To avoid alerting the Chiricahua, Chato recommended they enter Mexico from the Chihuahua side, crossing the mountains to a camp below Oputo, and then making their way north up the river past Oputo.[2]

Mexicans, thinking they were among the Apache who had been raiding the area, killed two of the scouts as Crawford made his way upriver past Oputo. The scouts were ready to go back and wipeout the village of Oputo but Davis and Chato managed to calm things down. A day later, scouts found a trail of eight to ten of Chihuahua's warriors who had taken livestock around Oputo. With Captain Crawford's blessing, Chato selected 30 scouts to accompany him and "Big Dave" a sergeant of scouts from the White Mountain scouts. They took three mules loaded with two days rations and a hundred rounds of ammunition for each scout and left that evening at moonrise. Crawford told Chato to find the camp and, if

The Chase
Painting by Herman Hansen, ca. 1910.

possible, hold their positions until the rest of the command arrived. The next morning it began raining about 9:00 a.m. washing out the trail the scouts had been following. Chato made camp and then slogged on the morning of the next day. He suspected he knew the area on the mountain where Chihuahua would make camp and didn't think he needed to worry about following a trail. On the way, they found the remains of eight butchered cattle reinforcing his view about not needing to follow a trail and just as the rain stopped, he saw through binoculars Chihuahua's camp about 500 yards away.[3]

Chato didn't wait for Crawford. He took five scouts up above the camp and Big Dave with the rest advanced from below. Chato and his scouts fired into the camp hoping to drive the escapees into Big Dave's group of scouts. The escapees scattered. A young sentry (Ulzana's sixteen-year-old son) and an old woman were killed. Fifteen women and children were captured including a son and daughter of Chihuahua later known as Ramona (who married Daklugie) and Eugene who became chief of Chihuahua's village at Fort Sill and was a scout with the Seventh Cavalry at Fort Sill. Chihuahua, seven warriors, four boys, and three women and children escaped.

Chato thought Chihuahua might be dispirited and sent a woman with an offer to either kill Geronimo or surrender (if Geronimo had been there it might have been his end). Instead, Chihuahua and his brother, Ulzana, knowing that Ulzana's son had been killed and their families captured, swore vengeance on Chato. Two days later, with an escort of ten troopers under the command of Lieutenant Hanna, an empty pack train and ten scouts, Crawford sent the prisoners back to Fort Bowie. Taking the prisoners to Fort Bowie was at the direction of General Crook who correctly anticipated that those warriors losing family members would try to take them back and assume they were returned to Fort Apache, site of their original camps. No one but the scouts on the Apache side knew the prisoners were being kept under close watch at Fort Bowie rather than Fort Apache. After the attack on Chihuahua's camp, Crawford's column headed southeast toward the Río Aros. The second day on the way north, Hanna crossed the trail of a large group of Chiricahua headed east across the mountains. The scouts warned Hanna that if they had been seen they might be attacked by the group at dawn the next day (it was the favorite time of day for Apache to attack). Hanna prepared his camp and waited, but no attack came.

NEAR THE END of June, the Chiricahua with Geronimo, Naiche, and Mangas left the Sierra Madre to raid towns to the west along the Río Sonora. The warriors brought their women and children with them to avoid them being captured by Chiricahua scouts who knew where the camps were at Bugatseka. There were about a hundred in the group including about thirty warriors and boys old enough to use firearms. Mexican nationals picked up their trail a week after they began raiding and led by Captain Leonardo Gómez stayed on it. They followed the Apache to the summit of the Carmen Mountains where the Chiricahua had located their base camp. Realizing the Mexicans were trailing them the chiefs broke into three groups. Geronimo, taking most of the women and children went northeast; Mangas went east; and Naiche with a group of about thirty-five went north and connected with Chihuahua about a week later. Gómez followed Geronimo's trail and on July 16 detected Apache fleeing their camp in the direction of the Pinito Mountains west of Río Bavispe where Mangas's group had brought horses and cattle for the others. Gómez's pursuit ended to refit and rest at Cuchuta. He sent word warning the residents in the villages along the west branch of Río Bavispe that Apache were raiding and killing.

Captain Wirt Davis left Fort Bowie around July 7, with two pack trains, two lieutenants, thirty-eight troopers from the Fourth Cavalry, and 102 Apache scouts including sixteen Chiricahua. Davis crossed the border July 11 and by July 20 had reached Huépari Creek about halfway between Oputo and Huachinera. The column had met neither Crawford nor Apache.

Late in the day on July 20, a mail rider from Moctezuma rode into Captain Davis's camp on Huépari Creek and informed him that the Apache had gone to north to the Teras Mountains. After consulting his scouts, Davis decided to leave at dawn in the hope he could surprise the Apache by coming up from the south. They rode all day for eleven hours and made camp six miles north of Oputo on the Río Bavispe.

THIRTY-FOUR

Geronimo's Family Captured

BY THE EVENING of July 21, Captain Davis had led his command up from the south to camp six miles north of Oputo. Along the way, the Mexicans had told him of sighting Chiricahua, and he had pushed hard to reach this camp. That evening a group of Mexicans from Oputo told him they had cut an Apache trail that went toward the La Jolla Mountains, the southern part of the Tigre Mountains inside the east and west branches of the Río Bavispe. It was a favorite Apache camping spot that offered protection from enemies, abundant game, and a bounty of mescal on the eastern sides of the mountains. One of the Mexicans offered to show Davis the trail. Davis sent six scouts under the lead of Bylas (whose uncle had been held by Geronimo at Ash Flat when Loco and his people were abducted in 1882) with the Mexican guide. Davis told Bylas that if they found the camp to send two scouts back, he would bring the rest of the scouts and soldiers up to surround the area. Bylas was finally going to get some payback for what Geronimo had done to his family at Ash Flat.[1]

The Mexican led the scouts into the canyon as far as they had dared travel. He shook hands with Bylas and told him that if the Chiricahua saw them they would kill them all—bad Indians—and then took off. Bylas seemed to know where the trail would lead, and he and his scouts easily found it. Bylas showed the other scouts how to descend into the canyon "on his back, using his hands and feet while resting his rifle on his stomach and chest." They saw two women on horseback riding toward them who stopped to gather fruit of the prickly pear cactus. They yelled up to the scouts that their men had seen them so they shouldn't try to hide, and that they didn't like it in Mexico and wanted to return to San Carlos. This was a common trick to get the scouts to

Geronimo's Wife Zi-yeh and Son Fenton, ca. 1886.
Photograph courtesy of the National Archives.

show themselves so they could be targets for marksmen and the scouts knew it. By midday, one of the scouts with binoculars saw warriors on a ridge of the highest mountain. Bylas knew the camp had to be nearby and sent two scouts to bring Captain Davis.

Davis had moved his camp back down river to be closer to Oputo after Bylas left, and it took the scout until 8:00 that evening to find the captain. The command left at midnight and went ten miles up the Río Bavispe where it rested at daybreak. The Apache were about ten miles to the northeast. That afternoon Davis sent his ninety-six scouts (including sixteen Chiricahua) to meet Bylas. At 7:00 p.m., Davis led his cavalry troopers on foot to join the scouts. The next morning before daylight the camp had been surrounded. As the sun rose and Davis's men readied to attack, they clearly saw the camp, but it had been abandoned. Years later it was learned that an old woman with Power had warned Geronimo that if they didn't leave that night trouble would be coming. Geronimo didn't believe her, but the others did. By the time Davis began his march to join Bylas, the band had gone to the top of the mountain above the camp to watch what happened. What they saw made Geronimo a believer and led him to immediately move their camp.[2]

CAPTAIN DAVIS AND his officers regrouped. Davis asked a scout medicine man to conduct a ceremony to decide where Geronimo's camp was. Only one scout, Gush-i-guu, agreed to use his Power in this way. After much singing and drumming, he went into a long description of where the Chiricahua had gone and finally said they were in camp near Bugatseka. On August 2, one of Davis's officers, Lieutenant Day, and Chief of Scouts Roberts with eighty-six scouts found Geronimo's trail. On the morning of 7 August, Bylas and fifteen scouts found Geronimo's camp on the southern tip of Bugatseka near where the scouts had attacked Chato's camp in 1883.

Lieutenant Day, with the rest of the scouts, were surrounding the camp in the early afternoon when a mule tied to a bush in the camp began to bray and run around alerting the Chiricahua. Bylas had to open the attack before all the scouts were in place.

Two women and a thirteen-year-old boy who was hit in the eye by a ricochet off a rock were killed. At the first salvos, Geronimo picked up his son Fenton and ran from the camp through an angry swarm of flying bullets. Both Western

Apache and Chiricahua scouts tried to bring him down. Some believed they had hit him as he escaped into the brush because he eventually put Fenton down in order to run on. Several men were away from the camp hunting or raiding. Others who escaped had to jump from a high bluff to safety. Fifteen women and children were captured. These included Geronimo's two wives, Zi-yeh and She-gha, and their children and the wives of Perico (Geronimo's "brother"), Beshe (Naiche's father-in-law), Dahkeya (who had married Geronimo's daughter, Dohn-say), and Mangas whose wife was Huera, the excellent tizwin maker who kept telling Geronimo that Lieutenant Britton Davis planned to put him and Mangas in the guardhouse. Geronimo's beautiful teenaged daughter, Dohn-say, was wounded along with two other prisoners. Lieutenant Day was the only Anglo in the fight.[3]

The attack scattered Geronimo's band. Mangas and his small group headed for Juh's old stronghold at Guaynopa and stayed apart from the others until he surrendered in New Mexico, October 19, 1886, six weeks after Geronimo surrendered. Geronimo and Nana, with about forty of their people, headed east toward Chihuahua.

THIRTY-FIVE

Retaking and Finding New Wives

IN THE EARLY afternoon of August 7, 1885, seventy-eight Apache scouts under the command of Lieutenant Matias W. Day and led by sergeant of scouts, Bylas, a White Mountain Apache, had attacked and captured fifteen women and children including Huera, the wife of Mangas, and Geronimo's entire family with the exception of his warrior son, Chappo. Only two warriors, Geronimo, and a woman escaped. The rest of the men had been out hunting and raiding.

The loses of the women and children were exceptionally hard on the entire band. Besides being devoted to their families, Apache society had a well-structured division of labor, so a man without a wife to maintain and prepare food supplies and clothing was in just as serious economic straights as a woman without a male for support. Women, sometimes stolen by lone outlaws hiding in the mountains, accepted the situation. There were cases of stable marriages formed this way. Geronimo and four of his followers ("brother" Perico, son-in-law Mike Dahkeya, son Chappo, Chinche, and Hunlona) decided that because of economic necessity and for love of their wives, they would slip across the border to bring back their families or if unable to find them, steal new wives.[1]

The Chiricahua who had not been part of the breakout in May (about 70 percent of the band) had been pulled into camps much closer to Fort Apache where they could be watched and "protected" from the "renegades" who had broken out earlier. With scouts and regular soldiers closely guarding the border, Geronimo avoided his normal path toward Fort Apache through the Peloncillo Mountains in New Mexico and during a night run entered New Mexico farther east than normal and made a wide loop across New Mexico and Arizona to come back into the Fort Apache camps. White Mountain scouts were patrolling ev-

Women taken on the Fort Apache raid in September 1885 to reclaim their wives or capture new ones. L-R is Ih-tedda the young Mescalero woman captured and taken by Geronimo. The photograph was taken about 1890 after Ih-tedda had borne two of Geronimo's children, Lenna (L) and Robert in her lap. Bi-ya-neta in the right two photos was the woman stolen from Ft. Apache and Perico took for his wife. She is often mistaken for Lozen, the warrior woman and Victorio's sister who never married. The Ih-tedda photograph is from Eve Ball-Lynda Sánchez Collection. Photographs of Bi-ya-neta, taken in 1886, Courtesy National Archives are (L) taken from a group pose of a few of Geronimo's band while they were detained for six weeks in San Antonio and (R) from a group photo while the group rested on a train berm near the Nueces River in Texas before they reached San Antonio on their way to exile in Florida.

erywhere, but running many miles on foot, Geronimo and the others managed to get close to the camps.

They stole some White Mountain horses and as they approached the camps in the dark found an old White Mountain woman living alone while guarding her farm. They asked her to lead them to the camp of Geronimo's family and point out its *wickiup*. Reaching it about 1:00 a.m. on the morning of September 22, Geronimo could only find and take She-gha and his sickly three-year-old daughter. The other warriors managed to steal another woman whose name was Bi-ya-neta Tse-dah-dilth-thlilth (Bi-ya-neta for the rest of this story) who had been part of the breakout and with She-gha had tried to hide on the Mescalero reservation to learn if the Mescaleros would allow Geronimo to hide on the reservation or join him in Mexico. But, they had been found and returned to Fort Apache.[2]

Perico, who had been Lieutenant Davis' second sergeant in his scouts could not find his wife, Hah-dun-key, who had refused to run with Perico when he left for Mexico, took Bi-ya-neta as his wife. They lived well together during the following months, through the prisoner of war years, and after they were released twenty-seven years later. They had five children together, three of whom are buried at Fort Sill. Bi-ya-neta can be seen in the famous photograph of the Geronimo band resting by the train tracks and is often mistaken for Lozen who was already in Florida at Fort Marion. She was also photographed when the group was held in San Antonio. Her photographs with the young Mescalero woman Geronimo took are shown on the previous page.

ON THEIR WAY back to Mexico, Geronimo and his men disappeared into the mountains toward the east of Fort Apache and evaded White Mountain scouting parties eager to catch them to get their horses back. In the southwestern New Mexico mountains, on the west side of the Black Range, the Chiricahua discovered a Mescalero group (on a thirty-day pass from their reservation) gathering piñon nuts and hunting deer that had grown fat on them. Piñon trees don't bear often and there had been no piñon crop in the Sacramento Mountains around the Mescalero Reservation for four or five years. There were forty Mescalero including men, but each morning they broke into small groups, the women to harvest the nuts, and men to hunt.

The group of Mescalero, Geronimo's warriors discovered, included Charlie Smith, then a young boy of four or five (Smith died in 1973 highly honored for his military service and leadership on the Mescalero reservation), Smith's mother, a young mother with her baby, and Ih-tedda, also known as Young Girl.

As Charlie Smith told the story, after spending the day collecting piñon nuts, the little Mescalero party started back to their main camp when strange warriors swooped down the mountain, and the Mescalero scattered. Charlie was heading to hide in some brush when a bullet nicked the calf of his leg, a rider charged up, leaned from his mount, and lifted him in front of him. Other riders forced the women to mount behind them, and they were carried to Geronimo's camp.[3]

Geronimo took Ih-tedda for his wife, giving him two wives (She-gha being the other) to support him and his family. Ih-tedda at the time she was taken would have been in her mid-late teens. Geronimo would have been in his early sixties. Apparently, they got along well. About four months later, Geronimo and his leaders met with Lieutenant Maus in Mexico and told him they would that they would meet with General Crook to discuss surrender terms in two moons. To prove his sincerity about coming to the meeting, Geronimo gave Lieutenant Maus nine persons from his band to hold as hostages. Among them was Ih-tedda, who was a month or two pregnant, and who Geronimo apparently didn't want running across sharp stones and thorns in the mountains carrying their child, not to mention the fact that, being pregnant, she was off-limits when they were under the blankets. They didn't see each other again for nearly sixteen months when they were finally reunited at Fort Pickens on Santa Rosa Island in Pensacola Bay in May of 1887. In September 1886, Ih-tedda had Geronimo's daughter. The Fort Marion Commander, Lt. Colonel Loomis Langdon named her Marion and so recorded her birth name. However, within a very few months the Apache had named her Lenna and that was the name she kept.

IN 1889, AS a prisoner of war at Mount Vernon Barracks, Alabama, Geronimo learned that the army had agreed to send Mescalero, who had inadvertently been caught up in the sweep of Chiricahua sent to Florida, back to their reservation. Geronimo divorced Ih-tedda to get her and Lenna back to Mescalero and out of the POW camps where far more Apache than normal were dying from disease. She didn't want to leave him and begged to stay, but he was determined to get her out and away from disease and, in his mind, possible execution at any time by the army. He didn't know she was pregnant with their second child, who she named Robert and was born seven months after she arrived in Mescalero. Robert and Lenna are the only known direct survivors to carry on Geronimo's name, all others, passed away before they had children or those who had children died before carrying on the family name.[4]

A few months after Geronimo's three wives returned to him at Fort Pickens, on Santa Rosa Island in Pensacola Bay, She-gha died. After Geronimo sent Ih-tedda back to Mescalero in February 1889, the only wife left to him was Zi-yeh. From that time on he had only one wife at a time. Zi-yeh died from tubercular lupus in 1904. He married Mary Loto around Christmas of 1905. He was then about eighty-two. She was fifty-eight. The marriage lasted three months before they divorced. Geronimo married again around 1907, this time to Sunsetso (Old Lady Yellow to the Apache), but she is remembered by her Spanish name, Azul (she had also escaped Mexican slavery and by herself walked back to her people with only a blanket and knife). Azul was about sixty when she and Geronimo married and apparently it was a happy union.

THIRTY-SIX

Ulzana's Raid

AFTER THEIR RAID to regain their first wives or find new ones, Geronimo and the others rejoined their people in Mexico late in the second week of October. Then moving toward Casas Grandes met Chihuahua and Naiche at a pine studded meadow high in the Carcay Mountains south of Casa de Janos. It was the first time they had been together since leaving Fort Apache on May 17. Despite having been hit hard by attacks led by Chato and Bylas with the Apache scouts, their own people, they weren't close to thinking about surrender. They knew Crook would probably turn the scouts who left with them over to the army for court marshals for probable hanging and the rest of the "hostiles" not scouts to civilian authorities for certain hanging. They didn't know where Crook was holding their families, except for a fact they had determined themselves—their families definitely were not at Fort Apache. They thought it most likely they were being held at San Carlos and decided to attempt a daring rescue. Chihuahua would lead a diversionary raid into New Mexico; his brother Ulzana (also known as Jolsanny) would lead a second group of twelve on a raid at Fort Apache and if it was determined that Chiricahua had been moved to San Carlos, then move on to San Carlos.

Ulzana's men included those wanting to reclaim their wives and children captured in the two raids by Chato and Bylas, which was the case for Perico and Ulzana. The second group of Ulzana's men were those who had left their families at Turkey Creek. These warriors included Cathla, Moh-tsos, Tah-ni-toe, Len-see, and Shoie. Others who were after revenge and information rather than family included Atelnietze (who stayed in the Sierra Madre long after Geronimo surrendered), Fun, Kanseah, Yahnozha (who all surrendered with Geronimo),

Ulzana at Mount Vernon Alabama,
ca 1890 from a group photo.
Courtesy of the National Archives

and teenaged Zachia. Six of the twelve had served as scouts during their time at the reservation, three had deserted on May 17. Besides recovering their kinfolk, they all wanted revenge against the scouts and to take prisoners Geronimo had instructed them to bring back to Mexico.[1]

Ulzana and Chihuahua's bands had a total of about twenty warriors and teenage boys when they left the Carcay mountains in mid-October. Geronimo, Naiche, and Nana, with about a dozen warriors and teenaged boys and about sixty women and children, left at the same time for a raid toward Yepómera, Chihuahua. After two or three raids for horses and supplies in Mexico while steadily moving north, Chihuahua and Ulzana split up near the Boca Grande Mountains south of the New Mexico bootheel. Ulzana took eleven men and entered the bootheel from the east planning to move north through the Animas Mountains. They made a hidden camp at the base of Animas peak. Scouts, looking for an opportunity to make a dash for Fort Apache, went out from this camp to probe the countryside crawling with cavalry and scouts.[2]

WHILE ULZANA PROBED west with his scouts, Chihuahua crossed the border east of Palomas (just south of where Columbus, New Mexico is now) at about the same place Geronimo and his four men had crossed two months earlier (ten miles east of Lake Palomas). His objective was a fast, diversionary raid that was supposed to draw the military's attention away from the path Ulzana wanted to take. After skirting the Florida Mountains, Chihuahua led his band straight for Lake Valley where they stole horses from ranches, attacked Jewitt's wood camp taking provisions, rifles, and ammunition, and then headed into the Black Range and Percha Creek. They took more stock and wounded a man over the next few days and then headed south crossing the tracks at a train water depot on November 6, 1885, crossed the border into Mexico on November 7, and headed for the Candelaria Mountains about fifty miles south.[3]

AFTER THREE DAYS of scouting, Ulzana backtracked into Chihuahua and took the same path into the United States Chihuahua had used. His first attack in the U.S. was in the southeast corner of the Florida Mountains where five warriors on foot ambushed two army couriers. There followed attacks on nearby ranches and attacking and trying to kill everything in their path, but there are some hero survival stories of back country ranchers surviving the attacks. Then Ulzana and his men suddenly seemed to disappear for two weeks as they worked their way west toward Fort Apache.

The territorial newspapers were filled with criticism and carping about General Crook. To many in Washington and the territory, every Apache at San Carlos was a potential hostile despite the facts that only 144 out of a little over 500 Chiricahua who were part of a total 5,000 Indians including Western Apache had actually left the reservation; the reservation Apache provided neither aid nor recruits for the hostiles; Apache on the reservation had become scouts to help track down the hostiles; and, Geronimo had few friends among the Chiricahua and even fewer among the Western Apache at San Carlos and Fort Apache. The White Eyes couldn't accept the idea that different Apache bands had their own allegiances. The belief in universal acceptance among the Apache became the guiding concept the Bureau of Indian Affairs and the Army adopted to exile all the Chiricahua east.

Remembering Geronimo's attack on San Carlos to abduct Loco's People in 1882, and believing he might attack again at Fort Apache to get his family members back, on November 16, General Crook sent the families of the hostiles to San Carlos where his orders were that they were to be treated as guests and that their transfer was for their safety and not punishment.

On November 17, Ulzana's raiders crossed the New Mexico line into Arizona and began raiding stock from ranches in their path. By early afternoon on

November 23, they were near Chato's farm, and they could see Chato and his wife working their crops. Ulzana was delighted. He had vowed to kill Chato. But Chato had Power and was on guard. As Ulzana was deciding how best to murder Chato, he saw him and his wife suddenly drop everything, jump on a horse, and head down river to Fort Apache. Ulzana and the others became alarmed thinking someone had warned Chato. Years later when one of them asked Chato why he had fled, he said his Power had warned (a muscular tremor sign) him something bad was about to happen. Chato brought his family to Fort Apache where they stayed until Ulzana left.[4]

Ulzana vowed to stay around the area until he killed Chato. He captured a Chiricahua boy and three women, but the boy escaped that evening and told the army what he had learned. Lieutenant Charles E. Nordstrom and ten troopers from the Tenth Cavalry followed Ulzana's trail until dark the next day when they had to give up. Ulzana was west of Turkey Creek. Late that evening the teenaged boy riding with Ulzana, Zachia, was sitting guard on a ridge with his rifle when a San Carlos Carrizo chief, Sánchez, shot him in the back, jumped on top of him and cut off his head to carry back to San Carlos for the hundred dollar reward Crook was offering for the heads of Ulzana's raiders. Zachia was the only man Ulzana lost during the entire raid. When the Chiricahua learned what Sánchez had done, there was nearly a war between the Chiricahua and the Western Apache at San Carlos, but Chato managed to calm the situation after the Chiricahua had attacked Sánchez's ranchería and killed his wife and several children.

Ulzana continued his raids well into December around San Carlos and Fort Apache looking for his wives and children, the missing wives of Geronimo and Perico, and family members of the other members of his raiders, but they never found them.

General Sheridan came from Washington as the new commanding general of the army, and he and Crook reorganized and refitted the commands of Captains Wirt Davis and Emmitt Crawford to break up the hostile Apache base in Mexico.

At the end of December, mounted on excellent horses, the Davis and Crawford commands crossed the border back into Mexico. General Crook, a stickler for accurate information, believed Ulzana and his ten raiders had traveled no less than twelve hundred miles, killed thirty-eight people, and captured and wore out about two hundred fifty head of stock.

THIRTY-SEVEN

Geronimo Agrees to Meet
with General Crook

AFTER ULZANA AND Chihuahua returned to Mexico they found Naiche and then Geronimo. There were apparently no hard feelings left from Geronimo telling Chihuahua and Naiche that Chato and Lieutenant Davis had been assassinated, which drove them to leave Turkey Creek. They camped together in the rough mountains about sixty miles south of Nácori Chico, a Juh stronghold Geronimo considered the best hidden and most impregnable in the Sierra Madre.

After a hard summer of tracking and fighting the "hostiles," Crawford and Davis had returned to Fort Bowie to refit and reorganize after the meeting of General Sheridan with General Crook. On December 11, 1885, Crawford returned to enter Mexico with five officers, two chiefs of scouts (Tom Horn and William Harrison), a hospital steward, an interpreter (Concepcion), one hundred scouts, and three pack trains of forty-five mules each and a dozen civilian packers. They climbed high mountains and crossed rough gorges and canyons to reach the Río Aros at a spot about sixty miles south of Nacorí, the area of Juh's best stronghold. Crawford's scouts found trails, campsites, and other indications of Apache occupation, but no Apache. On the evening January 9, 1886, scouts found the Apache rancheria ten or twelve miles away in a place with a good defensive location. Crawford decided to attack the camp the next dawn by doing a night march over mountains and across canyons so dark they seemed bottomless.[1]

Just before dawn, they saw the outlines of the rancheria location and were moving to encircle it when burros in the camp started braying and the Apache snapped awake to defend it. Shots were exchanged in the dim dawn light,

Geronimo's Camp
Painting by Henry Farny, ca. 1900.

but no injuries were taken on either side. The hostiles, who numbered about eighty including about twenty-three or twenty-four men, slipped away down the mountain sides leaving Crawford and his scouts to take possession of the horse herd and a stockpile of provisions. The scouts gave a haphazard chase for a few hours but were too disorganized and too wary to get close enough to engage. Some Chiricahua scouts were able to talk with the hostiles and learned Naiche said he wanted to come in and talk with Crawford.

That afternoon, an Apache woman appeared and told Crawford that Geronimo and Naiche wanted a conference. Crawford agreed to meet the following day (January 11) on the river below the camp. All the hostiles were to be there except for Mangas's small group, which never rejoined the others and was the last to surrender. Geronimo, with his usual deference to Naiche as chief, was their leader. He said the appearance of Crawford's force had convinced him that no refuge was safe from invasion.

CRAWFORD'S SCOUTS WERE exhausted from the hard days of march to get to the abandoned Río Aros camps, the difficult night march to get to the rancheria, and the fight that followed. Crawford camped about a hundred yards from the rancheria and let his command sleep around big fires to combat the bitter cold night. One Chiricahua scout on sentry duty became concerned when he saw most of the other sentries had fallen asleep. With Geronimo in the neighborhood, he was convinced that the medicine man had put a sleeping spell on them all. So, the scout, who may have been later known as "Jim Miller," employed his own ceremony to counteract Geronimo's power. He sang and sang until all the sentries finally woke up. When Geronimo saw the scout's ceremony had weakened his Power, he angrily yelled at the medicine man.[2]

Unknown to Crawford's men a Chihuahuan force of 128 men, Tarahumara Indians from villages south of Yepómera, had come up during the night with a few burros to carry supplies and ammunition for their .44–caliber Remington rifles. They had marched seventeen days from the eastern side of the Sierra Madre. By 7:30 the morning of January 11, they had taken positions in "white rocks" two hundred yards above the scouts. The Apache scouts thought they were scouts from Captain Wirt Davis's command and called to them in Apache expecting answers in Apache. Instead, the Tarahumara fired into the camp wounding three scouts, one of whom was sleeping. Thinking it was just a misunderstanding, most scouts didn't return fire, but the few who did, Chiricahua on a high east ridge, returned a heavy fire. The American officers who had been sleeping near a fire responded quickly. Crawford ordered his two lieutenants, Maus and Shipp, along with Tom Horn, to "see about it," and they raced to the scene. Crawford borrowed a white handkerchief from the hospital steward and followed them. The Americans called out to the Mexicans repeatedly identifying themselves as American soldiers. Fifteen minutes after the first volley, the firing stopped. Since only a few scouts had returned fire, the Mexican officers assumed Crawford's command had few men and were low on ammunition.

Crawford, Maus, and Horn, all unarmed, came out of the rocks to meet ten Mexicans, all armed, under the command of Major Mauricio Corredor, a Tarahumara who was famous in Chihuahua for supposedly killing Victorio (the Apache claimed Victorio had stabbed himself in the heart after running out of ammunition). Corredor's force didn't have peaceful intentions. They were hunting Apache scalps.

Horn walked out about one hundred feet in front of Maus and Crawford who was waving the white handkerchief as a peace sign. Corredor and three or four men walked past Horn ignoring his greeting in Spanish and toward the two officers who approached within about six feet of Corredor who now looked nervous and frightened. Maus said, "Don't you see we are American soldiers. Look at my uniform and my captain's." Corredor explained that they assumed the scouts were hostiles. The Chiricahua standing behind the Americans and Tarahumara standing behind the Mexicans were mortal enemies. The Tarahumara had helped defeat Victorio at Tres Castillos and wiped out most of Juh's band at Sátachi Falls. They were supremely confident they could take the Apache scalps for a big reward. Taunts about the other side's manhood began flying back and forth between the scouts and the Tarahumara. During the back and forth, the scouts had brought up a pack mule with ammunition and began to refill their cartridge belts.

The Mexican and American officers were unaware the two sides were near to firing on each other until they heard the sharp snaps of the scout's breech-loaders closing on cartridges. Corredor had seen the heads and rifles of fifty to sixty scouts in the rocks thirty yards in front of him and began to back away from open ground toward Horn. A group of Mexicans had moved to the left and above the parley which lasted about ten minutes. Crawford, aware things were fast getting out of hand said to Maus, "For God's sake don't let them fire." Corredor, realizing there were many more scouts and much more ammunition than the Mexicans had realized, begged Crawford to restrain his scouts, Maus turned and walked toward the scouts ordering them not to shoot. Crawford climbed on a "five-foot high rock, conspicuous above every other object," waving his flag of truce.[3]

About twenty-five yards away, a member of the Mexican peace party that had approached the Americans had taken cover near a little tree. Apparently the one designated to start firing, he shot Crawford in the forehead, mortally wounding him. Immediately, the Mexicans began firing at every American in sight. Corredor turned to Horn, smiled and shot at the unarmed American wounding him in the arm. Maus and Shipp escaped without being wounded. The scouts laid down a withering fire on the Tarahumara and Mexicans. Maus saw Corredor running for cover on the right side. However, scouts, unseen by Corredor, were hidden nearby. One was the warrior Binday, who took deliberate aim and shot Corredor through the heart. Dutchy, Crawford's orderly, killed the man who shot Crawford. Within a minute, nine of ten in the Mexican party who had come to "parley" with Crawford, fully intending to kill all the Americans and take Apache scout scalps, were killed. Firing went on most of the morning. Without Corredor, the Tarahumara seemed lost and disoriented, but on the American side, the Apache led by Maus and Shipp and the scout first sergeants, Noche and Tsedekizen, were in command of the situation.

The Naiche-Geronimo band had watched the battle from the bluff across the river. It is said Geronimo laughed to see the Americans and Mexicans killing each other off. They still wanted to discuss terms but not until the Tarahumara were gone. The next day, January 12, 1886, Maus who had been second in command under Crawford, gave the Tarahumara six mules to transport their wounded back to Chihuahua, and they were soon on the trail home.

ON JANUARY 13, MAUS decided to break camp and return to Nácori Chico, under a steady rain they marched four miles west before camping near a creek. Everyone had taken turns carrying Crawford and a badly wounded scout. That night, Geronimo sent a messenger to Maus asking for a meeting the next morning and insisting that Maus and his escort come unarmed. Early the next morning, January 14, Maus, Horn, Noche, and four scouts met with two Chiricahua (one was Nat-cul-bay-e) who promised that their leaders would come in the next day.

Geronimo, Naiche, Chihuahua, and Nana appeared the next morning with their lead warriors. Naiche was the nominal chief, but Geronimo did the talking and looking the officer straight in the eye for a full minute of silence asked Maus the purpose of his mission. Maus answered without blinking, "I came to capture or destroy you and your band." [4]

Geronimo smiled, walked over to Maus and shook his hand, saying he could trust him to report accurately to Crook. He then told the story of his grievances and why he left Turkey Creek, which according to Maus were imaginary or assumed. The band was ready to discuss terms. Their families captured the previous summer were still in army possession and the army had surprised them in their best stronghold. There was no place they could hide.

Geronimo designated nine members of the band he would send back with Maus and promised to meet Crook near the border in "two moons to talk about surrendering." Maus then returned to camp and Geronimo soon sent the nine "prisoners" as Maus then called them. The nine included: Nana and his wife (also the sister of Geronimo), a wife and child of Naiche, a wife and child of Geronimo, a man, a boy, and a woman. The wife Geronimo sent back with Lieutenant Maus was the young Mescalero woman, Ih-tedda, already pregnant, who he had taken in early October while returning from his raid on Fort Apache to take back his family.5

THIRTY-EIGHT

The Chiefs and Geronimo Surrender

T O UNDERSTAND THE thrust and maneuver of the peace talks that took place in March 1886 between Geronimo and General Crook it is useful to review major events that happened during the ten months after the escape from Fort Apache. The May 1885 Fort Apache escape of Geronimo, Mangas, Chihuahua, Naiche, and Nana led to a brutal war that was fought between Apache (scouts for the army and the "renegades" who had escaped the Fort Apache Reservation) across northern Mexico and southern Arizona and New Mexico for over eight months where no quarter was given and none was asked.

Major events in the fighting shows the renegades fought back hard against General Crook's strategy to force them to surrender. It was a strategy different from, but in many ways similar to, what he had used in 1883 to bring them back from the Sierra Madre to the San Carlos. Reservation. Rather than a single invasion force of about two hundred scouts supported by fifty troopers like he used in 1883, in 1885, he used two forces with about one hundred scouts each, a troop of cavalry to guard mule pack trains supporting each force, and two of his best captains, Emmett Crawford and Wirt Davis, to lead them while he, Crook, maintained his command center near the fastest transportation (trains) and communications (telegraph) to coordinate troop movements when attacks occurred in the United States. As Crook anticipated, his captains took advantage of the skills of their best Apache sergeants of scouts, Chato and Bylas, to track the renegades and lead attacks on the Chihuahua and Geronimo camps in the summer of 1885 when most of the camp's families were captured.[1]

The renegades often fought as Crook expected. For example, they tried to take back their women and children who had been taken in the summer raids. In

Geronimo talks peace terms with General Crook, March 25, 1886.
Photograph by C.S. Fly, courtesy of the National Archives.

September, the border and a wide swath of southern Arizona and New Mexico swarmed with White Mountain Apache scouts looking for renegades, who, assuming their captured family members had been returned to Fort Apache or hidden somewhere on the San Carlos Reservation, would come to free them. Crook, anticipating this would happen had ordered the families secretly kept under close guard at Fort Bowie over a hundred miles to the southeast from Fort Apache.[2]

Geronimo and four warriors in an attempt to get their families back, slid past White Mountain scouts guarding the reservation and in the dark of night quietly entered the Chiricahua camps at Fort Apache. He was able to find one wife, She-gha, and a three-year-old daughter he had sent to Mescalero to learn if the escapees could stay there (answer, not only no, but hell no). The raiders also found and took a White Mountain Apache woman, Bi-ya-neta, who had been with She-gha at Mescalero. On the way back to Mexico, Geronimo and his warriors unexpectedly found and abducted three Mescalero women with a young boy and a baby and made them wives, Geronimo taking the one called Ih-tedda (Young Girl).[3]

In late October and November, Chihuahua led a diversionary raid into the Black Range (Mimbreño Mountains) of New Mexico to detract attention from his brother, Ulzana, who used eleven men and teenaged boys on a raid to Fort Apache and San Carlos to find family members left behind when the renegades hurriedly left the reservation in May or who had been missed in Geronimo's September raid. They also planned to take revenge against scouts they believed had betrayed them. Ulzana was able to take a couple of women and a child, kill twenty-one family members of scouts, and wipe out anyone in his path. In November and December, his raid ended, with the loss of one man, a teen-aged boy shot in the back and beheaded by a Cibecue chief, Sánchez, for a hundred-dollar reward offered by General Crook. In addition to the twenty-one scout family members the raid killed, at least thirty-eight whites and Mexicans were killed, covered twelve hundred miles, and wore out two hundred fifty head of stock.[4]

After a few more small raids in Mexico, Geronimo, Naiche, Chihuahua, and Nana wintered near the Aros River in what they considered the best hidden and most defensible stronghold in the Sierra Madre. In the middle of January 1886, Crawford's scouts found the stronghold and in an early morning attack drove the Apache to the other side of the river and destroyed their winter supplies.

The attacks convinced Geronimo, the primary Apache war leader, that there was no place to hide in Mexico, and it was time to make peace with General Crook. He sent a messenger to Crawford asking for a meeting to discuss surrender terms the next day. Early the next morning Mexican paramilitary, Tarahumara Indians under the leadership of Mauricio Corredor (famous in Chihuahua for killing and scalping Victorio), appeared and attacked Crawford's scouts thinking they were low on ammunition and few in number. Although they had originally come to attack the Apache camp and take scalps for which the Mexican government paid a high bounty, and the scouts, friend or foe, appeared easy pickings. However, the Apache scouts were much more numerous and better armed than the Tarahumara originally believed, and they were soundly beaten by the scouts.

During the fight, Captain Crawford was the first one shot and Corredor was not far behind. After the Tarahumara retreated, Lieutenant Marion Maus, Crawford's second in command, sent the Tarahumara back to their villages on the eastern side of the Sierra Madre and began a march back to Nácori Chico for resupply. Two days later, Lieutenant Maus met with Geronimo, the chiefs, and fourteen warriors. Geronimo and the chiefs agreed to talk terms with Crook. Geronimo gave Maus what amounted to nine hostages including Nana and his wife (Geronimo's sister), a wife and child of Naiche, his own Mescalero wife he had taken the previous fall and who was newly pregnant, a three-year old daughter, an unknown warrior, a woman, and a child as surety that he would meet General Crook in two moons near the border at San Bernardino.[5]

DURING THE NEXT two moons, Geronimo, like any good leader, did his due diligence. He sent two women to the Prefect at Bavispe to learn what terms the Mexican government might offer if the Apache surrendered to them. The Prefect kept the women waiting while he corresponded with Governor Torres of Sonora. Torres wrote back recommending the Prefect arrange a meeting and then murder any Apache who attended. The Prefect released the women with assurances that the Mexicans were willing to discuss liberal surrender terms. When the women left Bavispe they were followed, but they were able to lose their pursuers.

They were expected back much sooner than when they finally returned. Geronimo, fearing the Mexicans might be torturing the women to learn where their camp was, moved north. The women found his trail and rejoined him south of the border. During the two moons Geronimo had wanted to wait, the Apache, expecting to be sent back to Fort Apache, had been raiding and taking as much stock as they could in preparation for their meeting with General Crook.[6]

THE FIRST WEEK of February 1886, General Crook ordered Lieutenant Maus to camp south of the border along San Bernardino Creek. Maus was to watch for Apache and to notify him when arrangements were made for a meeting place. On March 16, four Apache met Lieutenant Maus and said the band was not far away (actually about twenty miles) and would meet *Nant'an Lpah* in Cañon de los Embudos (so named by the locals as Canyon of the Funnels and which the Apache called Green Water Running) northeast of where Maus was camped.[7]

Maus notified Crook of the meeting place. Crook then brought Kaytennae, who had spent twenty months at Alcatraz, to Fort Bowie by train. After Kaytennae arrived three days later, Crook headed for Mexico with Naiche's mother, Dos-teh-seh, Alchesay, a White Mountain chief and lead scout, a White Mountain woman, Na-dis-ough, who had been taken captive and escaped from Ulzana during his raid, Nana, C.S. Fly, a Tombstone photographer who with the Mayor of Tombstone had asked to come, interpreters Montoya, Concepcion, José Maria, and Antonio Besias (all Apache), and his aids Captains John Bourke and Cyrus Roberts and

Robert's precocious twelve year old son. All the Apache, except Mangas, who had kept his little band away from the others to avoid being attacked for raiding, were to be there. Geronimo, Naiche, and twenty-two warriors who were later joined by Chihuahua, Ulzana and seven warriors, and about sixty women and children arrived at Maus's camp first.

Crook and his party didn't arrive until an hour before noon on March 25, and then Crook stopped to have lunch at the packer's camp. Every day Crook had not appeared and was much later than anyone expected, Geronimo had asked Maus where Crook was and if he was coming. The Apache had been drinking the mescal the bootleggers and beef contractors, Charles Tribolett and his brothers, sold in a tent saloon they had set up nearby to sell to mescal to the scouts. The Chiricahua were not in the best of moods and probably still suffering hangovers when, shortly after lunch, Geronimo, Naiche, and a few others came in for the meeting. Finishing lunch, Crook selected their meeting site by the creek in the shade of tall, slender white sycamores, tall shady cottonwoods, dark ash, and long-limbed willows. Twenty-four warriors watched and listened. Every man and boy among the Chiricahua wore two full cartridge belts and had brand new shirts and brightly colored blankets, and all carried a Springfield or Winchester rifle.

Crook picked a place to sit, assumed a business like, unsympathetic pose, and appeared clearly indignant with Geronimo. Crook spoke first. "What have you to say; I have come all the way down from Bowie?"

Before Geronimo answered Crook, he had short private talk with Naiche. Then he began an explanation of why he had left the reservation blaming Lieutenant Davis for listening to the lies of Chato and lies and poor translation of Mickey Free. Everyone was at fault except himself. He talked and talked telling of being warned by Nodiskey and Huera that he was going to be arrested and put in the guardhouse. All the while he clutched his little buckskin medicine bag and beads of sweat rolled down his cheeks. Crook stared at the ground, apparently not interested in Geronimo's long harangue and tapping the ground with a yucca stalk. When Geronimo finished, Crook looked him in the eye and said, "Your mouth talks too many ways." Geronimo, fed up with Crook's arrogance, said, "I want no more of this," causing a stir among the others until Naiche waved his hand to keep quiet.

Toward the end of the meeting, a sentry yelled that riders were coming. The riders were Chihuahua and Ulzana and six warriors driving a herd of stolen horses. It was the first time the White Mountain scouts had laid eyes on Ulzana who had engineered the slaughter of twenty-one of their people. Maus was concerned that the White Mountain might take their revenge against the brothers, but it didn't happen. When Chihuahua saw Crook, he walked over and shook his hand and the rage and anger he felt went away. Chihuahua and Ulzana stood on the edge of the watchers for the last part of the council and were included in the famous C.S. Fly photo of Geronimo meeting with Crook.

Crook ended the council giving his terms. He told them to make up their minds what they wanted to do: stay out on the warpath or surrender unconditionally. If they stayed out Crook said he would hunt them down and kill everyone if it took fifty years. Crook had offered nothing. They wanted to surrender and return to Fort Apache and live as they had before. He told them to return to their camp and think about it before giving him an answer. That evening he sent Kaytennae and Alchesay to their camp to talk them into going away until the uproar they had caused had calmed down. But even those two respected men had trouble getting them to listen.

THE NEXT MORNING Fly took most of his famous photographs and found Geronimo very cooperative. It was then that the White Eyes and soldiers first saw Santiago McKinn, the boy Geronimo had taken in his raid six months earlier. That afternoon, Crook met privately with Naiche, Geronimo, Chihuahua, and others about leaving the Arizona country for the east until they changed their ideas, and bad feeling about them in their homeland had dissipated. Kaytennae, once an angry war chief, helped pushed Crook's ideas for peace. To close the deal, Crook said he would limit their exile east to two years before allowing them to return to Arizona. That evening, Kaytennae told Crook that Chihuahua, who was desperate to see his family, would surrender the next morning.

AT NOON THE next day, March 27, 1886, Chihuahua, Naiche, Geronimo, Cathla, and Nana formally surrendered. Chihuahua offered his hand to Crook and as part of a long speech said, "I surrender myself to you because I believe in you, and you do not deceive us." Crook shook hands with Chihuahua and said, *"Enjuh"* which means in Apache "good" or "it is well." Naiche repeated many of the same things Chihuahua had said and then said, "When I was free, I gave orders, now I surrender to you." Geronimo was the last to speak and after a few words said, "Once I moved like the wind. Now I surrender to you and that is all.... My heart is yours, and I hope yours will be mine." Geronimo, Chihuahua, Cathla, and Tah-ni-toe asked Crook to send their families at San Carlos and Fort Bowie to meet them and the orders were sent.[8]

That night, the Chiricahua bought three, five-gallon demijohns of mescal from Tribolett for three hundred dollars. They got roaring drunk, yelling their war cries and firing their rifles toward the packer tents and those of Maus's soldiers but the shots were wildly off and no one was injured and nothing hit.

At 6:45 a.m. the next morning, Crook was in his buckboard and off to Fort Bowie to telegraph the news to General Sheridan that the Apache Wars were over and leaving Lieutenant Maus and the others to shepherd the Chiricahua back to Fort Bowie. A few miles north from the camp he ran into Geronimo, Cathla, and three warriors "drunk as lords" riding two mules. Geronimo embraced Captain Bourke, Crook's aid, saying he would follow "with my people in a little while." Bourke sensed "impending disaster."

THIRTY-NINE

Geronimo Changes His Mind

THE TRIBOLETT BROTHERS, Siegfried, Robert, Godfrey, and Charley were whiskey peddlers and cattle contractors who operated just south of the border and were likely part of the famous Tucson ring of contractors who were getting rich off contracts to support the army during the Apache Wars. It was to their benefit to keep the fighting ongoing. After Lieutenant Maus and his scouts had crossed the border in mid-February to watch for Geronimo, the Tribolett brothers had set up a tent four hundred yards south of John Slaughter's San Bernardino Ranch on the south side of the border that was a mescal saloon for Maus's scouts and which they frequented.[1]

The Blue Coat officers asked the Tribolett brothers not to sell their Mescal to the Apache. The brothers warned the Blue Coats they had no authority in Mexico and to stay away from their business. After agreeing to surrender, the Apache bought three, five-gallon demijohns of mescal from the Tribolett brothers and that night following the agreement to surrender became roaring drunk, yelling, and firing their rifles toward the packer tents and Crook's soldiers but hitting nothing or anyone.

Apparently, Charley Tribolett had done business with the Apache before, and Geronimo trusted him. As the Chiricahua started getting drunk, he pulled Geronimo aside and told him to be careful, that there was a plan to hang him as soon as he crossed the border. Nevertheless, Geronimo spent the rest of the evening getting drunk with everyone else.

Geronimo (center) poses with his warriors (Naiche far right) after meeting with
General Crook, March 26, 1886.
Photograph by C.S. Fly, courtesy of the National Archives.

The next morning at 6:45 a.m., General Crook left to race to Fort Bowie and telegraph the news that the war with the Apache was over. Lieutenant Maus, left in charge of bringing the Chiricahua to Fort Bowie, wanted to leave early too, but the Naiche-Geronimo group were so drunk and hungover they didn't break camp until about noon. Maus had gone ahead and broken his camp at the same time as Chihuahua's followers, who numbered about two-thirds of the Apache. He sent the pack train with Chihuahua's followers to his original base camp about eight miles up the little Río San Bernardino. Maus stayed behind with Kaytennae, Alchesay, and the scouts to shepherd along the Naiche-Geronimo followers who broke camp about noon. They traveled slowly before making camp at the pack train site. When Maus checked on them, the entire camp was heavily drinking again.[2] He also learned Naiche had, that dawn, shot one of his wives in the leg believing either that she was flirting with another man or that she was trying to run to Maus and tell him of plans to escape (both stories have been told, but only the latter makes sense; if he had thought she was looking for an affair, Naiche would have killed her).

The next morning, the Chiricahua all broke camp early and headed for the border eight miles away. Kaytennae and Alchesay told Maus the "good spree" was over. Maus issued a beef ration, and he sent Lieutenant Shipp with enough support to destroy the Tribolett whiskey operation that had been supplying the scouts near the border. Maus expected to cross the border that day and camp at Silver Creek that evening. But he discovered that the Apache had stopped for the day two miles south of the border with Chihuahua's fifty-one followers in one camp and forty-one in a separate Naiche-Geronimo camp. When asked why they had stopped, Geronimo told Maus their livestock were played out, and the people were still suffering from hangovers. Henry Daly, an old, experienced packer, tried to tell Maus that something was going on. He believed they had stopped because the Apache weren't going to cross the border.

At about 3:00 a.m. that night, Daly heard the tinkling of the little bell on a lead mare as she walked up to the camp. The next morning, Maus learned that Geronimo and Naiche, with twenty men, fourteen women, and six children, had slipped away during the night. Given when Daly heard the lead mare's bell, it was estimated they must have left around 2:30 a.m. The breakaways took only two horses and a mule from the Apache herd. After querying the Apache left behind, Maus wrote, "…and not a soul as far as I could ascertain, knew anything of the time they had gone, or that they intended to go."

The little breakaway group included Geronimo and his wife, She-gha, his son, Chappo, and Chappo's wife, "brothers" (actually second cousins) Fun and Perico, his brother-in-law, Yahnozha, and his orphaned nephew, Kanseah. Naiche had his wife Hah-o-zinne, her mother and father, her half-brother, and her first cousin. Not counting Kanseah, eight of the twenty warriors were related to Geronimo or Naiche and many were in their teens or early twenties. Plans for the breakaway were probably made the night after the camp had been moved the first time and Naiche had shot his wife. Four years later, Naiche was to tell General Crook that he thought everyone knew about the breakaway although there were no councils about it and that he left because, "I was afraid I was going to be taken off somewhere I didn't like, to someplace I didn't know. I thought all who were taken away would die…. Nobody said anything to me that night; I worked it out in my own mind."

Geronimo left because of what Charley Tribolett told him, which reinforced his belief that Crook was treacherous. Years later, he would tell S. M. Barrett, his autobiographer, of the argument between Crook and himself and his final decision to accept Crook's denial of any intention to arrest him—"It was hard for me to believe him at the time. Now I know that what he said was untrue, and I firmly believe that he did issue orders to put me in prison or to kill me if I offered resistance." He was certain that Crook's death four years after the surrender, "…was sent by the Almighty as a punishment for the many evil deeds he committed."

MAUS ORDERED AN officer and some of the scouts to escort the rest of the Apache whose leaders included Chihuahua, Ulzana, Nana, and Kutli to Fort Bowie. He took the remaining scouts and followed the trail of the breakaways into the mountains to the west, but they never gained sight of them. Low on rations and ammunition, Maus returned to San Bernardino where he was joined by two of the breakaway warriors. They had heard people leaving in the night and assumed something was wrong and had left too. In the morning, when they understood what had happened, they returned to the others headed for Fort Bowie.

The same day of the breakaway, Crook reached Fort Bowie and sent his telegram to General Sheridan stating the surrender and its terms. Sheridan answered the next day, and citing President Cleveland as his authority, rejected the conditions and instructed Crook to enter into terms of their unconditional surrender, only sparing their lives. He should prevent their escape and "insure against further hostilities by completing [their] destruction, unless these terms are acceded to," which were bureaucratic army instructions for surround and kill them if they don't accept the new terms. Sheridan was thousands of miles away, had no knowledge of the situation, and had given instructions impossible to follow. General Crook who had always been truthful with the Apache decided not to tell them of the surrender terms. He knew that if he told them the new terms, they would scatter back into the mountains, and it would be another fifty years before the Apache song of blood and fire ended in the southwest.

FORTY

The Naiche-Geronimo Band Raids
for Five Months Without a Loss

AFTER CAMPING WITHIN two miles of the border, Geronimo and Naiche had decided not to surrender. They left the main band with eighteen warriors, and twenty-two women and children around 2:30 a.m. in the middle of the night on March 30, 1886, and disappeared west toward Fronteras. Thinking something was wrong, two warriors, Nezulkide, a brother of Kaytennae and the other Shoie, the brother of Chepuede, left with the band when they heard people moving. After learning Naiche and Geronimo had left because they didn't trust Crook, they returned to the main band. At daylight the morning of the breakaway, Lieutenant Maus sent the remainder of the Chiricahua, who were under the leadership of Chihuahua, on to Fort Bowie, while and he and the rest of the scouts tried to find the Naiche-Geronimo band.

Thinking that Crook would assume they had headed for their camps in the Sierra Madre and would send Chiricahua scouts who knew the country very well to attack them, Geronimo and Naiche turned west toward Fronteras. By the time they reached Fronteras, they were all on foot and scattered in different directions making it virtually impossible for Maus to track them with his few scouts and fast dwindling supplies. Maus left off the chase and withdrew back to Fort Bowie. After reuniting at a rendezvous point, the Apache began stealing livestock for food and remounts and continued west to the summit of the Azul Mountains, which topped out at 8020 feet and rose southwest of Cananea. From the summit they could detect at long range threats coming from any direction including the rugged mountains and cañons in most of the country surrounding and far below them.

Nest of Rattlesnakes
Painting by Henry Farny, ca.1900.

BY APRIL 19, 1886, the band left their camp on the Azul Mountains summit and moved south toward Imuris attacking ranches for supplies and livestock and killing anyone in their path. They were pursued by a Mexican relief force of ten from Imuris who were ambushed during the chase and lost two men. By the next day, the Apache were on the eastern side of the Pinito Mountains about twenty miles southeast of Nogales. There, on April 26, they left their women and children under the protection of a few warriors at an abandoned ruin featuring a large stone corral.

Geronimo and Naiche with the rest of the men rode east and entered the United States from the Buena Vista Ranch where they had killed four men making mescal or wine. In the United States, they hit numerous ranches, murdered many of all ages, and took livestock and supplies. It was during this time that they wiped out the ranch of Artisan and Petra Peck and took captive her ten-year-old niece, Trinidad Verdín, who was able to escape two months later. They left the United States the end of April and reached the mountains on May 2, where their women and children were hidden.[1]

Geronimo and Naiche were aware that a company of American soldiers were about a day behind them. The soldiers were K Troop, Tenth Cavalry, led by Captain Thomas C. Lebo. These were Buffalo Soldiers, veterans of the Victorio war, who had heard about the murders of the men, women, and children in the raids and were after Apache blood. By the afternoon of May 2, after entering the

Cañon de los Negros (named in honor of troopers in the Tenth Cavalry), they had found evidence of a large camp and followed the trail until they found the Chiricahua concealed in impregnable positions on a semicircular cliff. Captain Lebo designated every fourth trooper to hold the horses, formed a skirmish line with the rest of his troopers and advanced toward the Apache. Corporal Edward Scott fired the first shot. The return volley shattered his kneecap, and Private Joseph Hollis was killed. Lieutenant Powhatan K. Clark rushed to pull Corporal Scott to cover with bullets passing within inches of his head and body. For this great act of courage, Clark was awarded the Medal of Honor and is memorialized in a drawing by Frederic Remington. The battle lasted about an hour, but there were no more casualties on either side. During the fight the Apache tried to outflank and take the trooper's horses, but Lebo ordered them to a site farther down the cañon. Officers and troopers thought they had battled eighty to one hundred warriors killing two and wounding one. Geronimo and Naiche's force actually included sixteen men and two teenaged boys and suffered no casualties. They had brought Captain Lebo's pursuit to a dead stop.

GENERAL MILES ARRIVED April 12 to replace General Crook, who had asked to be relieved of the Arizona command and had been assigned to command the Department of the Platt. Miles was anxious to show General Sheridan that he was superior to Crook as a general. Following Sheridan's hint that he thought the Apache scouts had let Geronimo and Naiche get away, Miles fired all the Apache scouts, keeping only a few for trackers, and he replaced Crook's experienced field officers with his own staff who knew, like Miles, little or nothing about fighting Apache.[2]

In order to impress General Sheridan, Miles wanted a strategy with new wrinkles Crook hadn't used that would bring the breakaways to captivity quickly and make his approach clearly superior to Crook's. To protect settlers north of the border he established signal stations with heliographs and telescopes to give notice when the breakaways were approaching. Miles thought this would serve as an early warning system so commanders could deploy troops to ambush threatening Apache. Between April 27 and July 24, he established thirty heliograph stations on mountain summits in southeastern Arizona and southwestern New Mexico. The stations might have been effective if Geronimo and Naiche were operating in the United States. However, during the period that the heliograph stations were functional, only one band under Naiche was in Arizona territory for about twenty days, and they usually traveled at night when the Heliograph crews slept because they couldn't see anything. The heliograph stations were innovative, but despite Miles's later claims, didn't contribute to the breakaway's surrender.

General Miles also had a policy of giving the breakaways no rest and sent one company of the Fourth Cavalry and five scouts under command of Lieutenant Harry C. Benson to relieve Captain Lebo's command. The scouts found the trail of the Chiricahua on May 5. It went south along the "worst trails imaginable." That day three pack mules fell off the narrow trails along canyon cliffs. The lead scout deserted, nervous the breakaways would attack. The breakaways set fires to further impede progress. Captain Henry Lawton and his command took over on May 10. Lawton believed they would continue south along the Magdalena River, but Geronimo and Naiche had reversed course and disappeared.

ON MAY 10, *vaqueros* reported the entire band of Chiricahua with seventy horses were in the Huscomes Mountains twenty-five miles south of Nogales. The following days saw raids near the border and attacks on Mexican National Guard soldiers and a battle with 150 men, many were Tohono O'odham (once known as Papago) Indians, from the village of Altar. The Apache, the Mexicans claiming to be fifty or sixty strong, were well hidden and fired down on them from ridges. The Mexicans and Tohono O'odham ran and left behind thirty-three horses and much of their supplies. Their commander later claimed they had run short of ammunition and supplies rather than leadership and courage.

On May 13, Naiche and Geronimo and their warriors began to probe the border for a vulnerable entry point they could use to enter Arizona. Naiche wanted to know where things stood if they surrendered. The Apache knew the border was heavily patrolled between Columbus, New Mexico, and Nogales, Arizona. Vaqueros spotted them thirty-five miles east of their last big fight (at Pinalta) with the Mexicans and rode to the San Pedro River where Captain Charles Hatfield was camped three miles south of the border to raise the alarm. Hatfield and thirty-four troopers mounted up and began a long cat and mouse game with Geronimo and Naiche. Eventually, the Chiricahua managed to ambush Hatfield and his troopers killing two, wounding two, recovered livestock and supplies that Hatfield's troopers had managed to take in a surprise attack on the Chiricahua camp in the Cuitaca Mountains, and took four additional horses one of which was Hatfield's own mount.

Geronimo and Naiche split their forces for a while. Geronimo to run circles around American and Mexican troops south of the border, Naiche with eleven warriors headed to Fort Apache.

SIX WEEKS HAD passed since Miles had arrived at Fort Bowie, and he had no idea if he was winning or losing. He tried to get the peaceful Chiricahua to send a chief to find and talk to Geronimo, but none would go. Then he offered $2,000 for Geronimo dead or alive and $50 for each of his warriors. Again, no takers. Naiche was able to slip into the Chiricahua camps at Fort Apache. There he saw his mother and other relatives and in a short time learned that Crook had sent his immediate family away and learned that Chiricahua scouts were no longer after him.

Miles had his Chiricahua liaison, Lieutenant Colonel James F. Wade, commander at Fort Apache, talk to the reservation Chiricahua chiefs about sending out someone to make contact with Geronimo. They refused. On the evening of May 26, two women agreed to go: Naiche's mother Dos-teh-seh and one whose name is not known but is thought to have been Bonita, mother of Fun, who was with Naiche. The message they carried from General Miles was that Naiche's band would be "treated justly."

When the women returned, Dos-teh-seh told Wade that Naiche had been nearly ambushed when he went to pick up hidden equipment and would be very cautious for a few days. This made Miles think the breakaways might be looking to surrender and telegraphed Wade specific terms beyond his original promise of them being treated justly. The women went out again, but Naiche only spoke to them from the shadows and thought Miles's offer a joke and left the area. About May 28, Naiche again joined forces with Geronimo in their camp on the summit of the Azul Mountains. The band stayed on the summit for a couple of days before going on the move again.

This pattern of run, fight, hide, was repeated often in the months of June, July, and most of August. Miles kept sending his troopers after the Chiricahua who followed Naiche and Geronimo, but in all this time with one quarter of the U.S. Army (5,000 men), 3,000 Mexican Military, and numerous civilian posses, none of the Naiche-Geronimo warriors were captured, wounded, or killed.

FORTY-ONE

Surrender to Lies

WITH ALL HIS unsuccessful effort over a period of four months in eliminating any of the Naiche-Geronimo band, General Miles still had reason to believe Naiche and Geronimo wanted a chance to surrender, but they first had to be found and offered terms. In mid-July 1886, Miles swallowed his pride and convinced Lieutenant Charles B. Gatewood, to contact Geronimo and Naiche to give them his terms for surrender. Gatewood was known and respected by Geronimo and was one of General Crook's most knowledgeable officers in the lifeways and fighting style of the Apache.

After his meeting with Miles, Gatewood ran into George Wratten on the streets of Albuquerque and asked the twenty-one-year-old to join him on the expedition. Although Gatewood spoke passable Apache, Wratten, who spoke Apache better than any known Anglo and was trusted and respected by the Apache, agreed to come. Miles had also recruited two trusted Apache scouts, Kayihtah and Martine, who had relatives among the breakaway band, to help Gatewood find and talk to Geronimo, Naiche, and the others into surrendering. It is said that Miles offered them a reward of $50,000 if they would go. They had no idea what that amount meant but agreed to go because the Army was paying them to be scouts, and it was their job to support their commanders. Of course, Miles never came through with the reward, and years later their supporters had to fight to make the army pay them the pittance of an $8.00 per month pension. Miles told Gatewood not to dare get near Geronimo without an escort of at least twenty-five troopers to prevent being killed or kidnapped. Gatewood knew the expedition would never get near the Apache with an armed escort and soon lost the troopers after Kayihtah, Martine, Wratten, and his mule packer, Frank

Huston, left Fort Bowie. He later added a rancher, Tex Whaley, to the expedition
to act as a courier.[1]

BY THE TIME Gatewood got into Mexico, the monsoon rains had started making it difficult to impossible to find and follow even a fresh trail. He eventually
found Captain Lawton over one hundred thirty miles south of the border near the
junction of the Nácori and Aros rivers. He stayed with Lawton until he learned
that Geronimo had sent two women into Fronteras to ask for an armistice and
to discuss a peace treaty with Geronimo. This was an age-old dance between the
Mexicans and the Apache where the Apache wanted gifts of supplies and mescal
and the Mexicans wanted to get the Apache in one place, get them drunk, and
kill them all. Both sides knew the game but still they played it. Geronimo had
no intention of surrendering, but he did want the gifts of supplies and a good
drink of mescal.

Using Kayihtah and Martine as his trackers Gatewood followed the women's
trail and then the main band to where the Bavispe River makes a great turn from
flowing north to south. Near the horseshoe of the turn are the Teras Mountains.
According to George Wratten's story years later, the Apache were camped on a
flat-topped mountain with the steepest slopes on the steepest mountain in Mexico.

KAYIHTAH AND MARTINE tied a white piece of cloth to a century plant stalk
and began approaching the camp. Geronimo didn't like Chiricahua working as
scouts for the army and considered them traitors. He knew Martine was close
friends with Chato and that made him even more disliked. He told warriors
watching the scouts to shoot them. However, Kayihtah and Martine had relatives
among the warriors. Perico, Fun, and Yahnozha, all cousins or somehow related
to the two scouts refused to shoot and said they would shoot anyone who tried.
Geronimo, who knew these men never made empty threats said for them to let
the scouts come on. Yahnozha yelled down to ask why they came. They answered
that they brought *Teniente* (Lieutenant) Gatewood with surrender terms from
Nant'an Miles. The scouts were led into the camp and held council with Naiche,
Geronimo, and their warriors.[2]

After to smoking to the four directions, Geronimo told the scouts to speak.

Kayitah said, "The bluecoats are coming after you from the east, west, north, and south. They have been told by their chiefs to kill every one of you even if it takes fifty years. Think on it. Everything is against you. If you are awake at night and a rock rolls down this mountain or a stick breaks you will be running. You even eat running. You have no friends anywhere in all the land. You are not at all like me. I get plenty to eat. I go wherever I want and talk to good people. I lie down to sleep whenever I want and get all my sleep. I have nobody to fear. I have my little patch of corn. I'm trying to do what the white people want me to do. There's no reason you people shouldn't do it. Don't you think my words are true?"

After watching his warriors listen to Kayihtah, Geronimo said to Martine, "You go to Gatewood and say, Geronimo wants to talk. You come back with Gatewood. Kayihtah stays with us until you return."

Naiche said, "Tell Gatewood if he comes, I give my word he will not be harmed."

The next morning, Naiche sent three men to tell Gatewood to come without soldiers to a canebrake on the river the messengers would show him. Gatewood, Wratten, and the mule packer, Frank Huston, went to the place and waited. 3 Soon warriors in twos and threes began appearing and lastly Geronimo showed up. Gatewood and Geronimo shook hands and then went into council with the others where they smoked to the four directions and got down to business.

Geronimo said to Gatewood, "We come to hear General Miles words. Give them to us!" Gatewood replied, "These are the words of General Miles. Hear them. Surrender, and you will be sent to join the rest of your friends in Florida. There you will wait until the President decides what he must do about you. Accept these terms or fight until you are all dead."

Geronimo had been drinking the mescal the women had been given in Fronteras after he had told the Mexicans he wanted to talk peace. He made his fingers tremble, said he felt shaky, and told Gatewood he needed a little whiskey, but Gatewood told him he didn't have any. Geronimo steadied and put it to him straight. "I leave the warpath only if we can return to the reservation and live as before." Gatewood shook his head. "General Miles's words will not change." Geronimo then told Gatewood all the trouble they had at San Carlos and why they left. Gatewood was not impressed. He just sat and listened. Then Gatewood left them to have a private council before eating a noon meal Huston provided.

Geronimo (center) waiting at Fort Sam Houston in San Antonio, Texas, with Naiche (seated) to his left, et al, September 1886 to learn if General Miles's terms of surrender. Photograph courtesy of Joint Base San Antonio.

AFTER THE NOON meal, the Apache met with Gatewood again. Geronimo looked Gatewood in the eye and said, "Take us to the reservation or fight." Gatewood looked around to see if any guns were pointed at him, but none were. Naiche who had been quiet during the council held up his hand palm out and said, "Whether we continue war or not, you will be allowed to leave in peace."

Gatewood nodded and said, "Hear me. You demand to go back to the reservation, but you have no reservation to return to. All your people have been sent to join Chihuahua in Florida." (Unknown to Gatewood, Miles was waiting until Geronimo surrendered to send all the Chiricahua east).

Geronimo and the warriors were stunned at the news. They went back into private council and decided to keep fighting. Still they desperately wanted to know about their families. Naiche sent Kanseah, the youngest warrior, off to find a beef so they could eat that night and pump Gatewood for all the information he had about their families, but there was no beef to be found.

They continued to sit in council while Geronimo grilled Gatewood about General Miles. He asked what kind of man now fought them in place of Crook. How old was he? How big? What were the colors of his hair and eyes? Was his

voice hard or easy? Did he talk much or little? Did he mean more or less what he
said? Did he have many friends among his own people? Did the soldiers and officers like him? Did he have experience with Indians? Would he keep his promises?
The warriors listened carefully to every answer Gatewood gave.

Geronimo believed Gatewood was an honest man with courage and respected
him. As Gatewood was leaving, Geronimo said, "We want your advice. Consider
yourself one of us and not a white man. Remember all that has been said today,
and as an Apache, what would you advise us to do?" Gatewood thought for a
little while before he said, "I would trust General Miles and take him at his word."

THE NEXT DAY the band agreed to meet General Miles in Skeleton Cañon a
few miles north of the border if Captain Lawton who had arrived the night before
the talks started would escort them north, Gatewood would ride with them, and
they could keep their weapons for protection (from Mexicans, civilian posses, and
U.S. soldiers looking for revenge). Lawton as the senior officer agreed to all this
and began moving north on August 27. The next day they had a brush with the
Mexican military which was peacefully resolved and continued on. A few days
later Miles informed Lawton he wouldn't meet with Geronimo unless he was
dead or in leg irons (and twice subtly suggested Lawton execute all the band).
He didn't want to risk being embarrassed like General Crook when Geronimo
decided not to surrender. Lawton sent Miles hostages (Wratten with Perico) and
had to beg him to come accept Geronimo's surrender as the Apache grew restless
wondering what was going on to keep Miles away so long.

Miles finally arrived the afternoon of September 3, around 3:00 p.m. Geronimo
came down from his camp on the mountain, introductions were made, and unlike
Crook, Miles listened patiently and respectfully to Geronimo. They discussed
Geronimo's reasons for breaking away and surrender terms. The surrender
terms included the Apache laying down their arms, going to Fort Bowie to take
and ride the train to Florida, in five days seeing their families in Florida with
Chihuahua, and all the Apache staying there until President Cleveland decided
what to do with them. No harm would come to them (Cleveland planned to have
Geronimo hanged by civilian authorities although Miles didn't know that), and
all the Chiricahua would be given a reservation of their own. Geronimo agreed
to these terms, but Naiche was still up in the hills waiting for Atelnietze to return
with some horse they had left in Sonora.

The next morning Geronimo and Gatewood rode to Naiche's camp and told him Miles's terms. Naiche agreed to the terms, and reluctant to be rude to anyone by keeping them waiting, brought his band to the army camp where Miles waited and formally surrendered. That afternoon Miles had a big surrender ceremony where a big rock was placed on blanket and both sides agreed to keep the peace until the rock turned to dust.

Early the next morning, Miles, Geronimo, Naiche, three men, and a woman left for Fort Bowie in Miles's ambulance while Lawton's command brought the rest of the Apache north to Fort Bowie where they arrived the morning of September 8, and all were put on a train headed for Florida that afternoon. The Chiricahua twenty-seven-year nightmare was beginning. Deceived by lies, Geronimo's song of blood and fire had ended, and the internment of the peaceful Chiricahua including the scouts who had helped bring him in, had begun.[4]

EPILOGUE

The Apache Iliad ended through deception just as the Greeks overcame the Trojans with deception in the Iliad. The Apache were prisoners of war for the next twenty-seven years. It was their Odyssey, a journey that preserved their tribal culture against congressional laws, the determined ignorance of government bureaucrats, and the siren calls to live life as second-class citizens in the towns and villages of the pindah lickoyee. The events that followed the end of the Apache Iliad tell as much about the victors as the vanquished. The details of the story of the Apache years in captivity is told in Geronimo: Prisoner of Lies. How the Americans dealt with their "victory" in the Apache Wars is sketched here.

General Crook accepted the surrender of the Chiricahua in late March 1886 under the terms that they would probably be held in the east for two years (this had happened to members of the plains tribes earlier) and then returned to the reservation. When the Chiricahua who didn't break away with Geronimo in March 1886 returned to Fort Bowie, they were immediately sent east and kept as prisoners of war at Fort Marion in Saint Augustine, Florida, and many of their children were separated from them and sent to the Carlisle Indian Industrial School in Carlisle, Pennsylvania.

When Naiche and Geronimo broke way after the March 1886 Crook agreement, General Sheridan told Crook, and is a reason Crook resigned, that the promise of two years exile was no longer appropriate. Only unconditional surrender would be accepted, but Crook didn't tell the Chiricahua that. When Geronimo and Naiche formally surrendered on September 4, 1886, Miles told them they would be held in Florida to protect them from white settlers until President Cleveland could decide what to do with them, knowing that was a lie; that the Naiche- Geronimo band would be reunited with their families in five days, knowing that was a lie; and, that the Chiricahua would get their own reservation with plenty of land, water, and grass, and that was a faint, desperate hope. Although Miles knew the land that he wanted for the Chiricahua was on the same lands controlled by the Comanche, Kiowa, and Kiowa-Apache, he hoped by some ironic twist of fate that the Chiricahua could live there too. It was a dream that soon vanished into the smoke of political reality.

Within hours after Geronimo and Naiche surrendered, in one of the most shameful episodes in American military history, General Miles, with the approval of the secretary of war, directed that the Chiricahua (about two thirds of the total band) still living at Fort Apache peacefully minding their business and tending their farms and even those who as scouts helped the army track and fight Geronimo and were still on the army payroll, be gathered up and also shipped to Fort Marion. They were now all prisoners of war, their fates also at the whim of the War Department and Bureau of Interior bureaucrats. Chiricahua with Geronimo were shipped east out of Bowie Station on September 8, 1886, and the Mangas band of eleven, the last to surrender, were shipped out October 30, 1886.

As soon as the train left carrying the Naiche-Geronimo band, the telegraph wires between Fort Bowie where General Miles was located and Washington began to hum. The President and War Department wanted to know if Miles had overpowered Naiche-Geronimo's band to capture them or had they surrendered under terms. Miles's answers were evasive and didn't directly answer the questions. President Cleveland wanted to turn Geronimo, Naiche, and their warriors over to civil authorities in Arizona and New Mexico, where after receiving a trial, it is certain they would have been hanged for murder, destruction of property, and stock theft. If the Naiche-Geronimo band had been forcefully taken by the army, then it was well within the President's purview to treat them like outlaws and hand them over to civil authorities. If on the other hand, the band had surrendered after agreeing to army terms, then the army was honor bound to treat them as prisoners of war.

General Sheridan, unable to get a straight answer out of Miles about what terms he offered Geronimo's band, ordered the train carrying the Naiche-Geronimo band stopped at Fort Sam Houston in San Antonio until the President and War Department could sort through the facts and determine under what terms, if any, the band had in fact surrendered. Still unable to get a straight answer out of General Miles after three weeks of evasive answers, General Sheridan had the Department of Texas Commander, General D.S. Stanley, separately interview Geronimo and Naiche on September 29 to determine their understanding of surrender terms. Their answers were remarkably consistent and reflected what Miles had promised on September 4. Eight days later President Cleveland announced his decision and the War Department and Department of Interior concurred, to wit the Apache were to have their lives spared, be sent to Florida and not turned over to civilian authorities in Arizona and New Mexico, and all, including Geronimo's band, were to be treated as prisoners of war.

The army kept the Naiche-Geronimo warriors at Fort Pickens in Pensacola Bay and sent their families on to Fort Marion with the other Chiricahua in Saint Augustine, thus already disregarding a term of surrender General Miles had made. Seven months later, the Naiche-Geronimo Band families were reunited at Fort Pickens, and a year after that all the Chiricahua were together at Mount Vernon Barracks thirty miles north of Mobile, Alabama. Six years (1894) later, the Chiricahua were all moved to Fort Sill, Oklahoma. Even then the Army had to play political games to get them there.

Fort Sill land, which the army intended to abandon "soon" as a military facility, had been part of the Comanche, Kiowa, and Kiowa Apache reservation. After the army abandoned the fort, the land was to revert back to the original reservation. The army planned to close Fort Sill a few years after the Chiricahua arrived. Knowing this, the Comanche, Kiowa, and Kiowa Apache had agreed to let the Chiricahua keep the Fort Sill land as their reservation after the army left (for a "small nominal fee" of course—Quanah Parker was no fool when it came to business).

As long as the army was responsible for the Chiricahua and their welfare, it had to identify them as prisoners of war in order to get budget money to pay for their support. It was also the reason the Army moved them to a different location three times. The Apache sent to Fort Marion were dying off at a death rate about three times that of the national average. Forty-three percent of the best and brightest of the Chiricahua children sent to the Carlisle School died from disease. The army was responsible for their prisoners, and they had to be held where it was safe for them to live. The extraordinary, high Chiricahua death rate put the army in the national spotlight in how it kept the Apache healthy and its decisions of where to keep them. In the meantime, reservation Indians under management by the Bureau of Interior continued to suffer theft of their reservation lands, shortages of supplies, and, often dishonest agents. In terms of long-

term management, the Chiricahua were probably far better off being prisoners of war than reservation Indians under the Bureau of Interior.

Until about 1904, the Army and Bureau of Interior had worked on various schemes whereby the Army could turn the Chiricahua over to the Bureau of Interior where they would be formally managed on a reservation, presumably at abandoned Fort Sill. However, each time an agreement drew near signing, the Bureau of Interior found some reason for delaying it or determining that it was unacceptable. In May 1903, a secret Army War College Board report emphasized the need to maintain Fort Sill for military purposes. Army management ultimately decided Fort Sill would become the Army's Artillery School, which meant the Chiricahua would have to give up the lands they had worked eighteen years to develop and be moved somewhere else.

By 1905, nearly all the great Chiricahua Apache leaders—Nana, Chihuahua, Loco, Mangas—had ridden the ghost pony and voices for use of Fort Sill as a military installation grew louder. Only Geronimo and the much younger Naiche remained and talk about setting the Chiricahua free began in earnest. In 1905, Geronimo begged Theodore Roosevelt to return him and the Chiricahua to Arizona. Roosevelt refused, saying that if he did, then the white Arizonans wanting payback for their suffering during the Chiricahua Apache Wars would attack the returning Apache, and for the safety and tranquility of the Apache it was better for them to remain prisoners of war.

When Geronimo rode the ghost pony in February 1909, the decision to free all the Chiricahua from captivity became a certainty. In 1913, their brothers on the Mescalero reservation in central New Mexico welcomed the Chiricahua, who as free men, wanted to return to the southwest. The Chiricahua who wanted to stay in Oklahoma were freed in 1914 and promised one hundred sixty acres for a ranch or eighty acres for a farm. They were lucky if any got close to 80 acres. The Chiricahua were free at last after twenty-seven years of unjust imprisonment, victims of ignorance and a self-serving bureaucracy. It was the end of an era, but despite ten years of war and peace, their years of imprisonment, and their children taken away for five to eight years to be trained in White Eye ways and to forget their tribal culture, most of the Chiricahua returned to the southwest and continued to live together as the Chiricahua Tribe.

END NOTES

Prefatory Note

1. *Geronimo: Prisoner of Lies, Twenty-Three Years as Prisoner of War, 1886-1909*, by W. Michael Farmer
2. *The Odyssey of Geronimo, Twenty-Three Years a Prisoner of War*, by W. Michael Farmer

Prologue

1. *Geronimo, The Man, His Time, His Place*, by Angie Debo, p. 13
2. Geronimo, His Own Story, The Autobiography of a Great Patriot Warrior, by S. M. Barrett, p. 38.
3. Ibid. pp. 43 – 45
4. Burbank Among the Indians, E.A. Burbank and Ernest Royce, p. 33.
5. Barrett, Op. Cit., pp. 47 – 54.
6. Debo, Op. Cit., pp. 86 – 89
7. Barrett, Op. Cit. p. xii.

Part 1: Captured

1. *From Cochise to Geronimo, The Chiricahua Apache, 1874–1886*, Edwin Sweeny, p. 84

2. *Geronimo, The Man, His Time, His Place*, by Angie Debo, p. 111

Chapter 1

1. *The Conquest of Apacheria*, by Dan Thrapp, p. 162

2. Ibid. pp. 162 – 163.

3. Ibid. pp. 164 – 165

4. *Geronimo, The Man, His Time, His Place*, by Angie Debo, p. 95

Chapter 2

1. *The Conquest of Apacheria*, by Dan Thrapp, p. 170

2. *From Cochise to Geronimo, The Chiricahua Apache, 1874–1886*, Edwin Sweeny, p. 58

3. Ibid. pp. 69, 70.

4. *Geronimo, His Own Story, The Autobiography of a Great Patriot Warrior*, by S. M. Barrett, pp. 124 – 127.

Chapter 3

1. *Geronimo, His Own Story, The Autobiography of a Great Patriot Warrior*, by S. M. Barrett, pp. 124 – 127.

2. *From Cochise to Geronimo, The Chiricahua Apache, 1874–1886*, Edwin Sweeny, p. 78

3. Ibid. pp. 81

Chapter 4

1. *Geronimo, The Man, His Time, His Place*, by Angie Debo, p. 105

2. *Geronimo, His Own Story, The Autobiography of a Great Patriot Warrior*, by S. M. Barrett, p. 131.

3. Debo, Op. Cit., pp. 105

4. "A Chiricahua Apache's Account of the Geronimo Campaign of 1886," Morris Opler, *New Mexico Historical Review*, Vol. XIII, No. 4 (October 1938) p. 379

Chapter 5

1.   *Geronimo, The Man, His Time, His Place,* by Angie Debo, p. 113
2.   "Geronimo," John Clum, *New Mexico Historical Review,* Vol. III, No. (part 1, January 1928) p. 34

Part 2: The War Begins

Chapter 6

1.   *From Cochise to Geronimo, The Chiricahua Apache, 1874–1886,* Edwin Sweeny, pp. 116 – 119
2.   *I Fought with Geronimo,* by Jason Betzinez with W. S. Nye, p. 47
3.   Edwin Sweeney, Op. Cit. pp. 119 – 120.

Chapter 7

1.   *From Cochise to Geronimo, The Chiricahua Apache, 1874–1886,* Edwin Sweeny, pp. 123
2.   Ibid. pp. 142.

Chapter 8

1.   *From Cochise to Geronimo, The Chiricahua Apache, 1874–1886,* Edwin Sweeny, pp. 147 – 148
2.   Ibid. p. 148
3.   Ibid. p. 162
4.   Ibid. p. 163

Chapter 9

1.   Geronimo, The Man, His Time, His Place, by Angie Debo, p.124
2.   In The Days of Victorio, by Eve Ball, p. 102
3.   Ibid. pp. 168 – 174.
4.   For a detailed story see Chapter 23.
5.   Ibid. pp. 120
6.   Debo, op. cit., pp. 126
7.   Debo, op. cit., pp. 127
8.   Indeh, by Eve Ball, Nora Henn, and Lynda Sánchez, pp. 53 – 54
9.   Debo, op. cit., pp. 129

Part 3: The War Expands

Chapter 10

1. *From Cochise to Geronimo, The Chiricahua Apache, 1874–1886,* Edwin Sweeny, p. 182

2. *Geronimo, His Own Story, The Autobiography of a Great Patriot Warrior,* by S. M. Barrett, p. 134

3. Edwin Sweeney, op. cit. p. 183

4. Ibid. p. 190

Chapter 11

1. *From Cochise to Geronimo, The Chiricahua Apache, 1874–1886,* Edwin Sweeny, p. 193

2. Ibid. p. 195

3. *Geronimo, The Man, His Time, His Place,* by Angie Debo, p. 139

4. Dan L. Thrapp, an Apache wars historian of major stature, believed, on the basis of army officer opinions, and that Nana was part of the raid to abduct Loco and his people from San Carlos, and Nana was seen close to the border near Corralitos a month before Loco was taken.

Chapter 12

1. *The Iliad of Geronimo, A Song of Blood and Fire,* a Novel by W. Michael Farmer

2. *Western Apache Raiding and Warfare* by Grenville Goodwin, pp. 143, 144

3. *From Cochise to Geronimo, The Chiricahua Apache, 1874–1886,* Edwin Sweeny, p. 208 – 210

Chapter 13

1. *Geronimo, The Man, His Time, His Place,* by Angie Debo, p. 141

2. *From Cochise to Geronimo, The Chiricahua Apache, 1874–1886,* Edwin Sweeny, p. 211

3. Some stories claim that Chato pointed his rifle at Loco and threatened to shoot him if he did not leave and lead his people.

Chapter 14

1. *Geronimo, The Man, His Time, His Place*, by Angie Debo, p. 151

Chapter 15

1. *I Fought with Geronimo*, by Jason Betzinez with W. S. Nye, p. 82
2. *Geronimo, The Man, His Time, His Place*, by Angie Debo, p. 160

Chapter 16

1. Most of the historical information recorded here comes from *From Cochise to Geronimo, The Chiricahua Apache, 1874–1886*, Edwin Sweeny, pp. 250 – 254 and 286, 287
2. *I Fought with Geronimo*, by Jason Betzinez with W. S. Nye, pp. 93 – 96

Chapter 17

1. Most of the historical information recorded here comes from *Geronimo, The Man, His Time, His Place*, by Angie Debo, p. 165 – 168
2. *I Fought with Geronimo*, by Jason Betzinez with W. S. Nye, pp. 97 – 101
3. *From Cochise to Geronimo, The Chiricahua Apache, 1874–1886*, Edwin Sweeny, pp. 290 – 297

Chapter 18

1. *The Truth About Geronimo*, by Britton Davis, pp. 57, 58
2. *An Apache Campaign in the Sierra Madre*, by John G. Bourke, pp. 14 – 40.

Chapter 19

1. Most of the historical information recorded here comes from *An Apache Campaign in the Sierra Madre*, by John G. Bourke, pp. 40 – 84.
2. *Western Apache Raiding and Warfare* by Grenville Goodwin, pp. 158 – 163
3. Goodwin, Op. Cit. p.164

Chapter 20

1. *Western Apache Raiding and Warfare* by Grenville Goodwin, pp. 165 – 167
2. Ibid. pp.165 – 167
3. *An Apache Campaign in the Sierra Madre*, by John G. Bourke, pp. 95 – 97.

Chapter 21

1. Most of the historical information recorded in this section comes from *I*

Fought with Geronimo, by Jason Betzinez with W. S. Nye, pp. 112 – 115

2. Most of the historical information recorded in this section comes from *From Cochise to Geronimo, The Chiricahua Apache, 1874–1886,* Edwin Sweeny, pp. 309, 310

3. *Western Apache Raiding and Warfare* by Grenville Goodwin, p. 169

Chapter 22

1. Most of the historical information recorded here comes from *Geronimo, The Man, His Time, His Place,* by Angie Debo, pp. 186 – 192

2. *I Fought with Geronimo,* by Jason Betzinez with W. S. Nye, p. 116

3. Ibid. pp. 118 – 120

4. *Western Apache Raiding and Warfare* by Grenville Goodwin, p. 170

5. *An Apache Campaign in the Sierra Madre,* by John G. Bourke, pp. 104 – 110.

6. Debo, Op. Cit. pp. 196, 197

Chapter 23

1. *In The Days of Victorio,* by Eve Ball, pp. 169 – 174

2. *Apache Voices,* by Sherry Robinson, pp. 27 – 29

Part 4: The Second Armistice

Chapter 24

1. *Indeh,* by Eve Ball, Nora Henn, and Lynda Sánchez, pp. 70 – 73

2. Most of the historical information recorded here comes from *From Cochise to Geronimo, The Chiricahua Apache, 1874–1886,* Edwin Sweeny, pp. 328

3. Ibid. p. 329

4. Ibid. p. 330

5. Ibid. p. 331

6. Eve Ball, Nora Henn, and Lynda Sánchez, Op. Cit. pp. 75, 76

Chapter 25

1. *The Truth About Geronimo,* by Britton Davis, pp. 96 – 101

2. *Geronimo, The Man, His Time, His Place,* by Angie Debo, pp. 205, 206

3. Ibid. pp. 207

4. Ibid. pp. 208, 209

Chapter 26

1. *Geronimo, The Man, His Time, His Place,* by Angie Debo, p. 221
2. Ibid. pp. 221,222
3. Ibid. p. 222
4. Ibid. pp. 233, 234

Chapter 27

1. *From Cochise to Geronimo, The Chiricahua Apache, 1874–1886,* by Edwin Sweeny, p. 372
2. *Geronimo, The Man, His Time, His Place,* by Angie Debo, pp. 226, 227
3. See Chapter 23 for the story of their escape
4. *In The Days of Victorio,* by Eve Ball, pp.157 – 158

Chapter 28

1. *The Truth About Geronimo,* by Britton Davis, p. 139
2. Ibid. pp 143 - 148
3. Ibid. p. 149

Part 5: Deception Renews and Ends the War

Chapter 29

1. Most of the historical information in this section comes from *Geronimo, The Man, His Time, His Place,* by Angie Debo, pp. 102, 103
2. *Indeh,* by Eve Ball, Nora Henn, and Lynda Sánchez, pp. 135, 136
3. Eve Ball, Nora Henn, and Lynda Sánchez, Op. Cit. pp. 45 – 50
4. Debo, Op. Cit. pp. 72,73
5. *The Truth About Geronimo,* by Britton Davis, pp. 145, 146
6. Debo, Op. Cit. pp. 71, 72

Chapter 30

1. *In The Days of Victorio,* by Eve Ball, p. 146
2. Ball, Op. Cit. pp. 136 – 39
3.

Chapter 31

1. *From Cochise to Geronimo, The Chiricahua Apache, 1874–1886*, Edwin
    Sweeny, p. 402
2. *Geronimo, The Man, His Time, His Place*, by Angie Debo, p. 345

Chapter 32

1. Most of the historical information in this section comes from *From
    Cochise to Geronimo, The Chiricahua Apache, 1874–1886*, Edwin Sweeny,
    pp. 433 – 435
2. Sweeney, Op. Cit., pp. 444, 445

Chapter 33

1. *From Cochise to Geronimo, The Chiricahua Apache, 1874–1886*, Edwin
    Sweeny, pp. 433
2. Ibid. p. 433
3. Ibid. p. 434
4. Chapter 34. Geronimo's Family Captured
5. *From Cochise to Geronimo, The Chiricahua Apache, 1874–1886*, Edwin
    Sweeny, p. 444
6. Ibid. p.b433
7. Sweeney, Op. Cit. pp. 444, 445

Chapter 35

1. *From Cochise to Geronimo, The Chiricahua Apache, 1874–1886*, Edwin
    Sweeny, pp.461
2. Ibid. p.469
3. *Indeh,* by Eve Ball, Nora Henn, and Lynda Sánchez, pp.102,103
4. Ball, Op. Cit., pp.262, 263.

Chapter 36

1. *From Cochise to Geronimo, The Chiricahua Apache, 1874–1886*, Edwin
    Sweeny, p. 479
2. Ibid. p. 480.
3. Ibid. p. 480.
4. Ibid. p. 487

Chapter 37

1. *From Cochise to Geronimo, The Chiricahua Apache, 1874–1886,* Edwin Sweeny, p. 493
2. Ibid. p. 499
3. Ibid. p. 502
4. *Geronimo, The Man, His Time, His Place,* by Angie Debo, pp. 251, 252
5. Ibid. pp. 252, 253

Chapter 38

1. Chapter 32
2. Chapter 34
3. Chapter 35
4. Chapter 36
5. *Geronimo, The Man, His Time, His Place,* by Angie Debo, pp. 251, 252
6. The Geronimo Campaign, by Odie B. Faulk, pp. 84, 85
7. Most of the historical information recorded here comes from Debo, Op. Cit. pp. 252 – 263
8. *From Cochise to Geronimo, The Chiricahua Apache, 1874–1886,* Edwin Sweeny, pp. 523, 524

Chapter 39

1. Most of the historical information recorded in this section comes from Debo, Op. Cit. pp.264 – 267
2. Most of the historical information recorded in this section comes *From Cochise to Geronimo, The Chiricahua Apache, 1874–1886,* Edwin Sweeny, pp. 524 - 526

Chapter 40

1. Most of the historical information recorded in this section comes *From Cochise to Geronimo, The Chiricahua Apache, 1874–1886,* Edwin Sweeny, pp. 536 – 540
2. Ibid. pp. 533 – 535

Chapter 41

1. *From Cochise to Geronimo, The Chiricahua Apache, 1874–1886,* Edwin Sweeny, p. 558
2. *In The Days of Victorio,* by Eve Ball, p.187

3. *Geronimo, The Man, His Time, His Place,* by Angie Debo, pp.283
4. Ibid. pp. 284 – 293

ADDITIONAL READING & INFORMATION SOURCES

Ball, Eve, Nora Henn, and Lynda A. Sánchez, *Indeh: An Apache Odyssey*, University of Oklahoma Press, Norman, OK, 1988.

Ball, Eve, *In The Days Of Victorio*, University of Arizona Press, Tucson, AZ, 1970

Barrett, S. M., *Geronimo, His Own Story, The Autobiography of a Great Patriot Warrior*, Meridian, Penguin Books USA, New York, New York, 1996.

Betzinez, Jason with W. S. Nye, *I Fought with Geronimo*, Bonanza Books, New York, NY, 1959

Bourke, John G., *An Apache Campaign in the Sierra Madre*, University of Nebraska Press, Lincoln, NA, 1987

Burbank, E[lbridge]. A[yer]. and Ernest Royce, *Burbank Among the Indians*, The Caxton Printers, Ltd., Caldwell, Idaho, 1946

Clum, John, "Geronimo," *New Mexico Historical Review*, Vol. III, No. (part 1, January, 1928)

Collins, Charles, *The Great Escape: The Apache Outbreak of 1881*, WESTERNLORE Press, Tucson, AZ, 1994

Davis, Britton, *The Truth About Geronimo*, Yale University Press, New Haven, CT, 1929

Debo, Angie, *Geronimo, The Man, His Time, His Place*, University of Oklahoma Press, Norman, OK, 1976.

Delgadillo, Alicia with Miriam A. Perrett, *Fort Marion to Fort Sill, A Documentary History of the Chiricahua Prisoner of War, 1886-1913*, University of Nebraska Press, Lincoln, NE, 2013.

Farmer, W. Michael, *Geronimo: Prisoner of Lies,* The Rowman & Littlefield
Publishing Group, Inc., Lanham, MD. 2019

Farmer, W. Michael, *The Odyssey of Geronimo, Twenty-Three Years a Prisoner of
War,* Five Star, Waterville, ME, 2020

Faulk, Odie B., *The Geronimo Campaign,* Oxford University Press, New York,
NY, 1969

Gatewood, Charles B., edited and additional text by Louis Kraft, *Lt. Charles
Gatewood & His Apache Wars Memoir,* University of Nebraska Press,
Lincoln, NE, 2005.

Goodwin, Grenville, *Western Apache Raiding and Warfare,* The University of
Arizona Press, Tucson, AZ, 1971

Haley, James L., *Apache: A History and Culture Portrait,* University of Oklahoma
Press, Norman, OK, 1981.

Hutton, Paul Andrew, *The Apache Wars,* Crown Publishing Group, New York,
New York, 2016.

Opler, Morris Edward, *An Apache Life-Way, The Economic, Social, and Religious
Institutions of the Chiricahua Indians,* University of Nebraska Press, Lincoln,
NE, 1996.

Opler, Morris, Edward, *Apache Odyssey, A Journey Between Two Worlds,*
University of Nebraska Press, Lincoln, NE, 2002.

Opler, Morris, Edward, "A Chiricahua Apache's Account of the Geronimo
Campaign of 1886," *New Mexico Historical Review,* Vol XIII, No. 4 (October,
1938).

Robinson, Sherry, *Apache Voices: Their Stories of Survival as Told to Eve Ball,*
University of New Mexico Press, Albuquerque, NM, 2003.

Sonnichsen, C. L., *The Mescalero Apache,* University of Oklahoma Press,
Norman, OK, 1973.

Sweeny, Edwin, *From Cochise to Geronimo, The Chiricahua Apache, 1874–1886,*
University of Oklahoma Press, Norman, OK, 2010.

Thrapp, Dan L., *The Conquest of Apacheria,* University of Oklahoma Press,
Norman, OK, 1967.

Worchester, Donald E., *The Apache: Eagles of the Southwest,* University of
Oklahoma Press, Norman, OK, 1992.